How Not to Live Abroad

How Not to Live Abroad

SURVIVING RUSTIC BLISS IN THE SPANISH COUNTRYSIDE

Shaun Briley

CITADEL PRESS
Kensington Publishing Corp.
www.kensingtonbooks.com

CITADEL PRESS BOOKS are published by

Kensington Publishing Corp.
850 Third Avenue
New York, NY 10022

All Kensington titles, imprints, and distributed lines are available at special quantity discounts for bulk purchases for sales promotions, premiums, fund-raising, educational, or institutional use. Special book excerpts or customized printings can also be created to fit specific needs. For details, write or phone the office of the Kensington special sales manager: Kensington Publishing Corp., 850 Third Avenue, New York, NY 10022, attn: Special Sales Department; phone 1-800-221-2647.

CITADEL PRESS and the Citadel logo are Reg. U.S. Pat. & TM Off.

First printing: February 2004

10 9 8 7 6 5 4 3 2 1

Printed in the United States of America

Library of Congress Control Number: 2003107969

ISBN 0-8065-2586-X

Contents

1

Unusual Capers

The stakes were high in the cobbled back alley behind the Restaurante El Rincón. Half a dozen swarthy mountain men waited anxiously. The bearded policeman, who was also the bookkeeper, closed the betting and pocketed his notebook. It was approaching noon on a Friday afternoon in an ancient whitewashed village. It was time for the rat race, Andalusian style.

The restaurateur, Enrique, peered out of the alley and then gave the thumbs-up. "No sign of the *padre*," he said.

"He's giving the St. Francis' Day service," a grubby farmer in a traditional peasant's cap reminded him. This was not a gathering of the village's most religious folk.

"Ah yes, the day of the animals. Let's hope he said a prayer for the rodents," said Enrique, now emptying a plate of scraps at one end of a deep gutter that bisected the alley. At the other end, his chef placed three shoeboxes containing the race's semi-tame competitors.

There was a time, not long before, when Helen and I would have brought this proceeding to a halt by our mere presence. As the only foreigners living in the area, we wouldn't have stuck out more if we'd just stepped off a flying saucer. That we were only in our twenties, and were furthermore an eclectic American-English combination, made us all the more unfathomable. But by then we'd been around long enough for the indigenous life-forms to realize that we'd come in peace. We stayed in the background and observed. Helen bent toward me.

"What do you think?" she said quietly.

"I think the skinny one. He looks lean and fast."

"No, what do you think we should do with the money from our capers?" Propped against my leg was a sack loaded with them. The ground beneath the almond trees on our farm was covered in caper bushes. Fortunately, someone pointed this out to us before we could mistake them for weeds and dig them up. Even when we knew what the bushes were, we didn't know at first that the bit you pick and eat was the unopened flower bud. The sad truth is, we didn't know anything about farming at all.

We had bought our dilapidated farmhouse in a remote corner of southern Spain to escape ordinary working lives offered by our American and English cultures. Back home there never seemed to be time to get off the treadmill and confront the nagging feeling that there should be something more to life. It was the search for that elusive "something more" that had brought us here. An unexamined logic told us that to get off the treadmill, we had to get off the beaten track. We followed that logic so ruthlessly that we ended up with no track at all—just a shack in the middle of a field, which also happened to have no wiring or plumbing. But since there was no electricity or running water for miles around, these things seemed perfectly logical too.

We greeted our new life with as much foresight as the Indians who rushed out to welcome Columbus. But there was no excuse for not guessing ahead of time that the differences in our personalities could doom the whole project from the start. Helen was a bespectacled redhead with a fondness for animals. She was into organic food and scorned anything invented after 1900. It's not that I didn't share many of her principles. It's just that in practice it's a lot easier to stop by the organic counter at Safeway than it is to grow the stuff yourself. She had a vague idea about rediscovering nature by living off the land. To me, "nature" meant bad weather and wild creatures eating each other. What I hoped to discover was a more laidback lifestyle. I wanted to cheat; to skip the treadmill altogether and go straight to a *very* early retirement. Here was a proposal to get there that I couldn't immediately see the holes in. What could be hard about growing almonds? They grew themselves, right? It's fair to say we were both in for the odd surprise.

As two young suburbanites, neither of us had any conception of how *unnatural* nature would seem when we finally encountered it. Especially the unfamiliar Mediterranean variety. We certainly weren't among that breed of escapee who already knows one end of a goat from the other. Nor did we have enough cash to live like colonials with our own army of local laborers. Before this, my only experience of roughing it was camping as a child in my parents' garden. Suddenly, we found ourselves in our farmhouse and it felt like we'd fallen three hundred years through time to the preindustrial age. I wanted to claw my way back, but it's not easy getting motivated in a culture that advocates a big boozy lunch followed by an afternoon nap. Lying there in the hot breeze, bloated with food and wine, the temptation to postpone digging a cesspool became damn near overpowering. If you're considering an alternative lifestyle of your own, our story will prove instructive only in that it shows how *not* to do it.

"I suspect the tab for Diego's drinks is going to match what we'll get for our capers," I said, pointing back into the restaurant, where our neighbor lay slumped over the bar. Diego was ostensibly there to help us sell the capers to a market trader called *Señor* Velázquez. We knew all along that his incentive was a trip to town and the chance to stop for a few brandies on the way.

"I don't see why we should pick up the bill; we've only had one black coffee between us," said Helen.

"We can't make *him* pay," I said. "After all, he's doing us a favor."

"Some favor!" She rummaged through her purse bleakly. "I want to buy seeds with this money, if there's any left." There was a stir as the chef and his two assistants prepared to simultaneously release the lids on the shoeboxes. We could hear the rats scrabbling to get out.

"Come on, my beauty!" the restaurateur called out, rubbing his hands together.

"Seeds? I was hoping we could take what's left and eat out for a change."

"Be serious," she said. "This is the only restaurant in town. Where do you think the rats come from? Besides, we need to start making our farm pay or we're in big trouble." Our attention was diverted by the uproar as the race began. In a matter of seconds it was over.

"I wonder if the fat one is fat because he always gets to the food first," I said. The skinny loser tried to take a bite out of the winner's tail as a consolation. We went back inside and at-tempted to stir Diego. He was snoring loudly and our efforts to rouse him only resulted in some mumbling before the snoring resumed.

"Fantastic. We'd better try this again another day," I said.

"No, we've got to sell them while they're fresh," she replied.

"But we need an introduction from Diego, to give us credibil-ity. Although in his current state, it probably wouldn't give us much. Without him I know we'll get robbed."

"Well, we could drag him along but they could take our house and car before he'd bat an eyelid," she said. "We know what this man looks like. Let's go meet him on our own."

"I'm in favor of postponing," I insisted. "Do *you* have any idea what a sack of capers is worth?" Her vacant look answered me. "Neither do I. In any case, lugging that sack around is turning me into a hunchback."

"So you don't want to bring it back another day then, do you?"

"Good point," I conceded. "You win."

We set off along a winding row of houses with red tile roofs and black iron balconies. The sun glared off the whitewashed walls under a blue Spanish sky. I give you this description from mere glances, because at the time I was bent double, staring at the ground with a sack on my back. I finally got to put it down when we reached a little square with a fountain and the cooling shade of some trees. At one end lay the indoor market, fes-tooned with sausages, cheeses, fruits, and vegetables. This was where we expected to find our man Velásquez. It was normally abuzz with bartering and sales pitches—but not that day. We stared in bewilderment through the closed gate at deserted stalls. There was no sound other than the languid movement of leaves in the breeze.

"It's never closed on a Friday," said Helen. We looked around and noticed there was no sight or sound of humanity in the vicinity. The whole village seemed shut up and deserted. "Even on a Sunday there's a few people about." There was a wobble of fear in her voice. It was one of those unnerving moments when it's scary to be a foreigner. Everyone knows something you don't. You can't help suspecting you're about to make a fool of yourself. Like the first time the two of us ate out in Spain and calmly ordered a set dinner for ten people by mistake. We couldn't think of a reasonable explanation for the evacuation of the village.

"Outbreak of the plague?" I suggested. A braying donkey drew our attention to a lane leading off the square. A hundred yards farther down there was a cross street where a family hurried by, driving its livestock. They certainly looked like refugees on the move. Helen and I exchanged a glance and then I heaved the sack onto my back and we set off after them. When we got down there the street was empty except for an impressive trail of animal droppings of all varieties leading away around a curve. Pinching our noses and trying not to step in anything, we followed this unpleasant trail over the crest of a hill and around several corners until we finally found ourselves outside the church. A large number of animals were tethered to every available railing and lamppost. A hubbub of braying, barking, chirping, and grunting filled the air. We'd been told this was a day to bless animals. What surprised us was that the animals were expected to show up in person. We hadn't guessed what a big deal it would be in this rural community. A hassled priest stood at the door talking to a few two-legged latecomers and shooing away the occasional four-legged stray. As we approached, he regarded my sack suspiciously.

"I'll bet *Señor* Velázquez is in there," said Helen. "It shouldn't take a minute to find him. The service isn't ready to start—look, other people are still arriving. Anyway, wouldn't it be fun to go in and see all the animals?"

"I can't take this sack in there," I told her. "It's a church."

"Why not? I just saw a *donkey* go in."

"Yes but it's St. Francis' Day, not harvest festival. We don't want to be disrespectful. We're not even Catholics."

"Oh well, leave it outside then," she said with irritation, "but for God's sake, let's find him and sell the damn things."

I leaned the sack against a wall and we went in, nodding apologetically to the priest, who had been watching us and our cargo with distrust. Every variety of farmyard animal was represented inside as well, and these delegates were all having their say. An organist struggled to stay on key in the background. The donkey chewed a hymnbook and a woman shrieked as her panicking cat dug its claws into her chest. An old man and a choirboy chased a pig around the altar. We scanned the pandemonium but failed to see our man.

"You cross the aisle and take the left side; I'll take the right," I said in an unnecessarily lowered voice. I hadn't gone far when I recognized his balding head, thankfully at the end of a pew. I tried to signal Helen discreetly but she was stuck behind an elderly lady dressed in black, who made the sign of the cross and slowly genuflected before moving on. When it was Helen's turn, she looked about uncertainly, crossed herself in a gesture resembling a karate chop, and then curtsied. Fortunately, she saw me waving and headed back, this time just dashing across the aisle with a bowed head. Judging by *Señor* Velázquez's faraway expression, he appeared to be transported to some higher place. He looked startled when I crouched beside him. "I sorry to break your prayer," I apologized in fractured Spanish. He told me he'd actually been looking at a pretty girl in the front row and thanked me for saving his soul.

"Bag caper outside," I said. He stared at me like I was some kind of moron. After several "whats?" from him and several repetitions from me, we brought in the neighboring pews for consultation. They told me to come to the market in the morning if I wanted to buy capers. "*Sell* caper!" I exclaimed, pointing to the door.

Finally he shrugged and got up to follow me. The woman sitting next to him twirled her finger against her head and then indicated in my direction. As we went out, the priest looked at his watch impatiently and then inspected us through narrowed eyes. Fortunately, another group of latecomers—some gypsies—was just arriving. Outside we couldn't at first find our lovely capers. Then we saw them—spilled out across the ground. Three goats stood over what was left, gorging themselves. "Ah!" *Señor* Velázquez's eyes lit up with understanding. He shrugged again and touched my shoulder sympathetically. "Maybe next year?" he said and turned to go back inside.

The priest and the gypsies were still standing there, staring at us. I suddenly began to wonder what I was doing in this strange foreign place. I could guess from their expressions that they were wondering the same thing. Normally I didn't contemplate life too deeply because I told myself I'd worked it all out a long time ago. But at moments like this, I realized with terrifying clarity that I hadn't worked out anything. We'd come to Spain on vacation. I could see that I needed to sit down and think about why we'd never left.

2

Running Away

I know one or two born optimists who can find something good in every situation and always have a positive outlook. Yet we were having an English winter so dark and grim that even these people were moping around filled with angst. It'd been so long since the sun had come out that we probably wouldn't recognize it if we ever saw it again. As I sloshed through puddles on my way home from the doctor one evening, I was already asking myself why I was putting up with it. I'd gone for medical advice about a bunged-up nose that wouldn't go away, only to be told that damp was the cause. "In a manner of speaking, you're allergic to England," my doctor had told me.

I could add this to the cultural schizophrenia the country had already given me, having been raised there by two American parents. My mother was a farm girl from Kansas who had spent her life trying to get as far away from Kansas as possible. She figured England was about far enough. She and my Michigan-born father first crossed the Atlantic so he could do a Ph.D. in Elizabethan Drama. They stayed on and he began writing screenplays for the dwindling British movie business. When big success finally came with *Gandhi* in 1982, he moved on to Hollywood and she remained in England.

The result of this mixed Anglo-American influence was that I never knew whether to react to the lousy climate with a stiff upper lip or a pouting lower one. I spent my youth wondering whether I was an American kid growing up in England, or an English kid growing up in an American house. My classmates called me a yank and mocked the way I talked. By my teens, I'd learned to talk with a British accent, just in time for my parents to ship me back to the States to go to school—where I was mocked for the way I talked all over again. I believe that "mid-Atlantic" is what people like me are called, and mid-Atlantic is what it feels like. Since I didn't feel wholly at home in America *or* England, I was quite ready to go to Spain or someplace else and not feel at home there either.

Feeling downtrodden and soaked to the skin, I finally reached the house Helen and I shared with her mother, Rita. In principle it was shared. In practice we lived in one room and made sorties into the kitchen and bathroom. Somehow Rita left her presence in the other rooms even when she wasn't home. Helen put it down to witchcraft. I walked in on a heated discussion. "I don't know how you dare complain about a lack of space," said Rita. "Frankly, I think it's disgusting the way you two insist on doing it where everyone can see."

"What's disgusting is you standing at the bottom of the garden and staring up at our window," said Helen. "I know you haven't had it for a while, but really . . ." I didn't like the sound of this so I closed the front door quietly and began to tiptoe toward the stairs.

"And the moaning—it's like living in a haunted house. I'm surprised I can get any sleep at all."

"You do exaggerate, Mother. You must be getting *some* sleep because you snore like an asthmatic bear. Oh hello, Shaun, we were just talking about you." I froze on the bottom step and slowly turned to see them both looking at me through the living room door.

"Evening," I murmured.

"Tell Helen she should listen to her mother."

"Tell my mother to mind her own business," said Helen.

"Well . . . I . . . Awful weather we're having, isn't it?" I offered hopefully.

"I was just saying that you surely have enough money now to get a place of your own," said Rita. "What was that thingamajig you did for that big company?"

"We built a database," I said.

"Since your business strategy seems to consist of sitting in the pub all day, it amazes me that you even got *that* job," said Rita.

"It amazed us too," I confessed. We'd met at university and found that our shared distrust for "the system" made us feel like comrades in arms. I can't vouch for what else she saw in me, but I fell for the way her hair hung over her face, the beginning of a smile always at the corner of her lips—profound stuff like that. Still together after university, our only ambition was to avoid following orders, so we made up our minds to be self-employed. Self-employed *what* didn't really matter, but ultimately we decided to pose as computer consultants. Actually, Helen was the computer whiz. Finding the "on" switch was about the limit of my expertise. I had just enough experience on the college paper to masquerade as a researcher and writer of support documents.

We were both determined not to have conventional careers, although we didn't have any firsthand experience of what a conventional career was. It was enough that our more industrious friends had warned us about them. Helen had some plausible-sounding objections to the workaday world, which had something to do with saving the planet from environmental destruction. I had no such excuse. I was just trying to save myself from grown-up expectations. I didn't get a lot of help choosing a future from my parents. Being a Hollywood player isn't something you realistically put on your list of career goals. And my mother was so down-to-earth that she didn't care what I did, as long as I was happy. I was happiest in the pub.

So far I'd done little more than drop out of every job and turn down every opportunity that was offered to me. At that time I had no idea what I was running away from; I just knew it was still there. It hadn't yet dawned on me that I might be trying to flee something that was inside. I was still young enough to philosophize that the idea in life was to do as little as possible, drink beer, go to parties, and get away with it for as long as I could. My lack of direction left a void in which Helen's only slightly less fuzzy ideas could reign. When we advertised our services we were very surprised, and not a little disappointed, when someone actually called our bluff and hired us.

"We could buy a mid-range sport utility vehicle with the lump sum we got," I suggested, "but it wouldn't stretch to a greenhouse with the price of real estate in this part of the world."

"A bank mortgage is ruled out on principle," said Helen indignantly. "We're not encumbering ourselves with those chains."

"Since we're now once more a couple of unemployed bums,"

I chipped in, "the bank's likely to rule *us* out on principle any-way."

"Well, just because I'm your mother doesn't mean you can take the rest of your life off at my expense." Rita turned from her daughter and glared at me. "It's time you sorted yourselves out and did something mature and responsible." With that, she marched out of the room.

"She wants us to leave, and I think she's serious this time," said Helen. I groaned.

"That means paying rent or stumping up for a mortgage."

"Either way, it means getting a sensible job," she said gloom-ily. My nose was bunged up again. I had a strong desire to be somewhere—anywhere—else. I could feel one of my periodic transatlantic migrations coming on, but I was attached to Helen and she'd be unlikely to get a green card.

"What I'd like to do is just pack up and go someplace sunny," I intoned nasally. There was a pause while her eyes slowly fo-cused on some faraway image.

"That's it!" she cried. "Before we commit ourselves to any-thing, let's take a vacation in the sun. It's off-season now—I bet we could rent a Mediterranean villa all winter for the price of two weeks in the summer. We'll sort out this mess when we get back."

"I hear Spain has the most reliable weather," I said dreamily. "And apparently the beer's dirt cheap."

"Then let's go to Spain until we've spent our money," she sug-gested. "I bet it would last right through to spring." I gave her a sideways look.

"If we spend *all* our money, things'll be ten times worse when we get back. Maybe this isn't such a good idea." I slumped down in the armchair, picked up the local newspaper, and began leaf-ing through the classified section. The paper was ripped from my hands and flew across the room. She eased herself seductively onto my lap.

"We could have a whole place all to ourselves," she said. "Just imagine it."

"I know I'm not exactly Dr. Livingstone myself," I said, "but to date, you've never been farther than Oxford. You don't know what it would involve."

"We could always work on the laptop." She wriggled playfully. "Listen to you, you sound like you've got a clothespin on your nose."

"It's a lovely idea," I said, "but it's out of the question. Take it from me—you can't just go off and live abroad like that."

A couple of weeks later, I was sitting in an apartment on the Costa Blanca, squinting at the sunny view. The building was in an unbroken stretch of vacation accommodation that ran along the seafront all the way from a fishing port about three miles away. Tourism was highly seasonal there, so at that time of year it was as deserted as Miami Beach during a hurricane warning. Nevertheless, birds sang and flowers splashed bright colors everywhere. These unseasonable springlike conditions and the eerie emptiness of the resort gave us the wonderful giddy sensation that we'd fallen out of step with the world we knew. Pretty soon we didn't just feel like the last people to surrender to the rat race, we felt like the last people—period. It was inevitable that our attention would wander from this ghost town to the living Spain beyond. So it was that we first began to stumble toward our adventure.

If anyone had told me then that within a couple of months I'd be growing almonds, I'd have said they were the one going nuts. Our introduction to the language, culture, and people began inauspiciously. I foolishly ate a bar snack, which are called *tapas*, that was composed of tentacled creatures I'd only seen before in

Helen's wildlife books. The rest of the night was spent sitting on the toilet making trumpeting noises loud enough to set dogs barking in the street. One aspect of getting ill in a foreign country is the certainty that you've contracted something fatal. To a hypochondriac's imagination, even the first stages of a cold are symptoms of a rare tropical disease. The next day we acquired a dictionary and traveled into the historic fishing port to see a doctor and at least put my mind at rest. The main square at that time of day was populated with dusty old men in traditional cloth caps and rope sandals. They sat on benches smoking strong black tobacco while they talked and gesticulated vigorously with each other.

At first these locals ignored us as we took a seat and I started to look something up in the dictionary. However, they soon began to give us horrified stares and several of them moved to the other side of the square. This baffled me until at last I realized I'd been saying "bowel infection, bowel infection" over and over in Spanish in a loud, carefully enunciated manner. We thought it would be wise to put the dictionary away and move on. Nevertheless, necessity had set us on the vital step of learning the language—the key that would eventually open a strange world that lay hidden behind this more familiar Spain. Without language we could only grunt and make crude gestures like a couple of Neanderthals. When you're foreign to a place, sometimes the simplest tasks are already beyond you. For instance, not knowing the etiquette for getting attention, how to mail a letter, or whether that prehistoric crustacean is a garnish or something you're supposed to eat. This combination of gibbering gestures and apparent retardedness produced unusual reactions in people. On one occasion a woman we'd just been communicating with tried to help me tie my shoelaces.

The initial isolation from the language barrier brought us closer together than ever. The ability to communicate with each

other on at least a Cro-Magnon level was suddenly something
rare that we had in common. We didn't have that much else in
common, except compatible sexual hormones and a reluctance
to surrender to steady employment. Neither of us was madly in
love with the other, but at that age these other things were
enough. We shared a view that was both cynical and romantic in
equal extremes. On the one hand, all married people seemed to
us to be old fogies whose idea of a good time was an early night
with a cup of cocoa. On the other hand, we were each certain
that one day some "true" love would enter our own lives like a
blinding light, and that thereafter all would be right with the
world. In the meantime, we were helping each other prepare for
this epiphany, especially with invaluable lessons in how to cope
with conflict. "You're not my knight in shining armor," she told
me.

"You're not exactly my princess in an ivory tower either," I
replied. It was the kind of frankness that only genuine friends
can get away with. But moving into a hovel in the middle of
nowhere is the sort of lifestyle choice that requires a committed
accomplice. We would never have got involved in a farming venture together if our relationship hadn't bloomed during these
early days, when to each other it almost seemed we were the
only man and woman alive. I defy anyone to avoid intimacy with
someone who has had little choice but to share every past incident and present bowel movement. I could never read her
mind, but on later reflection I think she started to fall in love
with the sunshine, with the orange blossoms, and a little bit with
me. She began to say our trip to this town was "meant to be," as
if a divine guiding hand had been at work back at the travel
agency. Everywhere she looked she started to see signs pertain-
ing to our lives. Personally, I never saw any signs, and found it
worrying that God had nothing better to do than leave little
messages for her. Despite this concern, I considered her enthu-

siastic outlook endearing. I'd never been more fond of anyone. Not being the most observant person, at that point I was blissfully unaware that her own feelings for me might also have intensified.

One portent of the future that did strike both of us was our accidental discovery of a ruined stately home. We'd gotten lost one evening while strolling among the small farms and orange groves that lay half a mile inland from our apartment. It amazed us how a different world began just a few blocks from the resort. We wondered what it would be like ten miles inland—or a hundred. Trying to find our way out again, we stumbled across the ruin. It had the ornate ironwork and decoratively carved wood of the Spanish baroque style. We both fell in love with the estate straightaway—she because it had gone wild, and I because it looked like the kind of place you'd live in if you were rich enough not to worry about a career. The grounds were overgrown with Mediterranean fruits that Helen said she wanted to grow and I said I wanted to eat.

We spent an hour picking our way through those ruins, disagreeing over what we'd do to them if they were ours. It's an understatement to say I'm no good at fixing things. If something needs repairing, my primary gift is to get someone else to do it. But this place lured me like a child to a sandbox. Against my better nature, I wanted to roll up my sleeves and get to work restoring it. Imagining ourselves living there started a dangerous train of thought. Had I known where it would lead, I might have run off to lie on the beach and pop open a beer instead—like the vacationer I was supposed to be.

Having no inkling of what lay ahead for us, I had only bothered to learn the Spanish I needed to keep from starving to death or getting botulism. However, trying to find our way back from the ruined *cortijo* that evening convinced me that this strategy was not, after all, sufficient for survival. We'd just got onto a vaguely familiar path when we had a strange encounter. Helen was the first to spot a bright blue exotic bird in the branches of a tree. My ignorance of handyman skills is matched only by my stupidity when it comes to flora and fauna—but even I could tell this bizarre creature was no European species. The Spanish are nuts about singing canaries and other caged birds, so we figured it must be an escaped pet.

The domestic pet theory was validated almost instantly because it suddenly took off and headed straight for me. Horrific visions from an Alfred Hitchcock movie flashed in my mind. Though I ducked and bobbed, the bird landed on my head. I shook it off frantically only to have it reland. The parrot, or whatever it happened to be, was determined. No matter how much I darted or swayed, it fluttered around me until it had found a landing area. Some people might find the idea of birds walking all over them delightful. For instance, as I was flaying at the thing, Helen said she wished it was happening to her. She couldn't do anything about it at the time though, because she was bent over laughing—at me, I believe. In the end, I was forced to run away with Helen hobbling after me, clutching her sides.

We hadn't gone very far when we came across a typical small farmhouse. I thought it reasonable to assume that the bird might have escaped from there since it was the only house nearby. It had the usual bright white walls under a terra-cotta tiled roof. A middle-aged woman in an apron happened to be sweeping the front patio, so I stopped with the intention of helping her recover her bird. Unfortunately, the only Spanish in my vocabulary that had any bearing on what I wanted to say was the word "blue." Having got the woman's attention, I proceeded to point back up the path and then flap my arms, saying "blue, blue." Pretty soon she was joined at an upstairs window by an old man who stared at me and scratched his bristly chin. I could see they weren't getting it so I elaborated my act to include jumping up in the air while flapping my arms for a more birdlike effect. This too had little impact other than to add a small boy and a barking dog to my audience. All four of them looked on in amazement.

A rethink was called for. I got Helen to pretend to be me while I ran from the orange groves and proceeded to dance around her, waving my arms and saying "blue, blue, blue" in the manner of a chirping bird. An ornithologist couldn't have done it better. Although the dog and the child thought this was great, the woman had clearly had enough. Under a babble of what I could only presume were obscenities, she proceeded to chase me off with her broom. For the second time that evening, I found myself on the run.

From then on I seldom went out without clutching our dictionary in my hand like some born-again linguist. I had to learn a couple of new words every day just to stay out of trouble. Despite the traumas of the bird incident, the lingering image in my head that evening was the abandoned *cortijo*. Helen must have been right about it being enchanted because for several nights all my dreams were set there. She told me she was having the same reaction. A few days later we spotted the office of an estate agent in town. "I wonder how much that ruin is worth?" I said.

"Why don't you go in and find out?" she suggested.

"Oh, right," I said, recalling the parrot fiasco, "I'll just walk in there, pretend to be a house, and then fall down on the floor, shall I?"

Fortunately, the agent's young secretary spoke some English. We inquired how much the tumbledown house cost and found out it might as well have been a Rothschild castle. Winning a house in a prize draw seemed more likely than being able to buy

even a ruined one with our budget. Then one day we were
strolling past a shuttered beach bar when something caught
Helen's eye. It was a faded poster that was written in English. "I
don't believe it," she said, cleaning her glasses and having another look. "This says there are rustic properties for sale from
fifteen thousand dollars."

"In London you'd be lucky to buy a parking place for that
price," I said.

"Why don't we go have a look?" she suggested. "It would be
fun if nothing else." With visions of the stately home in my head,
I called the number on the poster and spoke to an enthusiastic
Englishman called Ron. He lived in the city of Murcia, a couple
of hours to the south, but his cheapest properties were even farther south in the dry region called Almería, where Clint East-
wood shot his spaghetti westerns. This was our chance to see the
real hinterland. The next day we rented a car and set off for the
town of Albox, where we'd agreed to meet.

Like many towns in that part of the deep south, Albox possessed an impressive bridge. The strange thing about these
bridges was that they spanned nothing. In Albox, where there
should have been a river, there was in fact only a dirt car park. In
some towns we'd pass a bridge large enough for the Mississippi,
soaring over a trickle no bigger than the one I make when I wash
my car. I figured a band of unscrupulous door-to-door bridge
salesmen had passed through the area, convincing people that
what they really needed to put their town on the map was a fine
bridge. The natives told me to come back after the spring rains.

Albox showed few signs of having a tourist industry during
any season. We felt as if *we* were the sights, and I drew so many
looks that I checked to see that my trousers were zipped. Ron
was to meet us at a café that had as much charm as a truck stop.
There were plastic tables under bright fluorescent lighting, with
soccer team calendars and pictures of yet more local bridges on

the walls. But sitting at a table outside in the historic street and basking in the sunshine, it could have been the Ritz at Saint-Tropez.

The remoter the town, the more religiously old traditions are observed. One such tradition is that lunchtime should run all the way from one in the afternoon until five, and include a nap—the famous *siesta*. Now this was the kind of civilization I could appreciate. While the rest of the town ground to a halt, the café offered a three-course "menu of the day" to help pass the time. That's all they had, so there was nothing for the mustached waiter to ask except how many were in our party. The waiter was obviously the son of the man behind the bar inside, and it was his mother bringing out food from the kitchen. So, despite the decor, it was a bit like having dinner at home. This atmosphere was further enhanced by the lack of choice and the fact that the food was pretty basic. Mother seemed to be watching us to see if we were eating it all. I worried that if there were any vegetables left on my plate, I wouldn't get dessert.

Feeling stuffed and sleepy, I was settling the bill with the waiter when Ron arrived. An antique Land Rover coughed and sputtered to a halt in a cloud of dust in front of the café. The door opened and out squeezed a chubby, baby-faced man running with sweat. We could tell straightaway he was English because he clearly had no idea how to dress in this climate. He had on a tie, and although he wore shorts, they nearly overlapped the wool socks that were pulled up to his knees. I was disconcerted when he came bounding straight toward us because it confirmed that we must have stuck out just as much as he did.

"Stephen and Heather, isn't it?" he said, vigorously shaking my hand.

"Shaun and Helen," I corrected him.

"Quite, shall we get started then?"

As we piled into his Land Rover, the waiter caught my attention. He pointed at Ron, shook his head, and rolled his eyes up to heaven. I was puzzling over this gesture when the old Land Rover jerked forward. The vehicle seemed to go up and down almost as much as it went forward. This was unfortunate since I'd ridden bicycles with more seat cushioning. We seemed to be going very fast considering how much the vehicle shook, but a glance at the speedometer revealed we were barely clearing thirty miles an hour. Ron headed out of town on a narrow road, and pretty soon we were in a desert wilderness. There was a rugged beauty about the place, with broad vistas to sculpted hills reminiscent of the deserts of southern California. I expected a band of Apache Indians to come riding out of the shimmering haze at any moment. "Right, there are several farms in this area," he announced.

"There are?" I said, scanning the seemingly empty landscape.

"If it's a real bargain you're after, I've got five acres going for ten thousand dollars just a few minutes from here."

"Five acres!" Helen's eyes expanded to frightening proportions behind their lenses. "Shaun, we've got to see it." Ron turned the vehicle off the road and set out across the barren wasteland. Now we were really bumping along. Ron had the advantage of more natural padding in his derriere. Nevertheless, by the time we stopped, we were all so sore that even he could only limp delicately. We were deep into a lunar landscape. An abandoned stone shed stood in the middle of a rock-strewn desert.

"What exactly did they farm here, pebbles?" I said.

"Goats." Ron bent down and pulled up a handful of scrub. He spread his arms as if to show we were in an ocean of food. "They'll eat anything. I can just see you two here with a very successful herd." He was the only one who could see it.

"Er, where are the boundaries?" Helen squinted into the distance.

"Who cares about boundaries out here?" said Ron. "Any other questions?"

"Yeah," I said. "What else have you got?" Off we bumped to a succession of similar properties. Each time the stone shed was a little bigger and the price a little higher. "This is all great," I said, "but we imagined we might see something within a hundred miles of a water supply, and recognizably a farmhouse. I'm not expecting a little picket fence and a rose garden, but some windows and a door would be nice."

"Ah, now we're talking." He giggled gleefully. "I have exactly the place for you." Soon we found ourselves outside a small farmhouse with an underground water tank, a dozen gnarled almond trees, and a denser spread of scrub. By now we were all walking like people who have recently had hemorrhoid surgery. I'd just reached the door of the place when Ron said: "This costs thirty thousand dollars. Mind you, there's no land with it. The almonds belong to someone else."

"I think we've seen enough," I said dejectedly, and turned to begin the slow shuffle back to the vehicle. We bounced and shook back to the coffee bar in Albox as evening was drawing in. Despite his own discomfort, Ron's enthusiasm had not been dampened.

"Give us a call if you change your mind," he said and nudged me like an old buddy. "Remember, we're only two hours' drive from the sea!"

"You should get your suspension seen to," I said, nodding at the truck while I rubbed my bruised behind.

"Oh, that's nothing to me," he said, wincing unconvincingly. "I used to be an officer in the marines." I looked at his portly figure and had my doubts. He disappeared in a self-generated dust storm and I felt a touch on my arm. It was the mustached waiter from the café.

"The English *señor*, he is bad man," he said, pointing after

Ron. "He pays *nada* for desert land and sells to foreigner for big money." I asked him how much the land we'd seen should cost. "You buy in desert for nothing," he said. "A real farm with good land and water you can buy for twenty to thirty thousand dollars. My brother-in-law is estate agent." I accepted his card with weary distrust.

It was an uncomfortable journey back to the Costa Blanca. Having dreamed of discovering another beautiful stately home set in lush orange groves, you can imagine that we were a tiny bit disappointed. Nevertheless, we had to concede that it was still fun and interesting exploring a new part of Spain. Little did we understand that one day of looking at properties was like one "shot" of crack cocaine. We were already damned into an addiction. With little better to do, browsing cheap houses was to become our vacation hobby. And it was always tempting to try to see ourselves living there—even with only rocks and goat food around. Helen would daydream about growing her own food and living at one with nature; I would try to picture myself sitting with my feet up on the porch, safely removed from any challenges posed by others' expectations—or my own.

Brother-in-law or no, we decided to go back to the remote Almería region, and to our surprise the Albox waiter's assessment proved right. Not only could we afford a house, but also farmland—in places where we didn't have to imagine we were Neil Armstrong to want to be there. Now the dangerous train of thought really began to pick up steam. Helen started to believe that living off the land was seriously within her grasp. Meanwhile, I was quite happy to give full consideration to the life of leisure I envisioned. Having a marginally more practical plan, she tended to set the agenda. She also understood how I worked: I could be persuaded to go along with pretty much anything if it got me off a life of being told what to do and when to do it. She began to sell me on a self-sufficient farm as an alternative to going back to England to work. The way she explained it, all we'd have to do was sit back and nature would take care of everything. For all I knew, she was right. It certainly sounded great. There seemed to be plenty of other farmers around, so it couldn't be all that bad, could it?

If we'd still been in southern England, where even an attic garret costs well over a hundred thousand dollars, neither of us would've dreamed of making the commitment of buying together. But here the incredibly cheap prices and the "unreal" foreign environment meant we approached it with no more gravity than two students contemplating sharing the cost of a car. It seemed perfectly sensible to postpone the rat race and instead grow our own food while we tackled the great questions of who we were and what we wanted from life. Unbeknownst to me, one of those questions for Helen had become whether or not she wanted a future with me. She knew I had no plans to permanently settle down for at least the next fifty years, so she didn't dare tell me this at the time—fearing that if she did, I'd get on the next flight to America, or possibly China. She deflected suspicion by regularly joking that she was too young to hear her biological clock ticking and, until she did, was damn well going to enjoy herself. It was only much later that she confessed: "I thought I'd try you out."

We must have had some common sense left, because the only way we could justify our farming idea was to treat it as a big joke. There was an air of unreality about our actions, as though we both knew it would never happen. Nevertheless, we'd already started to go through the motions. Before either of us really knew what was happening, we were scrambling to set ourselves up in Spain while we still had some money left.

"There are only so many heartbeats in a life," said Helen, as if revealing a profound secret only known to her and a few Tibetan monks. "We've been using them up too quickly with all the stress in our lives." Having been on vacation for over a month, I couldn't recall what stress she was referring to. In hindsight, I think *lack* of stress may have been the problem. Normal rules of life don't seem to apply on vacation. The question of how we'd get by on a farm seemed a petty quibble. Someplace in the back of our minds we must have known the basic rules still did apply, even in Spain. But standing in the sun, looking at what could be "our place," we put them on hold. They would, of course, re-assert themselves with a vengeance.

Disturbing Nests

"**L**ook! There's a building over there," said Helen. "Is that Miguel's pickup in front of it?" She pointed at a vague shape in the dim light. The sun had just set and the winter twilight wouldn't last long.

"It'd better be," I said. "If we get lost out here in the dark, we'll never find our way back. This is the kind of place where killers come to bury their victims."

"I hope he's not going to be pissed off with us for being late. We shouldn't have missed that turn."

"We're the ones who should be pissed off!" I said. "His instructions were to turn left at the white house with the red tile roof. For the last hour *every* building we've passed has been a white house with a red tile roof."

The car bumped along a dirt track. I turned on the headlights but it wasn't dark enough yet for them to make much difference. The silhouette of the building disappeared behind rows of almond trees and then reappeared in front of us again. "Remember," she said, "it's not his fault if it wasn't on the map."

"Doesn't it make you wonder, after thousands of years of Spanish civilization, why no one's ever bothered to build a road out here?"

"He did say it was secluded," she said.

"Secluded? Columbus might have found America, but I'll bet he never could've found this place."

Thankfully, the figure leaning back against the pickup *was* Miguel. We'd met him by accident a few days earlier in a coffee bar. He worked in animal feeds and knew a lot of rural farms up for grabs in out-of-the-way places in southeastern Spain. Apparently, he was happy to drag us around for a day because he anticipated a rake-off from the owners if we bought one of these farms. Besides, he seemed to be entertained by our eagerness to grow our own food and our apparent lack of concern for any other considerations. So far we'd spent all morning looking at a variety of nondescript shacks that were about as inspiring as a lecture from Helen's mother. Finally around noon he raised his hands to heaven, cried out in exaltation, and announced that he'd finally grasped what we were looking for. Unfortunately, as it was siesta time, we would have to wait about five hours before he was available to show it to us. There was no way he was going without his lunch and a little nap.

Civilized as they might be, I was less in favor of siestas when they meant standing around half the day in a strange town where all the stores were closed. He dumped us in a dusty town where even the café was shut. We sat around near an apparently abandoned construction site and munched grapes from a paper bag. Helen wondered how Spaniards ever got anything done if they always took the afternoon off, even on cool winter days. When the sun started to sink and we got up to go, construction workers finally began to arrive at the building site. Presumably, they had let the afternoon slip by so they could come back after dark and clumsily grope around by flashlight. (And Spaniards wonder why their economy lags behind even the French.) Helen wanted to clear out before they started dropping things from the upper floors. Miguel had given us directions to meet him at the house around five-thirty. After getting lost, we were over half an hour late.

There wasn't much to see in this light but we could tell it was a two-story house with various outbuildings and almond trees stretching away on all sides. The fields were surrounded by low hills, as if the farm was in a bowl. Knowing that we wanted to plant things, Miguel was keen to tell us that the soil here was very good. Mind you, everywhere he'd showed us the soil had been "very good," regardless of how dry or rocky we could see it was.

He gestured toward the hills and invited us to be impressed with the location. As I was fast becoming a cynic, I suspected he was using the cover of darkness to sell us a dud. I'd also become cautious in what I said to him—mainly because he had the disconcerting habit of chuckling every time either of us opened our mouths. I knew our Spanish was still bad, but he reacted to even the blandest statements as though they were laden with wonderfully rude innuendos. I couldn't think of an explanation for this except that it fitted with his general amusement with us. We were foreigners and therefore weird. What we didn't yet appreciate was that our desire to buy an almond farm also marked us as slightly deranged. We'd noticed that everybody who already owned one was trying to sell it as fast as they could. This should have told us something, but we were as confident in our course as the crew of the Titanic.

There was an uncharacteristic chill in the air that evening. The countryside was silent apart from one eerie noise. Every few minutes there was a distant scream that sounded like a cat being tortured. Miguel said it was a bird. Whatever variety of bird it was, you could bet it didn't get too much trouble from cats. He turned over a rock and picked up a rusty old key that had a handle as big as a fist. This unlocked the two halves of a thick wooden stable door. "*Venga*, come," he said and led the way into one of the darkened outbuildings. I noticed that the beams of the ceiling were tree trunks—still crooked and with bark intact. Whoever built the place had been as determined to avoid unnecessary labor as I was. Some riding tackle lay on the uneven tiled floor but otherwise the room was bare.

"Be careful." Miguel tapped the low frame of the next doorway with his hand. I had to bend right over to duck through the opening. Was the place built by lazy midgets? It was so dark in the shuttered building that I could now only catch glimpses of his movement ahead of me. My hearing became extra sensitive to the sound of his steps and I noticed a strange scratching noise coming from upstairs. I was getting scared. Something touched me and I nearly lashed out in surprise. Fortunately, I'd been too stunned to do so because the touch was Helen's. She took my hand as we bowed under yet another low doorway.

"Can you hear that?" she whispered.

"Hear what?" I said, pretending to be calm.

"That noise like a claw dragging on the ceiling. I think maybe we should leave."

"Nonsense," I said bravely. "Besides, I need Miguel to guide me back through these low entrances or I'll decapitate myself." The shadowy figure in front of me had begun to mount a creaking staircase. I hesitated before following. It occurred to me that

I didn't know this man at all. Just because he looked harmless and worked in agricultural feeds didn't mean he wasn't a tourist-eating cannibal in his spare time. Jeffrey Dahmer had looked harmless too. I could feel sweat in my palm where Helen gripped me tightly. In my mind I was already trying to retrace the way out of there.

The scratching became louder as I began to climb. Miguel turned on a little flashlight and held it back toward us to show the way. The expression on his face was a mystery hidden behind the dazzling light. I noticed pellets with bits of fur and bone in them. Suddenly, the light ahead disappeared and my foot searched for a top step that wasn't there. My shoe came down with a thump and the scratching stopped.

The thin beam of Miguel's flashlight was searching out the sloped roof to our left. To our right I could see a gap in a wall behind which was a faint patch of twilight. I was relieved and Helen was reassured enough to release her grip. To give the impression that I hadn't been scared at all, I set off to explore on my own. At the gap in the wall I peered around the corner and saw weak strands of daylight coming through a hole in the roof. It took me a moment to notice two red eyes staring at me.

There was a chilling shriek and daylight vanished behind a giant pair of wings. In the sudden darkness I turned and ran. Helen echoed the scream of the creature and took flight before me. I stumbled down the stairs after her and—whack!—crashed into a low doorway and fell to the ground. For a moment I lay stunned, clutching my head. Then I realized something was chasing after me. I got up, groped around for the opening, and ran on. Finally, the dim light of the first room was visible in front of me. Then—whack!—I was lying across a threshold again, dizzy with pain. I scrambled up and staggered the last few feet. Helen watched me emerge into the evening, dragging a tangle of riding tackle around my ankle. She was already sitting on a

low wall and grinning nervously about the incident. I clutched
my bruised head and turned to see Miguel coming out behind
me with a look of puzzlement on his face.

"What happened?" he said. "You okay?"

"I hit my head," I said, hoping that would explain everything.

"There's a monster up there," said Helen.

"Oh, that's just *un águila,* an eagle," he said. To his credit, he
was gentleman enough to try to contain his hilarity this time, as
he helped free me from the riding tackle. "Nobody's lived here
for a while," he said between a grin and clenched teeth. "The
eagle's a good omen. It keeps vermin away." And potential house
buyers, I thought, as I finally shucked off my harness.

Miguel had one last chuckle as he offered to show us the
property again another day. Then we followed his taillights out
of the black emptiness of the area and back to civilization. We
hadn't seen much of the place but I found it hard to get it off my
mind. Not least because the headache lasted several days and it
was a full week before the bruises disappeared. We marked *El
Águila* on our list of visited properties and continued our search.
At that time, neither of us could predict the real impact that visit
would eventually have.

The incident nearly knocked some sense into me. For a couple of weeks I'd only look at modern apartments and only in
broad daylight. I even tried to sell Helen on a vacation trailer we
saw that had a great pitch right near the seafront. She wasn't
about to give up. "I don't want a mobile home. I want one that
stays put," she said. "Besides, we can't grow our own food in a
window box." She wasn't about to live in a broom cupboard
when she could have acres of open space. Now that we'd got the
bug, neither of us wanted to scale down our plan for a new life
as farmers. We both knew the only way we could afford the luxury of land was to head for the hills.

When the bruises had died down, I relented a little. It was
true the coastal plain was costly and had drawbacks associated
with overdevelopment. You've probably heard the refrain, "the
rain in Spain stays mainly in the plain." Well, in my experience,
the *drains* in Spain smell mainly in the plain.

We had a wonderful time going inland to explore unpopu-
lated points that had somehow succeeded in getting onto a map.
The crazy thing was that no matter how remote the area, there
always seemed to be an English, German, or Dutch Ron waiting
in the wings to offer us houses at inflated prices. When NASA finally lands on Mars, I expect they'll find one of these characters
already there and working some real estate angle. I suppose in a
land so far away from home, there was comfort in having an
English speaker give me familiar London prices. However, my
Spanish had improved enough by now to bring blurred signs
into focus and to turn incomprehensible babble into conversation. The small ads in local papers, where real bargains were to
be found, were no longer a forbidden text to me.

Since it was quantity rather than quality that impressed us,
we soon learned that the arid southeast was the only place to
look. Because of its ruggedness, it was one of the least attractive
and least accessible parts of Spain. It was a forgotten region too
far from airports and freeways to attract tourists. The European
Union had declared it an "underdeveloped zone," one of the
poorest areas on the continent. None of this mattered to us. The
lure of a big spread proved irresistible for two people used to
being confined to one room in someone else's house. This wasn't
really what I'd meant when I came to Spain in search of "something more," but by now the idea of buying a working farm had
gathered its own momentum.

Plan A was going ahead full speed; it was Plan B that should
have concerned us. We weren't at all agreed on what we'd do if
we didn't take to farming as readily as we expected. I thought

that we could always make some improvements to the place and
then either keep it as a vacation home or try to sell it for a profit.
Unbeknownst to me, Helen didn't have a Plan B and didn't want
one. Apparently, she was already beginning to feel this was our
one chance to free ourselves for all time from mortgages, commuting, and tyrannical bosses. For me, a farm would be a great
experiment; for Helen, *I* was the great experiment. She already
knew she liked gardening, so what could be so different with
farming? Personally, I'd never been interested enough in gardening to know whether I liked it or not.

For now, any potential differences between us seemed like
small matters we could deal with later. As long as we could grow
enough food to eat, we felt we'd be okay and everything else
would just work itself out. We were sure that farming would not
be beyond two graduates like us, and didn't stop for a moment
to consider that our degrees had been in somewhat unrelated
fields. Besides, we were confident that if worse came to worst,
we could fall back on our previous work. Driving down a dirt
track in an agricultural region, we felt we were probably the only
computer programmers for miles around. We were so sought
after in England it never occurred to us that there might be no
call for our skills in the remote outback of rural Spain. The
dogma of our generation stated that the geek shall inherit the
Earth. Yet most of these locals had never seen a computer and
needed us like they needed an igloo. Nevertheless, it would almost seem sensible when we'd see peasants shoeing their donkeys or shelling almonds that Helen would turn to me and say:
"I bet they'd like help computerizing their inventory."

On the question of location, as with so many things in our
lives, we scoffed at common sense. To us, the remoter, the better. Following a severe drought, there were bankrupt farms
aplenty in the hinterlands. Helen fell in love with all of them,
one after the other. She'd have happily thrown herself on the

first farm we saw. So it was down to me to be picky. Our pot of money that could have bought us a mid-range sport utility vehicle was shrinking in the direction of a subcompact. You get what you pay for, and nothing in our price range stirred anything in me except a desire to get the hell out of there as quickly as possible.

On one journey we realized we were again near El Águila. A macabre impulse prompted me to have another look in the safety of daylight. After all, Miguel had been sure this was the place for us. Miraculously, we found the turning where the dirt track branched away from the road. Our car cut through the almond trees, stirring up dust in our wake. Two peasants stopped what they were doing and stared at us with hostility. The track rounded the brow of a hill and there, spread out below us, was a beautiful basin of trees. The valley was hidden away within its surrounding hills like Shangri-la with a sprinkling of white houses amid the trees. Okay, it was too dry and brown to be Shangri-la and there was a tractor spreading manure at the time, but it was still pretty spectacular. The track descended to the valley floor, cut through fields, and there it was—El Águila.

The house itself was not dissimilar to others we'd seen. It had the usual whitewashed stone walls, clay tiles on the roof, and intricate black iron grills on the windows. However, there was something grand about this place. I think it was the way it sat in a wide space in the middle of a circle of hills. As we got out of the car, it was as if all the scenery had been laid out for our benefit. In the distance to the south, way above and beyond the near hills, were the snowcapped peaks of the Sierra Nevada. At their feet, through a small gap in the valley rim, we could see an ancient Moroccan fort glistening in the sunlight.

Helen took in my expression and beamed with pleasure. "Not bad," I conceded. I began to look around with unnecessary haste. Extending to the east side of the house was a series of outbuildings formed around an internal courtyard. The stable door we entered with Miguel had belonged to this part of the farm. Behind the house was a field of prickly pear cactus in neat rows, and in front was a circle of flat ground that we later learned was for threshing wheat. Otherwise the buildings were surrounded on all sides by hundreds of trees. These were mostly almonds but also olives, figs, pomegranates, and a few others we didn't recognize. Helen found the rock with the key under it and rolled it aside with her foot. "I dare you to open it up and look inside," she said.

"All right then," I replied and scanned the surrounding deserted fields to make sure we weren't being watched. We could see a far-off dust cloud that seemed to be getting closer. Nothing to worry about, you might think. But in such quiet and open countryside, a peasant could clear his throat a mile away and it would be hard to ignore. Helen and I both stood and watched as the cloud came closer and closer. In a few moments we saw there was a vehicle in the midst of it and Helen rolled the stone back over the key. A dilapidated white car came to a halt behind ours. The driver sat for a moment to light a cigarette and then got out. He was red faced, scowling, and slightly unsteady on his feet.

"What do you want?" he demanded in Spanish.

"You is the owner?" I replied in kind, nodding at the house.

"Who's asking?" he said. He puffed up his chest menacingly but then a look of surprise and panic came over his face and he doubled over in a coughing fit. When he'd recovered, he took another drag on his cigarette and tottered toward me. I could smell a cocktail of brandy and garlic.

"I hear the house is for sale," I said.

"So it is." He nodded to himself as if just remembering. "It's *Señor* García's house."

"You is related?" I asked.

"I'm Diego, the son of Diego." He pointed away in the distance and staggered slightly. "I live in the next house. In the country we look out for each other. So when I saw a car at Pedro's house, I came." He lifted his head proudly, thumped his chest, and appeared to be close to tears for a moment.

"We can look?" I said, gesturing to the house again.

"You can what? I can hardly understand you." He inhaled some smoke and studied me. "Are you from Barcelona?"

"No, England."

"Is that near Barcelona?"

"Not really. Two countries to the north."

He nodded his head. "I went to Madrid once," he said. "Couldn't understand them either."

"We go in the house?" I pointed at the door.

"You can't stay here!" he said, scowling again. "What do you think this is, a hotel? This house belongs to a very fine man. Just because he's now too old and frail to live here doesn't mean you can come and go as you please. I'll give you the number of his son." Diego scrawled a number on the back of an old lottery stub and waited until we'd gone. We would be back.

Despite the neighbors, seeing El Águila had the same effect on me as the ruined stately home. In my mind I was already living there. Which is odd when you think that after my first twilight visit I'd have sooner eaten slugs than gone near the place again. We met the owner's son and visited the house on two further occasions. The eagle must have decided that the neighborhood was going downhill because we never saw the bird again. The inside of the building was dusty and empty except for some broken furniture, but we didn't care. As far as we were concerned, the less already there, the more we'd put our own stamp on it. We walked the perimeter line, which was marked only by piles of rocks on each corner. There were just over ten acres of land with the house and about five hundred productive trees. We were an hour from the sea but in another world.

It seemed foolish to imagine we could afford such a glorious place. Perhaps that's why it felt safe to open negotiations. Anything above twenty thousand dollars and we could return to England with our honor intact, having been spared the commitment our fantasies demanded. When we came to the all-important discussion of price, the owner's son chewed his lip and I knew I should prepare for the worst. "Twenty thousand and not a penny less," he said. I was stunned that all this was going so cheap and stood there with my mouth open. He registered my disbelief—but completely misinterpreted its cause. "I can come down to fifteen but that's as low as I'll go," he said. "There's a small return on the almonds and you'll never have to buy olive oil." I've never been brilliant at math and I was frantically trying to see where I'd got the conversion wrong. I hadn't. It seemed such a fantastic bargain that I was literally speechless. He observed my silence and puzzled expression with growing panic. His face saddened. "Okay, I can drop to twelve thousand," he continued, "but that's my final offer—I've got elderly parents to take care of."

"We'll think about it," I croaked. It took Helen and me all of three seconds to decide we wanted to buy the place. At that price we'd even have enough left to actually live in it for a while. Hopefully for long enough to get it going as a viable farm.

On the day appointed for signing the deeds, we met the owners for the first time. Pedro García and his wife, Isabel, were an archetypal sweet old couple. I already felt guilty about how little we were giving them for their home, but I only felt worse when I saw that they were at least a thousand years old and poor as dirt. To compound my shame, they insisted on being extremely charming. Pedro was delighted to meet us and wished us the very best in his ancestral home. The implication was that we would be assuming the mantle of a long tradition. This sounded great until he told us that all of his six children had been born in the house. I suddenly wondered if I was up to the responsibility of maintaining traditions.

As we were walking into the notary's office, Pedro caught my sleeve and pulled me close so he could whisper in my ear. "Eh, young one, we have a custom here when a house is sold."

"Oh yes?" I thought he was going to mention something quaint like the throwing of rice at the new couple.

"We've put only five thousand as the price on the deed, to fool the notary," he said. "That way we both pay him less fees." He winked at me and followed the others in. I did recall reading that deed prices in Spain rarely reflected actual worth. We were beginning to learn that corruption in Spain was part of the culture, as it is in Italy. If a prime minister, the head of the country's biggest bank, and the chief of national police had all been either implicated or convicted for corruption at one time or another, then why shouldn't Pedro García get his ten cents' worth? I took my seat next to Helen, who was looking nervous. Since we were two feet from the notary, I didn't risk whispering the old man's words to her. The notary didn't waste any time getting down to business. At the pace of an auctioneer, he sped his way through the reading of the deed. When he got to the price of sale, Helen sat up suddenly in her seat.

"Five thousand? Did he say five thousand?" she said loudly in English.

"Don't worry," I whispered. "It's not a problem."

"He definitely said five thousand. We're not being swindled, are we?"

"No, I've read about this before. It's normal," I assured her. The notary was looking at us. He cleared his throat and continued.

"Wait a second," said Helen. "I'm not putting my name on anything fishy." The notary raised an eyebrow but carried on. "Twelve thousand we're paying, not five." The notary put the deeds down and looked at Helen with a hangdog expression.

"Look, I know you're not paying five thousand," he said in good English. "I'm not stupid. But please, if you want me to continue, you must at least pretend." Helen looked at me, baffled. I nodded and thereafter she didn't speak again except to confirm her name.

Before the ink could dry on the signatures, we were on the way to our very own farm. Never had I seen anything as wonderful as that gleaming white house set against rolling hills and a deep blue sky. Helen hugged me tightly for a moment and then excused herself to go to the toilet. The notary visit had been traumatic for her and she still hadn't quite recovered, despite my explanations. Besides the recorded price being different from what we'd paid, there were other disturbing things about the deed. For instance, the boundaries were only defined by who our neighbors were, so it read something like "to the north Mr. and Mrs. Jones and to the south Mr. and Mrs. Smith." You had to agree with them where their boundary ended in order to know where yours began; a pile of whitewashed rocks wasn't much of a legal guarantee. Also the deed didn't describe the land in acres or hectares but in some archaic form of measurement that nobody under the age of ninety could explain.

I was sure the eccentricities of the deed were only an aspect of endearing old Spain. While Helen was gone, I just stood there in awe while it sank in that I was part-owner of this splendid house. I could hear her opening and closing doors inside. Staring up at the sky, I noticed a few tiles missing from the roof and thought it odd that I hadn't spotted them before. I suddenly wondered what other faults I might have overlooked in my infatuation with the place. Then I saw her wave at me from a window and I waved back before she disappeared again. This drew my attention to the grill on the window, which I noticed was loose—and furthermore in desperate need of some paint. I was thinking that we would have our work cut out for us when I realized that Helen was dashing from one room to another at an ever-increasing speed.

"Are you all right? Did you find the toilet?" I called out. Finally, she appeared panting at an upstairs window.

"There is no bloody toilet!"

4

All in a Day's Work

We eventually found the toilet around the back of the house. In a thicket of bamboo, we discovered a dining chair—minus the seat—positioned over a bucket. By this time, Helen had relieved herself behind a tree. She said that had she known about the facilities, she'd have picked the tree anyway. For the first time, we began to realize what we'd got ourselves into. This house looked like a house, but it wasn't a "house" as we understood the word. There appeared to be no kitchen, no bathroom, no running water, and no electricity.

Just because we couldn't recollect seeing these things didn't mean we weren't expecting them to be there *somewhere*. It was news to us that there were houses in Europe that didn't have them. Surely we'd uncover a little cupboard containing a water pipe and an electrical fuse box? Perhaps through a door we'd missed, or behind the broken furniture? Alas, no. The couple of times we'd seen the place, we'd been seduced by the big rooms, the fireplace, the windows with decorative shutters, and clear signs that it had long been lived in. It's not that we thought we were getting a piece of suburbia; we knew it would be a little basic. After all, it was over a mile to the nearest road. And even the road was in the middle of nowhere. There were almond and olive trees in the valley, but beyond its rim was a hilly wilderness that went on as far as the eye could see.

Buying the place had been like a naughty prank that we'd dared each other to do; the first one to blink would be chicken-livered. No one had blinked and here we stood. Helen had received a letter from her mother, telling her that if she went ahead with the purchase, she'd cut her off without a penny. "She says here that if I buy a property with that irresponsible young man then I'm clearly not of sound mind."

"Oh, so it's not the fact it's in the middle of nowhere in a foreign country that bothers her," I replied. She read on:

"She also blames you for the idea of living off the land. Apparently, it's typical of your complete disregard for reality."

"Haven't you told her that was *your* idea?"

"Yes, but she doesn't listen, you know that. Mind you, I can take *some* comfort from this letter. She says that I can always count on family if my life turns into a total disaster. Although she does add that I'm not to bother her before then."

We wondered what mama Rita would say when she found out we'd already gone ahead and bought the farm. I think, like me, she never believed it would really happen. After all, it was only a vacation diversion; a game that would probably stop before it got out of hand. I now believe this is why employers restrict va-

cations to a few weeks a year. Any longer and a lot of people
would never come back. For the equivalent of about four thousand English pounds each we'd managed to buy a farm. It had
almost been too easy, except that now we were stuck because we
would need all of the money that was left to make it habitable.
As we searched for the kitchen—surely even a *very* rural house
would have a kitchen—the eccentricity of what we'd done
began to hit home. How would we ever find anyone to buy us
out? Could one actually survive on almonds and figs?

Despite this post-purchase hysteria, a part of us remained ex-
cited. As the place wouldn't be fit to live in for months, the sensible thing was to rent nearby while we fixed it up. Not being
sensible—and suddenly no longer particularly solvent—we
moved in straightaway. First we dashed up to the coast to collect
our belongings and surrender our rental accommodation. Then
on the way back we stopped off at the nearest town to the farm.
The notary had advised us to call in at the local government office to sort out our taxes. Behind the counter was a man with a
loosened tie around his neck and beads of sweat on his balding
head. In my best Spanish I said: "We buy a house and we like to
pay our taxes, please." He gave me a puzzled look for a second
and then replied:

"Yes, certainly. Do you have a tax slip from the previous
owner?" I looked at Helen. She shrugged. "Can you give me
their name in that case and their national identity number?"

"Pedro García is the name," I said and pointed to his ID
number on the deed. The man jotted this down and walked behind a frosted glass screen. We saw him pull out a file, check
Pedro's details, and then go to another file and repeat the procedure. After a couple of minutes he returned looking hassled.

"I can't seem to find the records," he said. "What's the address?"

"It has no address," I said. "There's no mail."

"No address?" he said incredulously. "Where is it then?"

"You go out of town about six miles and then turn off the road by the house on the bend. Then go along a dirt track for about—"

"Wait. This is a *casa de campo,* a rustic property?" he asked.

"It's difficult to find a house more rustic than this," I assured him.

"That explains it," he said. "Most of these households have never paid any taxes."

"Well, we want to pay," I said.

"We want to be legal," said Helen. The man sighed.

"To be honest, it's not worthwhile," he said. "If we collected from you, we'd have to collect from your neighbors. There'd be a riot. Never mind the work involved. These places are scattered all over and you've probably noticed that half of them aren't even on the map."

If I'd walked into an American or British tax office and asked to pay, I'd have been lucky to get out of there with the clothes on my back. I couldn't believe what I was hearing, but a glance at the plaque on the wall confirmed that I was indeed in the tax office. "You don't understand," I said. "We've come from England; if we don't pay our taxes, we're going to wake up at night in a cold sweat. Now, I know I'm supposed to pay and I want to pay, please."

The taxman looked annoyed with me. "It's you that doesn't understand," he said. "We can't start taxing rural properties. Most of these people are very poor. What would happen if we tax them and they can't afford to live in the country anymore? I'll tell you. The *campo* won't be tended and it'll turn to desert. What good does that do anyone? We want to encourage people to stay in the country."

"Ah, so the farms are tax free?" I said.

"I didn't say that! My advice is that you don't pay the tax." I was beginning to wonder whether this man belonged behind the counter in the local asylum.

"So you're telling me to forget my taxes?"

"That's it." I noticed he had a name badge, and the other staff in the office weren't reacting to what he was suggesting.

"So you, an official of the government, are telling me that I just walk out of here and never pay any tax?"

"More or less correct." I looked him in the eye. "Correct," he confirmed.

"Right. So I'm going now," I said, taking Helen's hand and slowly backing away, "and I'm not going to come back. Ever. And no one's going to come after me in ten years to ask for back taxes?" He shook his head with certainty. "Well, good-bye then."

"Good day."

With our taxes sorted out, we just had time to buy a few provisions and get out to the farm before dark. Being several hundred dollars richer than we expected, we bought a small gas cooker, a heavy gas bottle to fire it, and our pride and joy—a chemical toilet from the camping store. The unexpected outcome of our visit to the tax office had thrown our concentration and we were overeager to get home. As a result, we failed to buy half the things we needed. For instance, we had a blow-up camp bed but no sheets, cans of food but no can opener, and nothing to see with besides the car headlights. Our foresight was such that the absence of these essentials only occurred to us when the need for them arose.

When we got home, there was still about an hour of light left. It would've been better if it'd been moonlight—then our fantasies might have remained intact. As it was, when we really looked at it, we realized the inside of the house appeared to have been pillaged and then abandoned for ten years. There were scraps of paper on the floor, an item of broken furniture in most rooms, and a good half inch of dirt covering everything. There was no way we were going to make an impression on the mess in one evening, so we decided to pick one room to clean up and sleep in.

I've heard it said that when you move into a new property, you can generally expect a couple of surprises. It was soon clear that this place would far exceed expectations. One of dozens of surprises was the discovery that while we could fry an egg on the patio tiles at midday, we could then deep-freeze it on the same tiles at midnight. I don't know if it was the slight altitude or the proximity of the desert that was responsible for the huge temperature swing. All I know is that I had thought I was buying a house in a warm climate. We'd started to sweep out a large upstairs room that we figured would make the ideal master bedroom. After half an hour, we'd cleared a good spot. "The floor's now clean enough to eat your dinner off of," Helen announced.

"Good, because we haven't got any plates."

"Quit the wisecracks and break out the food," she said. "I'm starving."

"Let's blow up the camp bed first—then we'll have something to sit on." The instructions said "easy to inflate" but they must've been written for someone with Pavarotti's lung capacity. Lacking a foot pump, we took turns blowing into the rubber valve until we were both on the verge of passing out. Finally, we had something roughly the right shape with just enough air in it to wobble like a water bed. It was only when we stopped to catch our breath that we realized a terrible chill had descended. Helen shivered and then quickly sat up.

"Oh my God, we haven't got any sheets," she said. "We'll freeze."

I thought for a moment. "What about the small room downstairs with the fireplace?" I suggested. We both looked despairingly at what had at last become a nice wide bed and then at the low and narrow door through which it wasn't going to fit. Helen reopened the air valve, to the mocking accompaniment of a loud farting noise. While she tried to squeeze as much as possible through the door, I raced out into the sunset to gather twigs from under the trees. When I came back, she'd just finished sweeping the new room. The fireplace had a thick layer of soot and the lingering aroma of previous cozy fires. In the encroaching darkness, it wasn't hard to imagine the ghostly presence of Pedro and his family, gathered around the hearth. I placed a bundle of sticks and put some newspaper and a match under them. The dry twigs burned quickly but gave off a surprising amount of heat. The glow of their embers was the only light we had. Helen had started blowing up the bed again but paused with her finger over the valve. "We haven't got a flashlight either," she said. "How are we going to see at night around here?"

"We'll have to eat a lot of carrots," I said, handing her one. It was a testimony to how exhausted we were that we slept at all that night. The half-inflated bed offered little protection from the cold, hard, uneven floor. Even after eating, I couldn't get the taste of the bed's rubber valve out of my mouth. With no can opener, all we'd been able to do was munch on some fruit and vegetables.

When our stomachs were no longer rumbling and the fire had stopped crackling, we huddled together in a darkness and silence deeper than I'd ever experienced. If the room were drifting in outer space, it could hardly be blacker or quieter. It was so bizarre to be there in that old stone building, so far from the lives we'd always known. So far from anything, in fact. The isolation called to mind a wilderness adventure movie I'd seen; then my mind began to wander to movies about ghosts and deranged killers.

It suddenly became a little too quiet for my taste. Maybe I should at least barricade the door? Finally, I decided I had to get up and have a look outside. Helen didn't particularly want to come with me but she preferred that to staying behind on her own. Hand in hand, we groped walls and tripped over furniture until we'd found the door. We stepped out into a world before streetlamps and cars were ever conceived. There was no moon but the sky overhead was almost white with more stars than I'd imagined could be seen with the naked eye. We were both awestruck. Beneath the sky there was no sound and no light except one faint glowing point in the direction of Diego's farm. The light went on and then off, then on and off again in a quickening rhythm and finally went out for good. We puzzled over this and gazed up at the heavens until our teeth chattered with the cold.

Having shivered all night, I at last had the dreamy sensation of a warm blanket covering me. It was so real that I awoke and realized I was bathed in bright sunlight. Helen was already gone and I couldn't wait to start exploring for myself. I wanted to know just how close we were to the total disaster Rita had referred to as a prerequisite for family assistance.

There being no facilities, one room was much the same as another. I couldn't say with any certainty which was supposed to be a "living room" or which a "bedroom." At that point, I could say no more than that there were three large rooms upstairs and four downstairs; all interconnected by an assortment of smaller alcoves, anterooms, and corridors.

Before we bought the place, it seemed fairly empty. On closer inspection I discovered a lot that was revealing about those who'd lived there before. Let's just say that the Madonna picture on the wall wasn't of the pop star. It wasn't only junk and dust that Pedro had left behind; at least, not in the perspective of two kids trying to save money. I found the pieces for a wooden bed, which was fine except that one leg was shorter than the others. Once assembled, a precarious balance was maintained by the three longer legs. However, I would later discover that the weight of bodies could unexpectedly shift this balance to the shorter leg—with a loud crash. Many nights in the future, I would suddenly awake, sleepily convinced that a gun had gone off in the bedroom. That first morning I also found a pine table pockmarked after a woodworm infestation, and some rickety bamboo chairs that had clearly been made by Pedro himself. We weren't going to get an entry in *Town and Country* magazine but it would do for us.

I went around opening the shutters to let in the sun and got my next big surprise. Old stone houses in Spain seem to have been designed to keep the sun out, not let it in. I recalled a certain dinginess when we had looked around before, but figured the place just needed to be opened up. Apparently, it was already "opened up" at the time. The windows were tiny and set back in thick walls, so the large rooms remained dim. Cold nights and dark rooms? No travel guides about "sunny Spain" had mentioned this. Although shutters and doors were intricately carved and decorated, no unnecessary effort had been expended on the rest of the construction. The way the ceiling was put together was far too rudimentary for my liking. Looking up, we could see bamboo mats laid over roughly hewn logs. Upstairs, plaster had been poured over the bamboo to make an uneven surface. What particularly troubled me was the way this floor seemed to bounce as I walked on it. For a long time, I only had the courage to walk around upstairs on tiptoe.

The floor downstairs was much sturdier, with beautiful terracotta tiles—although it was disconcerting to lift these and see they'd been laid directly onto soil. Gradually, it dawned on me that the house was built by one of Pedro's ancestors and that this ancient had not been a professional builder. There wasn't a single straight wall in the place. If you picked away the plaster coating on the walls, you could see they were made of rocks with straw stuffed in the gaps. It was only a short step up the evolutionary ladder from a termite mound. Yet he wasn't taking any chances on his handiwork falling down. In fact, being nearly a yard thick at the base, the walls probably could have withstood an artillery attack.

While I inspected the house, Helen had rushed straight to the land. I went outside and found her at the edge of the patio, lovingly pushing seeds into tiny finger holes in the soil. "I thought this would be a good place for the vegetables," she said. Being only ten feet from the door, it was at any rate convenient.

"You couldn't have gone a bit farther away?" I said. "Why spoil this majestic view with a scruffy old vegetable patch?"

"Don't come on like the lord of the manor with me," she said. "Why should it be where *you* want it?"

"We've got ten acres! But this is our only patio—it would be nice to eat dinner out here without the smell of fertilizer."

"Listen buster, I can decide where to put things as much as you can."

"All right, but couldn't we at least discuss what we're going to do to the place?" I said. "If we each do our own thing, it's going to end up looking ridiculous."

"Let's talk about it over breakfast," she said. "You're always grouchy before you've eaten." We brewed up some coffee and brought a table and two chairs onto the patio. Spreading off to our east was the drunken neighbor's land, the bulk of the valley, and its spring. In the other direction there was nothing but our own fields and a ridge of hills. This ridge eventually curved around us to both north and south. We knew there was one house between us and the hills in either direction, but we could only see these other farms when we were descending the track into the valley.

The trees were fairly spaced out but there were enough of them across the valley to give the impression of a canopy of green spreading out in all directions. In the background, the cicadas provided their nonstop daytime accompaniment; well, almost nonstop. Cicadas were like an intruder alarm because if they fell silent, you knew someone or something was approaching. The only other noises came from the occasional singsong call of a distant goat herder, or the grasses, which moved and sounded like gentle waves on the sea. Otherwise, the solitude of the valley was as complete by day as it was by night. There were no roads, no cars, no electricity pylons, and no other houses in sight. Just trees against a backdrop of rugged hills. We could have been in any century of history since the Stone Age. A light breeze rippled through the valley but time hardly seemed to move at all. For the first couple of days, our lives went in slow motion. It was a dramatic contrast with London, where standing still for a moment made me fear that I was missing something terribly important.

Unfortunately, the scene of tranquility only lasted about five minutes that morning. We agreed on a compromise spot for the vegetable patch and were just about to eat some sticky rolls when the flies found us. After several minutes trying unsuccessfully to swat them away, I was getting so agitated that Helen suggested it was better for my health to retire indoors. Having found us, it appeared the flies would not leave us alone until the last sweet crumb of breakfast had disappeared. Despite her advice—and the unfavorable odds—I decided to kill them all. I determinedly chased one fly around the yard with another three sitting on my back. Finally, I realized they were winning and gave up. We finished breakfast inside.

If life moved slowly for me those first couple of days, then it had ground to a complete halt for Helen. She decided that half an hour's planting was enough to start off with and sat down with a good book to appreciate her new surroundings. Having quibbled over where our vegetables should grow, I gallantly took up the task of digging over the new patch. Since our plan called for feeding ourselves within the next few months, I felt we'd better get started. But any notion that I was in for a day of leisure was soon dispelled. The ground was like concrete, except concrete usually has fewer rocks embedded in it. By lunchtime I was coated in a paste of dirt and sweat. What I really needed was a shower.

Let me be quite clear on the plumbing situation: Not only was there no toilet, but also no taps to wash your hands, no sinks to clean dishes or clothing, no bath to wash yourself, and no drains to take waste water away. We had walls and a roof. That's it. Every drop of water had to be lugged in from a well and carried out again when used. The best substitute for modern sanitation that we could quickly come up with was an odd variety of plastic containers. We even bought a plastic tub for bathing, which was just big enough if we stood to attention and didn't move. Otherwise, it would topple and take us with it. This small tub suddenly seemed huge when it was time to empty out what felt like a couple of tons of soapy water.

The well was a white structure with a tiled roof and a blue wooden door like a dollhouse version of the main building. The door was just big enough to lean through but it was too dark inside to see anything. I was instantly struck by the humidity, which caused the walls to be slippery near the top. Opposite the door was a ceramic bowl, into which you were supposed to pour your buckets of water. This bowl fed out through a hole into a trough for watering animals.

I'd been told to gauge the water level by dropping a pebble in. I dutifully heard the pebble plop a second or so after dropping it—and realized my instructions were incomplete. What the hell did it mean? Eventually, I just tied a bucket to all the rope we had and threw it over the edge. I pulled it up again to find there was just an inch or two of water in it. I repeated this several times before realizing that the bucket must be lying on its side and floating. At this rate, it would take me a month to bring up enough water to wash my hands. So the next time I tried dragging the bucket over the surface of the water. I felt a tug on the rope and began to pull. Now it was as if a sumo wrestler were hanging on to the other end.

"Come have a look at our very own water," I called to Helen as I heaved the bucket up.

"What could be more natural and pure?" she said, excitedly hurrying over. "None of that chlorinated city junk." The previous owner had told us the well drew from a natural spring and that the water was quite drinkable. But when I finally got the bucket to the top, we found the "spring water" also came with an old sandal, a strip from a car tire, and several stalks and leaves.

"You couldn't see the bottom of a coffee cup with this in it!" I said as she peered into the well. A frog croaked in the darkness down below.

"There's something living down there, which shows it must be basically quite healthy," she said defensively. "You don't find natural life in city water—that should tell you something."

"It tells me something all right. You also don't find sandals and car parts."

"This is a natural environment. It's going to take some getting used to, that's all."

"What's natural about a tire?" I mumbled as she headed back off to the shade with her book. I could see that washing in this stuff would almost certainly make me filthier than I already was. At this point, I was ready to give up on the well and go back to England for a shower. No doubt a person with a good head for these sorts of problems would've thought of a simple solution. I managed to take an already long process and slow it down to a task of mind-boggling tedium. My idea involved straining the water through a tea towel stretched over a funnel. I poured the water through this filter into the neck of a gallon bottle gripped between my legs. Naturally, half of it ended up on the ground. Look, if I were Einstein, I wouldn't have been in a house with no running water in the first place.

I was aware that Helen was watching me with amusement from over the top of her book. Every now and then the sun would glint off her glasses when she looked my way. My pride was being bruised. I became determined to haul the heavy buckets with the minimum show of effort. Filtering the water and filling all the bottles we'd need was going to take awhile. Several buckets later, I was heaving and groaning in a tug of war with the last one when she strolled up. "Why didn't you use the pulley?" she said casually. I tightened my blistered grip on the rope, braced my leg against the edge of the well, and said through gritted teeth:

"What pulley?"

"There," she said, pointing to a smooth beam running across the ceiling of the well house. "You're supposed to pass the rope over that so it takes the strain." I figured I had just enough strength left to wring her neck, but she'd already retreated once again to the shady spot and opened her book.

By the time I had enough water to wash, I was covered in yet more dirt and sweat. Since there was no bathroom, it seemed sensible to strip off outside in the warm sun and do it there. I stood precariously with my legs together in the plastic tub, held one of the gallon bottles over my head, and poured. Only an Antarctic penguin could have taken water that cold; my scream echoed across the valley.

It's one thing to stand completely naked in a bucket in the middle of open countryside and quite another to then yell at the top of your voice. Suddenly feeling self-conscious, I quickly scanned the horizon for possible onlookers. To my horror I saw one. At the very edge of our land there was an old man crouched on his haunches beneath a tree—staring at me. I grabbed a towel, but when I looked back, he'd vanished. There and then we designated one of the rooms to be our bathroom. By the time it was ready, the bottles had been sitting in the sun for a long time and the water was warm. This was one lesson I wasn't going to forget. Thereafter we always washed up in the mid-afternoon, after the bottles had sat in the sun for a while.

In our new bathroom we had our tub to wash in while standing to attention, a table with a plastic basin and a jug of water, and finally the chemical toilet. There was only one tiny window deeply recessed in the fortresslike wall. In the winter it was chilly but it matched a cell in the Tower of London for privacy. The camping toilet was a great luxury, apart from the fact its water tank had to be filled up every day and a fresh hole dug for its output. Emptying the toilet was the worst job of all, and one that Helen left to me "because it's heavy and you're the man." A few days before, when I went to the toilet, I had simply to touch a handle and that was the last I would see of that. No more. From now on I could be seen at dusk staggering about under a heavy box that was the size of a laundry basket and smelled like a sewer. There were usually one or two flies around whenever I was outside, but I only had to come lumbering through the door with the day's effluent and a swarm would appear from nowhere.

By the time I'd swept out a couple of rooms that first day, it was getting dark and I was so worn out I could barely stand. Helen closed her book and said: "What's for dinner?"

"Are you expecting me to make dinner as well?" I said.

"As well as what?" she replied, sounding surprised. "I've nearly read this entire book while you've done nothing except muck about all day with bottles of water. If you think I'm cooking because I'm the woman, you've got another thing coming." I wondered silently if women's liberation had hit this part of Spain yet.

"Okay then, if you think I'm pulling up the water every day because I'm the man, you can forget it."

"Fine."

"Fine."

We ate cold tuna out of the can in silence that night. Later, as the chill and dark set in, necessity forced us into a truce. I could sense looming around me the hundreds of trees, the rocky ground, and all the labor that farming it would involve. We'd bought some candles that day and in their dim flickering light we scribbled out a roster of jobs. When we looked at it, there was much more to do than either of us had imagined. To fit everything in, we had to devise a military-style schedule that was enough to shatter any dream of a relaxed life. Even sharing the load, it was clear that simple things that took a couple of minutes in a modern house were going to occupy half a day here. How mankind had found the time to advance beyond the prehistoric was beyond me.

The roster didn't last too long. I found it was easier to chop the wood or pull up the water myself than it was to watch Helen's dainty efforts. Partly I think she behaved this way on purpose, just as a man who doesn't like to cook deliberately prepares something inedible when it's his turn in the kitchen. But because I had a great deal of affection for her, I quickly stepped to the rescue. In fairness, she wasn't your typical strapping peasant girl. Some of the local women looked like they could go into wrestling if the farming didn't work out. Compared to them, Helen looked like, well . . . a skinny, bespectacled computer programmer.

So we tried a new division of labor. She would keep an eye on the plants while I would take responsibility for everything else.

This seemed very fair—to her. From my end, it looked like I was spending all day doing nasty chores while she communed with nature. It's not that she didn't do anything at all; she spent a lot of time walking around the farm, stroking the trees and talking to them. I began to feel like she was the High Priestess of Mother Nature and I was the human sacrifice.

It was clear to me from Day One that my life of leisure was going to be damn hard work. I'd started that first morning feeling nostalgic about Pedro García and wondering if he was sorry to leave his ancestral home. Now all I could do was picture him in his son's house with his feet up in front of a television, a cold beer from the fridge in his hand, and a sly grin on his face.

5

Love Thy Neighbor

Apart from the old man who did the disappearing act while I showered, we didn't see any evidence of other occupants in the valley for a couple of days. Certainly no other houses were within half a mile and none were readily visible through the trees. We thought we'd found perfect peace, but it was an illusion. Our neighbors were just giving us a chance to settle in.

In such open countryside, it's impossible to sneak up on anyone—so at least we had warning when they did come. Our first visitors, Emilio and Pepe, removed any danger of surprise by singing loudly as they approached on foot. Having a combined age of over 170, they walked so slowly that we not only had time to dress but could've got some decorating done before they reached us.

Emilio greeted us with a firm handshake and a smile so warm and genuine that I felt an instant liking for him. He stood tall and upright with the bearing and manner of a gentleman. In one hand was a walking cane and he wore a dark suit and rimmed hat, both of which were dusty and worn. "Good day," he said. "You've picked a spot blessed by God to make your home. There's nowhere with finer air."

I inquired where he lived and discovered that his house was behind us toward the northern valley rim. He introduced his companion as his cousin, who was also our neighbor, but to the south. Apart from the gray hair and wrinkles, Pepe was very different from his cousin. Although naturally tall, he was stooped and his clothes were untidy. While Emilio had been extending formal greetings, Pepe was leering at Helen with a toothless smirk. When he finally gave me his attention, it was to rub his forefinger and thumb together in the international sign language for money and say: "How much did old Pedro skin you for?"

Before we could offer them a seat on our patio, and without waiting to be invited, the two of them entered the house and began to look around. "My father helped build this place," said Emilio. "All the neighbors came together to do it." He pointed his stick at the ceiling beams. "Still solid as a rock, I see. No one's lived here for over a year, you know."

"It's nice to see young blood in the valley again," said Pepe. As they went from room to room, they picked up our things and examined them. If they'd been less brash about it, I would have taken greater offense. "Is this all you have?" said Pepe, regarding the sparseness of our belongings.

"We're getting the rest of our stuff shipped from England," I said.

"We'll come back and have another look then," he said.

"Ah, what's this?" said Emilio, prodding the chemical toilet with his stick.

"It's a toilet," said Helen, and she proceeded to indicate how it worked. We left the two old men staring at it with wonder. Out in the hall I heard Emilio explain it again to Pepe, who was a bit deaf.

"You mean they go to the toilet *indoors*?" said Pepe. "Disgusting!"

Emilio gave us a tour of the rest of our house, explaining what each room should be used for. There was no question of us showing them around. When I got thirsty I found myself asking for his permission to get a glass of water. He said the cupboard under the stairs was only to be used for storing vegetables. To prevent them from rotting in the heat, he instructed us to preserve them in jars of olive oil. Things that needed to be kept very cool were to be put in a bucket and lowered into the well. I didn't have the heart to tell him I had my eye on a secondhand butane-powered refrigerator. He'd already moved on and was telling Helen that the thick walls of the house kept the heat out in summer and the cold out in winter. It was an education to hear this ninety-year-old talk, and I hoped his wisdom would change the way I looked at the place. My wisdom, based on living here one winter day, had been that the walls kept the cold in, not out.

Back outside, the two of them began quizzing me over an area of turned soil. "And what's this?" said Emilio.

"A vegetable patch," I said, rubbing my sore back at the memory of digging it.

"No, no. You can't put it here," he said. Helen and I looked at each other. "The soil's no good. The only place vegetables will grow is over there." He pointed to a field at the side of the house, far from any of the sites we'd argued over putting it. The field was empty but for one big olive tree in the middle. I could see now that the land there was shaped in hollows for irrigating and there did seem to be fewer rocks. "You must come up to my place and see for yourself how things are done," he said, tutting at my pitiful first foray into agriculture. I gratefully accepted the invitation, assuming he meant some other day. He meant straight-away and walked off, signaling for us to follow. We looked back with anxiety at our open house as we traipsed after him. "You don't have to lock up around here," Emilio said, hobbling on de-terminedly.

"So why all the bars on the windows?" I asked. So far, every place we'd seen had resembled Fort Knox. But there didn't seem much point in having jailhouse windows if you were going to go out leaving the front door wide open.

"They were put on in the civil war of nineteen thirty-six, be-cause you never knew what to expect back then."

"You haven't got anything to steal, anyway," Pepe said.

About halfway toward the valley edge, two scruffy dogs came bounding and barking toward us. By the way they leapt all over Emilio, it was clear they were his. I noticed with some jealousy that Emilio's almond trees looked neater than ours and the land beneath them was freshly ploughed. As we approached his house, there was a straight row of pines leading to the entrance. The majestic trees towered over the humble stone cottage. "Let's walk through my garden," he said, cutting across the line of trees. We entered what was almost a formal garden. A stone path led away from the front door toward a well similar to ours. The well was covered by a grapevine, and the land on either side of the path was laid out in tidy squares containing orange, lemon, plum, and other fruit trees.

"Oh, Shaun, this is what we've got to have," said Helen. I had to agree it was nice but couldn't help thinking that even if we started now, I'd be Emilio's age before our garden looked any-thing like it. I was expecting a similar abundance when we went inside, only to find the house almost as empty as ours. In the hall was a gasoline-powered machine for shelling almonds and a pile of sacks. There were pictures of saints on the wall and a small amount of handcrafted furniture. It was all a bit dusty and grim. The only room that was pristine and completely furnished was clearly unlived-in.

"This is where my son and his wife stay when they come to visit," said Emilio. "They live in Cartagena. My wife and I used to sleep here before she passed away." It had been touchingly preserved. He beckoned us to move on and sit in another room that turned out to be both the kitchen and living room. It was a small, sooty room with a stone floor, two chairs, a small table, and a massive fireplace. Pots and pans hung around the mantelpiece. A couple of stools were gathered from other rooms.

"Don't you have a butane cooker?" I asked. Emilio made a gesture of contempt.

"My son bought me one of those." He indicated behind a curtain. "Every six months when he visits, he brings me a full butane bottle. To keep him happy I use it until he's gone and then I return to the fire." He offered us a glass of strong wine made from his own muscat grapes. He poured generously from a bottle that looked as if it had been recycled many times. The glasses were filthy but I wasn't about to insult his hospitality by wincing at them. Soon we all felt much more relaxed and the conversation became animated. "Would you like another glass?" he asked. I was already reeling slightly from the first but I said "yes" because I didn't want to offend him. When the first bottle was finished, he fetched another. I tried to decline. "But I insist," he said.

Emilio was delighted that we were curious about life in the *campo*. It must have been a long time since anyone else had asked his opinion. In fact, the place was so remote, it had probably been a long time since he'd even *seen* anyone else. He rose to each question with the glee of a performer called for an encore. The almost perfect circle of the flat threshing area outside our house had been baffling me. It was the kind of oversized geometric shape that got quacks talking about alien visitations. I recall him explaining that wheat used to be spread out on the ground and a donkey tethered to the middle by a forked device that tossed the grain as it went around. Later a stone mill was placed in the center to grind flour. If there was no donkey on hand, people walked in circles turning the mill. It was, in short, a treadmill—a phrase that made me shudder with unpleasant premonition. Although Pedro had been too frail to use the circle for many years, it was so firmly trod that nothing grew there anymore. Emilio told me many other things too, some of which I thought would be useful to keep in mind. Unfortunately, we consumed so much alcohol that the next day the only thing I could remember was that there was something terribly important I was supposed to remember. Fortunately, Emilio's habit of repeating himself over the coming months eventually brought it all back. Despite this repetitiveness, he always spoke excitedly, as if sharing a secret or unfolding a fresh revelation. It's just that it would often be the same "fresh" revelation he'd given us a week before, and sometimes one we'd most recently heard just that morning.

As it began to get dark, he lit a fire and a simple lamp that consisted of a wick dangling from a tray of oil. While he talked he roasted us each a potato over the fire. "More wine?" he asked. "I have one bottle left."

"No, thank you. We must get back," I said in a voice that was beginning to slur.

"But I insist."

"We can't drink your last bottle," I protested.

"But that's what it's for—to share with neighbors. Here in the *campo* your neighbors are your family." How could I resist? The evening chill had settled outside and here we were, warm in the bosom of our new family. Nevertheless, I reached out to put my unsteady hand over my glass but he was already filling it and spilling a good deal in his own drunkenness.

Pepe dominated Helen while I talked with Emilio. I tried to listen in on their conversation and soon realized they were talking nonsense. I later discovered that Helen was too drunk to concentrate on his rough dialect and simply couldn't understand him. It turned out Pepe was deafer than we thought and was happily chatting away in the belief that Helen's nods and grins were affirmation of what he was saying. She caught my eye and said in English: "What did he just say? He keeps trying to put his hand on my knee."

"I think you just agreed to sleep with him," I said. Helen turned back to Pepe in horror to catch him gesturing the figure of a woman with his hands in the air and winking at me.

"Have more wine," said Emilio, nearly falling off his chair.

"I suppose resistance is futile?" I tried to say.

"You're welcome here," he said.

As the final bottle came to an end, we were a sorry bunch; Helen was draped over the table feeling sick, Emilio looked on his last legs, and Pepe had nodded off and half-fallen from his chair.

I don't remember how we got home. Perhaps the cold revived us because when I woke up in the middle of the night, bursting for the toilet, there were embers of a fire we'd somehow managed to make. Even at the best of times, trying to find the toilet in the dark in our place was a nightmare that made *The Blair Witch Project* look like a kindergarten picnic. Still drunk, I lit a candle and staggered off in a desperate search for the bathroom. I hadn't gone very far when a gust extinguished the light. I thought I could handle alcohol but I'd never experienced anything with the disorienting aftereffects of Emilio's potent home brew. It took me several minutes to locate the bathroom by touch alone, having first visited every other room in the house and some of them more than once. When I finally arrived, I had to piece the bathroom's components together using the blurred vision of my inebriated mind's eye. Searching around, I knocked over the table and upset a bowl of water. Finally, I stubbed my toe on the toilet and could tell by the way it sloshed about that it was already full. I just made it outside in the nick of time to relieve myself under the stars. Pepe would have been proud of me.

The next morning we were sitting inside away from the flies and nursing our hangovers when a car began to move across the valley. Such was the inactivity of the place that this rated as an event to go to the window and watch. I'm glad we did, because it was heading our way. It turned out to be Diego, the first valley resident we'd encountered when viewing the house. As he pulled up in the middle of the threshing circle, he honked his horn urgently and staggered from the car.

"Quick, you've got a fire!" he shouted, his eyes bulging from his puffy, red face. My first thought was that Helen had left her glasses outside; since the lenses were so strong, you only had to put them down on a sunny day and smoke would start rising. But when we ran outside, I instantly knew that I was the culprit. The flames were where I'd sleepily emptied the embers from the previous night's fire just minutes earlier. It didn't take long to put out but it was just as well that he'd showed up when he did. We were so dopey that day that half of Spain could have been toast before we'd have noticed anything awry. The last time we'd seen Diego, he'd come to stop us from snooping around Pedro's house. This time he was here to welcome us to our new home. He'd brought with him a small bottle of brandy that made me go green just to look at it, and a canary.

"It sings all the time," he said proudly. Sure enough, when he set the cage down, the little yellow bird started off a head-splitting trill that would give us no peace until sundown. "It's for you—a gift for your home." My hangover went into meltdown. Although it was still breakfast time, he cracked open the brandy bottle, poured himself a glass, and set about further destroying any hopes I'd had for a lazy life. "These need to be pruned," he said, surveying our ten acres of trees. "The almonds must be tended every year for a good crop, but no one did it last year so they need it all the more now. You have to do it before the spring. And they could use some mulch around the bottom. At the very least, you must plough in these grasses."

He went on to outline a series of jobs from grafting through cropping and shelling that might easily escalate into a full-time occupation. All the jobs involved with one tree could take an amateur the best part of a day, and we had more almond trees alone than there were days in the year. "Now then, when are you coming to visit my house?" he said and lit a cigarette. I didn't think I could face another boozy encounter for at least a decade, but gallantly suggested the weekend. "Nonsense," he roared. "It's the custom that you visit all your new neighbors as soon as you move in. We're at home this afternoon. Come after siesta."

"Quick, I've forgotten the word for generous," said Helen in English.

"*Bandolero*," I said. She told him he was *bandolero* for inviting us. He looked surprised and insisted he wasn't.

"Yes, very *bandolero*," she assured him, indicating the remaining brandy and the canary.

"No, really, I'm not at all," he said. "It's one of my canaries. I breed them."

"You're still *bandolero*, though," she said. He twiddled his mustache pensively, gave a puzzled smile, and left. "These people just don't know how to take praise, do they?" she said.

"I think you'll find that wasn't the problem," I said, staring down at the dictionary in horror. "I don't understand why that word leapt into my head. Must be a combination of my hangover and that mustache of his. *Bandolero* means bandit. You've been calling him a bandit."

Helen snatched the book away from me. "You idiot!" she snapped. "There's absolutely no connection between the word you gave me and the one I asked for."

"I'm sorry. It was the first word that came to mind when I looked at him."

"Please leave me alone," she said.

By that afternoon we were feeling vaguely human again when old Emilio stopped by on his way to Pepe's. It was a journey he made every day and from then on he always broke it with a small visit to us. Without fail he would materialize after the heat of the day had faded and sit with us to have a coffee and chat. On this occasion he looked extremely old and fragile, and I was quite concerned about him. "The wine," he croaked. "Usually I have one glass with dinner . . . but last night!"

The visit reminded us of our duty to call in on Diego. When Emilio had gone, we cleaned ourselves up, got in the car, and set off to navigate the dirt tracks as best we could—which wasn't very well at all. I knew how difficult it was to ignore a car moving across that empty countryside. I could imagine them watching us with bafflement as we needlessly crisscrossed the entire valley several times before finally bumping to a halt outside their house. Since Diego was in his mid-thirties, I expected him to be head of the household. In fact, he was the lowest in a pecking order that started with his father, also called Diego, then his mother, Virtudez, and finally his own plump new wife, Anna.

When English people meet for the first time, they politely shake hands and say "how do you do?." In Spain they handle things a little differently. Helen and I had barely freed ourselves from the car when various family members fell upon us, one after the other, with tight hugs and a barrage of kisses. Even the family dog joined in by trying to have its way with my leg.

Their house was next to a shady orchard of silver-leaved olive trees. On the terrace was a large pottery urn spilling over with flowers. Virtudez had already spread out her best tablecloth and laid out a couple of cakes. She seemed thrilled to have visitors and explained that it was very rare to see young people moving to the *campo*. It was disconcerting to hear that not only were there no other foreigners in the area, but even the Spaniards were moving away. I naturally wondered if they had information that we didn't. Or perhaps, like us, they'd gone in search of "something more." The elder Diego put my mind at rest by congratulating us on our farm, saying our olives produced the finest oil for miles around. In the presence of his father, the brusque Diego junior was unusually subdued, although he reeked of brandy as usual. He scowled throughout his father's lengthy praise of country living. It took me a while to catch on to the family subplot that was being enacted.

"Diego and Anna want to leave the country and live in the town," said Virtudez, inviting us to be surprised at her son's foolishness.

"At least there I can have a job that pays decent money and an apartment with electricity," he replied.

"We have electricity," said the father.

"Two lights and an hour's television a day!" scoffed Diego junior. I didn't want to be in the middle of a family quarrel so I interjected to ask about their electricity supply. "We've got a solar panel," the younger Diego continued. "Come, I'll show you around." All six of us set off in a troupe as Diego junior led the way, fresh brandy glass in hand. For someone with my limited experience of animals, it was like a trip to the zoo. In addition to their trees, the family had a herd of goats, which the father tended. In the outbuildings they kept pigs, rabbits, and chickens to eat, and the younger Diego bred canaries to sell at the market. A glance through the barn doors would have sufficed for me but he insisted on leading us through the muck and flies to inspect each beast. Helen loved it and insisted on stroking all the animals she could, and babbling to them as if they were infants.

"One day all these will be mine," Diego said, eyeing her with suspicion.

"Only if you don't move away to the town," said his father.

The house was similar to ours in construction: terra-cotta tiled floors, whitewashed stone walls, and beamed ceilings. Geraniums in pots tumbled from windowsills through the ubiquitous iron bars. They had a rudimentary kitchen with the colorful ceramic tiles the Spanish are famous for on the walls, but no bathroom. A solar panel on the roof fed a car battery that in turn lit one naked bulb in the kitchen, one in the main bedroom, and a small black-and-white television. As a concession to Diego and Anna's recent marriage, they had the master bedroom. "A new bed," said Diego as he sat on it. The headboard was pressed up against the wall and partially covered the light switch. When he bounced on the bed to demonstrate its quality, the light flashed on and off. I suspected I'd found the cause of the mysterious dim light we'd seen flashing in the distance on our first night.

The last stop was a dark room where two legs of pork were hanging from the ceiling to dry. "Each year we kill a pig to eat," said Virtudez. She went on to give us a graphic description of how they gutted and prepared the animal to make a variety of sausages using the intestines. My own intestines still hadn't recovered from the night before. Her description alone made me woozy, but things were about to get worse. "You must try our homemade sausages," she declared. Since we didn't want to offend them or do the wrong thing, there seemed no way out. I did try protesting lack of hunger but that approach didn't get me very far. We were given sausage after sausage until I felt sure I'd

be sick. As we slowly chewed each one, we got an explanation of
its grisly, gristly contents and which part of the stomach lining
had made the skin. The episode turned into a repetition of the
night before, only this time pig entrails were the offering rather
than wine. As soon as I'd finished one dish, they put another in
front of me, no matter how sincerely I declined.

"I really couldn't eat any more," I would say with an involun-
tary groan.

"We insist. You're our guest." I would guiltily cram another
one in. Finally, I could take no more, even though they were
nearing the end of their supplies. I decided it would be less rude
to walk out now than to vomit all over their kitchen. Nevertheless, despite their hospitality, I thought I registered a sigh of relief from Virtudez when we got up to go.

On the way to Diego's house, we'd passed a tidy farm of
young trees in neat rows. This we heard belonged to a retired
army colonel who divided his time between here and Murcia.
"You won't have to visit him because he's in Murcia at the moment," Anna had said. My stomach was thankful. The only other
immediate neighbor was Pepe and we felt we'd done him the
night before. So the next day we set off to catch up on a massive
pile of laundry that had built up.

"We've got to do it today," said Helen, "or it'll be unbearable
around here." Virtudez had told us about the *fuente,* or spring,
that was about a mile away. This was where all the locals did
their washing and drew irrigation water for their land. As it was
in the middle of nowhere and far from any road, I was surprised
to find a traffic jam in front of us. This consisted of two groups of
women that had come to wash clothes, one farmer, and a herd of
goats.

"Let's come back tomorrow," I said.

"No, we've got to do it today, no matter what," she insisted.

Ourselves, the goats, and the second group of women all stood around while the first group of women did their washing. After twenty minutes, they moved off and as many goats approached as would fit by the trough.

"This is ridiculous," I said. "These people may not have anything better to do, but *I* have."

"Yeah, like what?" she said. I was still working on an answer when we were joined by yet another group of women behind us. They were fascinated by us and wanted to converse. You'd think their chief interest would have been the fact we came from a totally different culture thousands of miles away. But what they found really bizarre was the sight of a man come to do the washing. This was the cause of much giggling for them and embarrassment for me. It seemed like an eternity before we finally reached the front of the line. We stepped through goat droppings and swatted flies to reach the spring, which gushed from dry rock like a biblical miracle. From the speed of the water, I could see it was going to take some knack to scrub our clothes on the rock without them getting washed away down the muddy irrigation ditch. I was conscious of the small crowd watching us, and *me* in particular. With my pride at stake, and having stood in line for hours, I wasn't about to give up.

"Shaun, don't look behind you," said Helen. It was the one thing she could've said that was guaranteed to make me look. Add to this the fact that she'd gone pale and her eyes were bulging. I turned just in time to see an enormous snake coming straight for my ankle. I froze in sheer panic, convinced I'd be bitten. Instead the snake slithered over my right foot and into the irrigation channel—apparently without noticing me at all. Helen was already packing the laundry back in its bags. "Let's go," she said. "We don't need to do this today."

I was a little peeved about the time we'd wasted and very shaken by the snake incident. We decided to drive straight into

town, get a fix of civilization, and do our washing at a laun-
derette. We'd both had enough nature for one day. It wasn't
until we got into town that we realized how grubby ourselves,
our clothes, and our car had become. After just a few days, we
managed to look like a couple of peasants having a day out.
Nevertheless, we had such a good time sitting in cafés and using
proper toilets that it was early evening before we headed home.

In the dusk I must have missed a vital turning on the track. I
knew I was close to home and could see the shape of a house up
ahead but didn't recognize the route we'd taken to get there. As
I approached the building, the barking of a dozen angry dogs
confirmed this was not our house. But before I could turn the
car around and get away, we were once again pulled from our
seats and set upon by hugging and kissing natives. We'd accidentally stumbled onto Pepe's house, where he lived with his
fifty-year-old daughter, Maria, and two granddaughters who
were in their twenties. Pepe nudged me and pointed to his
granddaughters.

"A lovely pair, eh? Which one do you fancy most?" he said.
Even though one of them had buckteeth and the other was
cross-eyed, Helen kicked me in the shin as a warning not to
reply. The next few hours followed a predictable pattern. There
were the usual questions that seemed to come from a standard
set of instructions on dealing with foreigners. One of the girls
asked us if we knew David from London, an English guy she'd
met for thirty seconds some years ago down at the coast. As
there are some sixty million Britons, it was a bit like asking an
American if they knew John from California. This illusion, that
we'd come from a land populated by a handful of intimately ac-
quainted chums, led Maria to ask us what Princess Diana had
really been like, as if we were bound to know. Pepe had heard of
Manchester United football club and was almost adamant that
we must be supporters. They were all convinced that Margaret

Thatcher was still prime minister and wanted to know why the queen wore hats that looked like teapot covers.

However, the most embarrassing questions were the elementary ones like "what do you do?" and "how long are you staying?" These should have been simple enough for any grown-up to deal with. It said a lot that we didn't know the answers. All our reasons for being there sounded like nonsense as soon as we put them into words. We didn't have much of a plan. The farm wasn't meant to be as big a commitment as it was turning out to be. So we "ummed," "ahhed," and pretended that we'd be able to explain everything if only our Spanish were better.

However crazy we appeared to be, our neighbors were happy to welcome us among them. Again the welcome included a tour of the farm, and in this case, Pepe proudly displayed a gasoline-powered electricity generator that could light the whole house. At his insistence, Maria started it up and the peace of the *campo* was shattered by a noise like machine gun fire. For half an hour we sat there under bright lights that dimmed and surged with the engine, but were unable to talk in its deafening roar. We could only stare dumbly at each other while it shook the clearly illuminated room. Eventually, it coughed and sputtered and then we were plunged into total darkness and silence. "Of course, we don't use it that often," said Pepe's disembodied voice.

The girls lit lanterns and set about making pastries that were the size, shape, and consistency of cow manure but tasted like donuts. When they brought out a bottle of wine, Pepe took fright and went off to bed. I could envision a glut of hospitality again and determined that this time I would not accept more than one round of food or drink.

"Eat, eat!" said Maria, thrusting a second plate at me.

"No, I couldn't. I'm full," I said.

"But you're my guest. You must eat."

"Really, Maria, I can't."

"Nonsense. I insist." I looked at Simona, one of the girls, for help. She laughed.

"It's the custom here to insist that guests take hospitality," she said. "But don't worry, it's also the custom for the guest to refuse."

"But I *am* refusing," I said.

"Yes, but you mustn't eat. As long as you eat or drink, we must bring you more until you're full. If you empty your glass or plate, then your host will insist you have another."

"You mean I'm not supposed to eat or drink?"

"You should have a taste but it's rude to take too much." I had visions of Emilio passing out his last bottle and Diego's family handing over a year's supply of sausages. I realized we'd made ourselves sick committing the social blunder we'd been trying to avoid. In our bid to make a good impression, we'd cleaned out one family and nearly killed two old men.

We went home and sat outside in the stars with a blanket wrapped around us for warmth. We'd only been there a few days but our conceptions of the place had completely changed. The quiet country home I was hoping for looked set to become a rural workhouse. We even had a real-life treadmill. On the other hand, the same peasants who had stared at us with hostility when we came as tourists now treated us as family. Helen summed them up like this: "They're like a woman who guards her celibacy," she said. "Cautious and cold at first, but when they finally give their love, it's total and unreserved."

Our neighbors were to play a major role in our time at El Águila. If we needed help of any sort, they were always there to give it. Without their guidance, we wouldn't have cropped and sold our almonds that year or got a fair price for them. We would never again sit on our patio and feel we were living in isolation. Indeed, it turned out that everyone in the valley knew what everyone else was doing. The lack of walls in all that openness gave me less sense of privacy than I'd known in the anonymity of an apartment block. We had all the space in the world and yet none at all. As if to confirm my thoughts, the dim light started flashing on and off over at Diego's place. We had one last glance at the stars and went inside.

6

The Way Ahead

Helen pulled up a chair on the patio and started to read another letter from Rita, the first since hearing that we'd bought the farm. "It looks like she's taken it rather well," she said blithely, and then read on a bit further. "I don't get this—she says that she's written to the hospital where I was born." Her eyes suddenly focused angrily on the page. "She's '*convinced I took the wrong baby home, because no child of mine could be this stupid.*'"

"What did the hospital say?"

Helen glared, but Rita was the real source of her indignation.

"She can be so hostile. I'd never say anything horrible about her—the demented old cow!"

"She thinks we made a mistake, that's all," I said. "Maybe she has a point."

"What do you mean?"

"Well, it hasn't exactly turned out to be the restful arcadia we thought it would be," I said, swatting at a fly.

"Speak for yourself," she replied.

"I was."

"Show some confidence that nature will provide," she said with annoyance. "And don't complain so much about the chores."

"I complain because you seem to think nature has provided you with *me* to do them all."

"Forgive me for believing I was involved with a *real* man. Since you're so smart, I'm sure you can figure out a way to make things easier."

"Well, we could modernize the house a bit. *That* would make life easier and we might also be in a position to sell it for a profit some day."

"How can you talk about selling? We just got here!"

"I'm only looking ahead to the future," I protested, "I'm not talking about selling it tomorrow."

"And it's so charming as it is. Modernizing would ruin it."

"Well, it doesn't have to be twenty-first century, but couldn't we at least upgrade to the eighteenth?"

She huffed dismissively, but in the light of how things were shaping up, I personally felt it was time to look at Plan B. In my view, that meant improving the value of the buildings so we'd have a financial safety net if we had to sell quickly. She didn't think we needed such a plan because she'd read somewhere that one acre of land was enough to feed one person; how could we fail with *ten* acres? The fact these were mostly rocks and scrub hadn't yet entered our conscious calculations. But nagging visions of our neighbors' poverty were starting to wake me up in the middle of the night. While Helen said she'd be content to herd goats and grow vegetables for the rest of her life, I would gladly have given it up that afternoon. I hadn't left England in search of a third-world lifestyle. Relaxing, yes—but primitive, no.

I felt her attitude was endearing but not to be taken seriously. I looked at the dusty pile we'd encumbered ourselves with and decided she couldn't possibly mean it. Tackling the place for a couple of years would be an adventure, like climbing Everest— but no one who climbed Everest moved there permanently. Other than what she told me, I could only guess at her motives. But it was about this time that I first began to suspect she was putting me to some sort of test—and that so far I was failing miserably.

Despite her objection, I started to think of what we could do to "civilize" the house. If I was going to be a farmer for a while, what came to my mind was landed gentry, not peasant. "Imagine how much easier it would be with electric light," I said. "In fact, think what someone could do here with power tools!" Before long, I was talking about gutting the former animal section to expand the human quarters. I couldn't help it. When it came to dreaming up big ideas for building projects, it turned out I had a lot in common with Nero. Except I wasn't the richest man in the known world and I couldn't operate a violin—much less power tools.

Helen, on the other hand, remained opposed to any "improvement" on the grounds it would ruin the natural charm of the place. A primitive life, close to nature, was precisely what she wanted. The battle lines were drawn. The way the deed was arranged, neither of us could lift a finger without the other's agreement. "We'll discuss what we're going to do in a minute," she said, screwing up her mother's letter and laying out a fresh piece of paper and a pen. "But first I'm going to reply to my mother and challenge her to come see the place for herself before she criticizes it."

I lifted my eyes to heaven. "Please, God, don't let her take up the invitation."

"I'm sure if she did come at least *she* would be persuaded by the beauty of our secluded spot."

"It's even turning out a lot less secluded than we thought," I said, pointing off to the edge of our fields. Maria was coming our way in the company of about seventy goats and the half-dozen dogs that helped her shepherd them. Even from that distance, we could make out her flustered gesticulations as she was swept along in the midst of this chaotic crowd. At intervals she called out hoarse reprimands, like a schoolmistress in charge of an outing that had turned to anarchy. We watched, helpless, as this marauding band headed straight for us. When she was in earshot, she called out:

"Your fields are so overgrown. Now that we've met, I hope you don't mind me taking advantage of the grazing!" We were glad to see her on her own, but the arrival of a herd of hungry and mischievous goats outside our house was as welcome as a plague of locusts. While I sat and talked to her, Helen was busy shooing them away from her newly planted seedlings. Maria was oblivious. "It must seem so empty here without animals," she said, nonchalantly accepting a glass of water from me.

"We do have a canary," I said defensively as I booted away a goat that was trying to eat my sandals. Even the canary was one singing bird too many for me. It sounded like a cross between a ringing telephone and an alarm going off. I'd already got so sick of the damn thing chirping all day that I'd hung its cage in the farthest outbuilding.

"One of my dogs had a litter of puppies a couple of months

ago. I haven't got room for any more dogs so, if I can't give them away, I might have to drown them. Would you like one?" She should have been a used car salesman. I was sickened by the possible fate of the puppies, of course, but honestly felt that lumbering ourselves with a ten-acre farm was probably enough baggage to take on for a while.

"I don't really think so," I said. "A dog is an awful lot of responsibility."

"Responsibility?! A dog?" She laughed. "Now children— *that's* responsibility."

"There's another thing that hasn't worked out the way it was supposed to," I said to Helen when Maria and her pillaging horde had finally gone. "We've barely been here a week and already people are lecturing me about 'responsibility.' "

That evening, we still hadn't gotten around to our discussion about improvements when Maria's daughters, Theresa and Simona, showed up with a wriggling puppy. "It's for you," said Theresa. She put it in my hands before I could hide them in my pockets. "It's a gift for your house."

"But I'm not sure—" I began.

"Mother says you need the practice in responsibility," said Simona. "One day you'll want children with Helena or someone else. The dog might teach you something about that." The dog gave me my first lesson in parenting as they left: it pissed all over my hand and halfway up to my elbow.

"I don't like the way those girls look at you," said Helen. "What did they mean, you might want children with me or *someone else?*"

"I'm sure they didn't mean anything," I said. "Anyway, Simona is cross-eyed. You can't assume she's looking at me at all."

"All the same, I don't want you going to their place on your own," she said. "I don't trust them." She became convinced there was a plot to marry me off to Theresa or Simona or, for all she knew, both of them at the same time.

"Doesn't the fact that they're both ugly as hell reassure you in any way?" I said.

"I know what you men are like—anything in a skirt will do." As a result of her suspicions of ill intent, she was determined to dislike their gift, so neither of us really wanted the puppy. However, the idea of sending him back to be drowned was out of the question. As we stood there, contemplating what this thing would do to our lives, he was scooting about licking our hands and faces when he could get to them. He would stumble over himself, our feet, or a rock in his enthusiasm to get near us. Needless to say, we soon capitulated to his charms. We named him Bobby, and within hours Helen was indeed treating him like a baby. Until that point, the closest we'd come to the patter of tiny feet was when we had cockroaches. But now I didn't sleep a wink, as she kept getting up through the night to put the puppy out. I figured it was just my luck to end up with the only native of the valley that did believe in relieving himself indoors.

At that time, I didn't realize this little bundle of fur would be an ally in my campaign. He spent his first night shivering with nerves but by the time Emilio came for his usual coffee the next day, Bobby was so at home he'd put himself in charge of security. He showed amazing aggression for an eight-week-old, but the only real danger he posed was that the old man would trip over him. We asked Emilio which of Maria's dogs were the parents.

"The mother's a hunt dog, but the father—who knows? Your puppy's ten percent this, twenty percent that, but I can see he's a hundred percent dog."

Thanks to the distraction of a new and unhousebroken puppy, Helen was able to continue evading my demand for a modernization plan. It's not that we didn't start arguing about what we were going to do, now that we were officially peasant almond growers. It's just that having a demanding third party around, even a furry one, kept cutting us short. I could hardly get started before Helen would put her finger to her lips and caution that raised voices upset the dog. We had to be particularly sensitive, she claimed, because he was a genuine native of the valley. "Be careful what bad things you say about this place in front of him," she admonished me.

After one of these brief quarrels, we were more likely to get a response talking to Bobby than talking to each other. As a result, the dog was fast becoming the most popular member of the household. Pretty soon he was as much a part of El Águila as the walls and trees. He followed us around our land, marking it as his own personal territory. If we went into town, we could leave him free to roam outside and he'd always be waiting there for us when we came back. This loyalty was no wonder, considering his lot was so much better than that of other dogs in the valley. In this farming community, dogs were beasts of labor that lived permanently outside and were lucky to be thrown a few scraps. They had to supplement their diet by fighting over fallen almonds. They'd sniff them out, expertly crack the shell with their teeth, and spit it out before consuming the nut. Bobby, on the other hand, lived a life of leisure, gorging himself at our expense and sleeping on the sofa.

Our novel treatment of him began to raise eyebrows among our neighbors. Most of them joked about how we spoiled the dog but Maria thought it was no laughing matter. She blamed herself for our "strange" behavior. She looked particularly concerned when she saw us cook him a meal of perfectly good chicken giblets. When she heard that we regularly bathed him, it was almost too much for her and we thought she was going to ask us to give him back. "It's an animal!" she said with exasperation. "When I said it'll teach you about children, I was only joking!"

What he did teach us was that a stomach of his pedigree was better suited to some other diet after all, or at least an outdoor life. The first time we noticed this, Helen and I spent several minutes looking sideways at each other before realizing the smell was emanating from the dog. The instant we established that politeness was not required, we both leapt up to throw open the windows. But Bobby took to his new life as easily as an aristocrat coming into his rightful inheritance. Indeed, his droopy jowls only lacked a pipe to complete the picture of an old-school English gentleman. He even began to act aloof from his poor cousins, trotting along with his head held high and growling if they got too exuberant in their greetings.

After dark his favorite hangout was right in front of the fire where, on one occasion, he managed to frizzle a patch of his fur. Apparently, this experience wasn't enough to put him off. He continued to lie inches from the logs until he was on the point of bursting into flames himself. Then he'd retire panting to the farthest and coolest corner of the room to recover. Ten minutes later, he'd be right in front of the fire again. This back and forth activity was enough to end the disconcerting nighttime scrabbling noises made by unknown creatures, which were either in the next room or the unseen corners of the one we were in. Until he came along, these other inhabitants had hardly been bothered by our arrival. This was hardly surprising, when we were so far from any lights it was like living on the dark side of the moon. If we lit a candle, it only cast enough brightness to see the candle itself. Bobby's sense of smell meant he wasn't as limited as we were. One night he chased what might have been a mouse for several minutes, and in general we felt his odd growl or two were keeping us safe.

So he was good company for us—at least, until the fire had died out. After that he became as invisible as all the other creatures. One night I was carrying the candle as we headed off to bed. Within moments there was a canine yelp underfoot, and the candle went out as I flew through the darkness into a room full of bruising furniture. I landed in a clatter with Helen in turn tumbling over me. For a few seconds we lay there in the dark and silence, trying to feel if we'd broken any bones. "Right, that does it!" I cried. "I want lights in here."

I admit that when we first moved to the farm, there was a sense of adventure as darkness fell. Groping around in total blackness actually seemed like fun. But within a fortnight the fun had already begun to wear a little thin, as the stubbed toes and banged foreheads grew less and less amusing. Trying to use a toothpick was like playing "pin the tail on the donkey" on yourself. But the issue of bringing light back into our lives didn't get a hearing until we fell over Bobby—heaven forbid that *he* should get hurt. So after a short but barbed discussion, we agreed to upgrade from huddling around a candle to huddling around a hissing gas lamp. This was still pretty dim, so to make the place more cheerful we sometimes set up an array of candles that could match any cathedral's. The fumes created when we put them out nearly choked us to death, and there were black marks all over the place where toppled candles had come close to burning the house down. Helen found the situation very romantic and couldn't be more satisfied. She wasn't enthusiastic when I suggested getting electricity connected. "It's like Chartres," she sighed dreamily one night.

"Exactly," I said sourly, "but when I came in on this project, I don't remember agreeing to live in the Dark Ages."

"But this is so lovely," she replied.

"We can always turn the lights off and sit around in the dark if we miss it," I reasoned irrefutably.

"It wouldn't be the same," she insisted, and I certainly hoped she was right. The dispute brought out the stubbornness in me and the militancy in her. An angry scowl came to her face that reminded me of the first time I saw her. I'd been passing a student demonstration on my way to the university library when I saw this fiery redhead trying to beat a Rolls Royce with a placard. At the time, I was turned on by the thought of a passion so unfettered that it spurred her to lash out with a piece of wood at the trustee's hundred thousand dollar car. But now I felt it was *me* in danger of getting clobbered.

"How are we going to live here?" I said. "We've got nothing in common."

"In fact, when I think about it, I can't stand you," she hissed.

"If it's any help, you irritate the hell out of me too." Seconds after this outburst, we were inexplicably in each other's arms in an embrace of unprecedented passion. Bobby couldn't understand why we'd rushed off to bed so early. This wouldn't be the last time a fight about the farm would end this way. The more intense the disagreement, the more intense the making up afterwards. I guess it was the only way we had to bridge the gap that was opening up between us. I think Helen believed that after moments of such intimacy, I couldn't say "no" to her. At least, she always picked that time to lie with her head on my shoulder and then, in her gentlest voice, hit me with some particularly thorny question I'd rather avoid, or else ask for a favor that she knew would kill me. Luckily for me, she never discovered that the real time I couldn't say no to her requests was in the moments immediately *before* we got intimate. So I was able to turn the tables as we lay back in the afterglow. "What harm would it do if we just had an electrician come out and look?" I said sweetly. I could see by the stifled irritation in her affirmative response that she knew what I was up to—but couldn't say so without admitting that I was playing her own game.

The electrician was a fat, sweaty man called Manolo, whose belly and part of his backside spilled over the top of his trousers. The first thing I needed to ask him was whether an electricity connection was possible in this location; after all, no one else had it. "Of course it's possible," he said. "Anything's possible, but don't expect electricity tomorrow." I tried to measure his voice. Did he mean we could get it in three weeks or three months, or was he talking about when my grandchildren took over the place? Helen read my fears and enjoyed a private smile at my expense.

"We *will* get electricity?" I asked penetratingly.

"One day the electricity company will come to this area," he replied circumspectly. In the meantime, he said his Catholic conscience wouldn't allow him to wire a house so many miles from the nearest electric pylon. The most I could persuade him to do was draw a very basic circuit on the wall in colored crayons. If I felt like channeling grooves in the walls in preparation for wiring, that was up to me. I made him promise that he would return "one day" to install wires and fit switches in this diagrammatic circuit. "You could have a solar panel," he suggested just before he got in his car and drove off.

"Novel decorative touch." Helen sneered, looking around at Manolo's patterns. "Some people put up pictures but we have lines and shapes in colored crayon." As far as she was concerned, my plans were already messing up the rustic ambiance. Admittedly, it did look like visiting aliens had covered the place in graffiti. But I couldn't get used to waking up with the birds and going to bed earlier than my five-year-old nephew. I wasn't ready to admit defeat.

"What could be wrong with a solar panel?" I asked. "Even Diego's got one." She muttered dissent but it was hard for her to take issue against something environmentally friendly that had the blessing of our neighbors. In the hope of shutting me up once and for all on the subject of modernizing, she agreed.

I fear electricity so much that every time I change a lightbulb, I worry I'm going to get fried. So I got Diego to come and install our new panel. "You can't kill yourself with only twelve volts," he shouted to me at my safe vantage point several yards away. He stuck the panel on the roof of an abandoned stable, and joined it to a car battery in the manger underneath. From there, a cable with a lightbulb on the end was draped over meat hooks and through cracks in the walls until finally arriving in our living room. "Just be careful how much you use it," he said. "It's only good for a few hours' light a day."

That evening, life on the farm was transformed. This may sound like an exaggerated claim on behalf of a single lightbulb. But what could be more simple than fire or the wheel, and look what those things led to. For me, this wasn't just a light—it was a beacon of hope. Thanks to the long cable, we could carry our little bulb into most of the downstairs rooms. For the first time in weeks, we actually saw what we were eating and the washing up resulted in clean dishes. I was able to read without endangering my eyesight or singeing my eyebrows on a naked flame.

As ever, progress came at a price. Helen found the naked bulb crude and registered her feelings on the matter by sitting in a distant corner with candle wax dripping over her book. Another side effect of the brightness was a constant thudding barrage of beetles and other bugs against the window. "Now look what you've done," she said. "You've brought a biblical plague on our house." Only Bobby seemed not to notice the change, though his chewing on the cord or trying to run through it like a finish line constantly threatened to plunge us into sudden darkness. Yet for me, this little puddle of electric light was a miracle—partly because I couldn't understand how it worked (I'm one of those people who marvel every time they see an airplane lift off or hear music through a radio), but mainly because it brought our farm into the early twentieth century.

While I sat right next to this light, drawing up plans for my next assault on the primitiveness of the place, Helen clung to the dark corners. She became a figure moving in the shadows, mumbling disapproving comments about me and my bulb. "For God's sake, stop hiding from the light," I said moodily. "It's like living with a vampire."

"I feel like *I'm* living with a giant firefly," she retorted. "The way you walk around dragging your spotlight with you. There's no escape from you."

"On second thought, stay in the dark—I prefer you that way." The argument soon escalated until, without warning, we suddenly stopped fighting and raced upstairs for another unscheduled early night.

As I lay there afterwards with Helen asleep on my arm and Bobby snoring across my legs, I contemplated the state of our finances. When we bought the farm, an hourglass had been turned over and the sands were quickly running through. Even though there was no mortgage and no bills, it would still be a close thing whether or not we could hold out until the cash came in for our almond crop—which presently amounted to a few tender-looking buds. In the meantime, we tried to minimize expenses by eating like fasting Buddhists and letting our clothes get threadbare. To keep us alive, we were counting on an extensive vegetable garden that would be producing its first crops within a couple of months.

But despite all our efforts to reduce our expenditures to zero, we knew there would inevitably be a few more major purchases to get the farm running smoothly—each of which brought forward the date of our bankruptcy as effectively as tearing a page from the calendar. This made me feel all the more that I was in

a race to turn our peasant shack into something we could sell or
borrow on, while we still had a choice in the matter. The only
danger in my plan was that, with my handyman skills, I might
actually lower its value. Helen's take on the matter was that the
less spent on the house, the less danger we'd end up broke in
the first place.

Our neighbor Emilio was becoming something of a mentor
with his afternoon visits to rest on the way to his cousin's house.
The next day we sat with him on our patio with its majestic view
of mountains and the hill fort. Usually he would regale us with
tales of the war of 1936—the only time in his life he'd been outside this area. Or we'd hear about his departed wife or the children who had moved to the city. He frequently bemoaned their
efforts to get him to join them in some apartment somewhere,
far from his beloved trees and hills. This led Helen to believe
she had an ally in Emilio when it came to our dispute over what
to do with our farm. His love of nature, and desire to preserve
the valley as it was, were obvious. Not only was he living proof
that it was possible to get by, but he was always lecturing us on
the traditional ways of doing it.

It was one of those afternoons when time slowed to a stop
and all the problems I'd been juggling the night before seemed
to fall away. It was impossible to feel anxious while filled with a
sense that some essence of this scene would go on forever. For a
moment, even the wind paused for breath and the air grew hot-
ter. It was so silent that I could hear a fly approaching at some
distance, buzz past us, and then disappear away in the other direction. All the colors were bleached in the bright heat so that
even the sky had faded to a milky blue. There was nothing in the
scene that was not totally natural to it. Except perhaps me. Even
this far under its spell, I found I had an instinctive urge to touch
the valley, to order it, to build something.

The last thing I wanted was for Helen to break the silence by challenging me to explain this deep-rooted urge. I wasn't keen to air our disagreements in public because I knew they would then form the subject of teatime conversation at Maria's, and from there spread far and wide. Everyone in the valley yearned to know our every move. But Helen could see that I respected this elderly gentleman and that he and I enjoyed a certain rapport. Convinced he would support her, she chose that day to relate her views on the simple life and then invited Emilio to be amazed that I could want to change it. His reaction took us both by surprise. "But Helena, he is the man, the head of the household." He indicated me. "If you can't persuade him, you must accept his decision." This concept was alien to both of us but objectionable only to her. "The simple life is indeed the best," he said, consoling her with a fatherly hand on her shoulder. "But be careful not to embrace poverty, which is rarely dignified and never simple." After he'd gone, Helen made it clear there was to be no patriarchal hierarchy in this house. Thereafter, she treated all Emilio's counsel with suspicion. She went back to her plants and I went back to my solar light.

Even Helen had to admit that it was hard to apply the phrase "rustic charm" to the chemical toilet. So I had little trouble persuading her to let me start digging a cesspool. I think she considered it a harmless diversion. Not just because there was no plumbing to connect it to, but mainly because I couldn't do any damage digging a hole outside. This noble concession actually gave her two victories. One, her principled opposition to change had not altered, thereby allowing her to continue to claim the moral high ground. And two, thus enshrined, she could sit back and allow me to do all the digging.

I expected to be halfway to China by lunchtime and had optimistically laid out some bricks and a bag of cement in readiness. But the ground proved so hard that by the time Emilio came by that afternoon, I'd only managed to rearrange some topsoil and a few boulders. He surveyed the building materials sitting beside my grave-shaped excavations. "Why?" he said, shaking his head.

"Shaun misses cement," Helen explained.

"Do you want me to help?" he said.

"No thanks," I said. "I'm sure I can handle it on my own." The next day he offered again and I had to laugh that a frail ninety-year-old should even think of helping with this physical labor that was killing me. After two days, the only perceptible change was that even the bag of cement had now turned to rock.

Again the following day he stopped by. I'd progressed by about a foot. "Do you want me to help you with that?" he said. I slowly straightened up my sore back.

"Look, Emilio, I can hardly dig this myself. You're not going to be much use at your age."

"Oh, I'm not going to dig," he said. "Only a fool would dig. I've got a friend in the village with a tractor who'd gladly do that for you in half an hour. If you want me to help, I'll get him to come over."

Even with a vast new hole in our backyard, putting the cesspool together was going to take me awhile. I knew as much about cementing as I knew about brain surgery. So with my usual unflagging thoroughness, I abandoned it after the tractor left and moved on to a new scheme. I took a drink of water over to where Helen was basking in the sun. "When we were in town the other day, I saw a small fountain pump on sale for not much more than a hundred dollars," I said.

She sat up. "A fountain?! This is a tumbledown almond farm! Not the palace at Versailles!"

"It's a twelve-volt pump, so we could run it off our solar panel, and I don't want it for a fountain—I want it to bring water up from the well."

"I really must draw the line somewhere. So far, after all your efforts, what have you achieved? One light bulb and a bloody great hole in the ground."

"Exactly! There's so much more to do to make this place livable."

"Until you came along, it'd been perfectly *livable* for hundreds of years. Next you'll be wanting an elevator to the bedroom."

So I insisted we take turns hauling water up from the well. Within two days, she'd softened her line on the pump. "I suppose if it works off solar power, it'll be all right," she conceded magnanimously.

Unfortunately, when we got the pump, we learned it was too delicate to work on the dirty water in our well. It would spurt out a cupful and then clog up. Either we were going to have to give up drinking and washing, or else somehow clean the muck out of the water. Once again, this was a job that required help, and Diego was the only man with time on his hands—whose hands weren't half-crippled with arthritis. I had a hunch that I only needed to mention my difficulties and he would volunteer. I was right. Getting our well cleaned started as a good neighborly deed and after a few brandies became a matter of family honor. "My friend, you can count on Diego, son of Diego," he told me, his voice full of emotion.

We started early the next morning when Diego showed up scowling and bad tempered. He seemed to regret his offer of help but a little booze in his coffee restored sociability. He'd brought a rope ladder and a powerful gasoline pump with him. This reassured me that at least one of us had a vague idea of what was required. I even needed him to tell me that our well wasn't really a well at all but a giant underground reservoir. Rather than being porous and filling from a water table, it was made of plastered brick that was coated with lime to keep it sealed and "hygienic." It was filled every year during the wet season by rainwater. If we ever needed a top-off, we could divert water from the spring, to which we had a right confirmed in our deed. This was brought to our reservoir by a network of irrigation ditches, along with every bit of mud and debris along the way.

Diego rigged up his pump and began to empty out the water that was left in there. I raced around with the end of the pipe soaking the vegetable patch, nearby trees, and myself. This went on for longer than we expected, partly because he regularly had to stop and clean the filter, and partly because the reservoir was bigger than we imagined. Diego estimated ten thousand gallons. When the pump got down to mud he turned it off. "From now on, it's buckets," he said. "You go down and I'll haul up."

"You want me to actually get *in* the well?" I said.

"It's your well, isn't it?" he said. "Besides, I'm too fat."

I peered into the darkness and felt my chest tighten with fear. "What do you think is down there?" I said.

"Oh, nothing much. Maybe some snakes, maybe not," he said. "Just pick them up with a stick and put them in the bucket. But warn me first before I pull it up, okay?"

"Don't worry," said Helen. "It's only an hour to the nearest hospital."

"I don't suppose you'd like to go down there?" I asked her.

"Certainly not," she said. "You're the one who insists on meddling with everything. You do it." Diego lit a cigarette and kicked the rope ladder over the rim. I heard a distant splash as it hit the bottom.

"You won't go away, will you?" I said to him.

"Me? Desert a neighbor? Never!" I drew some comfort from his look of offense at my suggestion. He handed me a bucket and a powerful flashlight. Helen helped me tie the light to my baseball cap so I looked like a miner poised to enter the bowels of the earth. "Just tug on the rope when the bucket's full," he said. "I'll throw the mud on your vegetable patch—it's great soil."

I directed my gaze and the flashlight downwards but saw nothing. Helen was hanging around to watch this one and Diego was getting his first beer out of a cool bag. The start of my descent must have been anticlimactic for them. It took a full five minutes for my head to finally drop below the opening. I tested each wobbly rung of the ladder before letting it take my weight and scanned the darkness below for the fangs of a serpent monster. After a few feet, the narrow neck of the entrance began to open out with a gradual curve and the tank lay below me like a giant pot. It was probably less than twenty feet deep but it seemed to me like two hundred.

At least there was no sign of snakes. I could only see a small circle of light in front of me but I systematically scanned the walls and floor for movement in the slimy mud. When I saw the floor, I realized that I didn't need to bring a bucket with me. I've never seen so many buckets in my life. I thought of Emilio's advice to store food down there in the cool and wondered how many times Pedro had gone to fetch his dinner only to find a loose end of frayed rope. Then, as I neared the bottom, something leapt from the darkness and I turned in terror. The rope ladder began to spin and I fell the remaining few feet and landed with a squelch. As I scrambled to pull myself from the sludge, I saw a three-inch frog staring at me—more confidently than I was staring back. During the rest of the day, I worked around my slippery companion as I scraped that reservoir clean. There were old coins, shoes, car tires, a hat, and various other bizarre items—but no creatures bigger than an insect. By the time I'd finished, it was me that looked like a riverbed monster. When the walls were washed, Diego lowered down buckets of a lime solution for me to paint them with. I finally emerged in the late afternoon to the accompaniment of his drunken singing.

We had to wait a day to refill the reservoir from the spring. Helen was mourning over the year's rainfall we'd just thrown away. "It's been a dry winter," I reasoned. "The plants needed watering."

"They didn't need drowning. And you could've saved some for the washing up—now it's covered in ants." But in a couple of days, we had a tap outside our back door that we both agreed was pretty handy. There was no more hauling buckets up from the murky depths. But we still had to lug the same amount of water in and out of the house—it's just that we had less distance to carry it. My big plans to plumb the whole house hadn't quite gotten off the drawing board yet—to Helen's relief. But my biggest folly was failing to consider how power hungry the pump would be. The tiny amount of electricity we produced now had to go that much further. The result was frequent blackouts, usually just as Helen was using the light to thread a needle or carry out some delicate maneuver in the bathroom.

I was pleased that she'd come to accept what little modernization I'd gotten away with so far. Once she got used to our one dim bulb, she realized it didn't really disrupt the natural ambiance all that much—certainly not as much as I would've liked. Meanwhile, she started to feel quite smug about the "renewable energy" aspect of our solar outfit. "Do you realize we're getting a taste of the way ahead for mankind?" she proclaimed over dinner one night. I surveyed the gloom from my rickety bamboo chair and wondered what the hell she was talking about. "What could be more up-to-date than solar power and green self-sufficiency?" she explained.

I tried to see it her way. After living in a premodern state, it made a nice change to entertain fantasies of a futuristic lifestyle. As I slopped out our commode, I tried to delude myself that our farm was on the cutting edge. Anything seemed possible, especially after a glass or two of the latest batch of Emilio's wine. She discovered that we could run our laptop computer off our panel, and I added a mobile phone and satellite television to my mental shopping list for some more prosperous future date. Apparently, there is even such a thing as a sun-powered refrigerator, which made as much sense to me as an ice-powered heater. At last Helen and I felt we could once more share a vision of the way ahead. It looked like I could eventually have my modern conveniences without violating her environmentalist credo. We were together again and reaped the benefits with cozy, if sedate, evenings spent snuggled together, or toasting the *campo* beside Emilio's fire. Perhaps the farm would work out after all. Then we had a cloudy day. Five cloudy days in fact.

This was when I discovered the fundamental flaw with things powered by the sun: The sun has to show up for work. Having lived so many years in England, I should have known that anything dependent on the weather would be doomed. The first night, we only managed an hour of electricity before blacking out for days. I checked the stable for vital signs but found that the battery was dead. Another problem with sun-powered things is that you need them most when the sun isn't shining. Only electric light could have lifted the dark gloom of those cloudy days. In the accompanying chill, we'd have greatly appreciated water that had been warmed by the sun before bathing. Leaving the bottles outside now only made them colder. We tried not washing, but by the second day even a cold soaking seemed preferable. I had to spend a couple of hours a day chopping firewood to heat the house or we'd have gotten pneumonia. In a region with three hundred sunny days a year, you'd think we could make do with the sunshine we were getting. All I can say is that it's amazing how long the other sixty-five days seem. Renewable energy had lost its charm, and global warming suddenly had a lot of appeal to me. Helen knew our vision had really clouded over when she heard me start channeling paths for the wires the electricity company might or might not need in our lifetime. The solar dream—and our truce—were over.

As we again started to argue, the only good thing was that making up afterwards was a great way to keep warm. I discovered that taking a hammer and chisel to walls is another fine way to vent frustration and warm up. Manolo had drawn nice straight crayon lines on the walls where the wires might one day go. But since there were irregular rocks underneath the plaster, these lines proved impossible to follow. My channel zigzagged around boulders or became a gaping hole where hammering resulted in a landslide. Poor Helen was stuck indoors with me pounding away in a dust cloud, at the end of a meandering trail of rubble. "Why don't you just get a bulldozer in and knock the whole place down?" she said dejectedly.

My application for electricity disappeared into some bureaucratic void and eventually Helen agreed not to stand in the way of other improvements. She knew she didn't have to. I didn't know which end of a hammer to hold and was too broke to hire someone who did. So she figured I'd soon see reason and come to appreciate this basic lifestyle with all its appeal. She also thought she could count on my innate laziness. As she put it: "The only thing you put any effort into is the avoidance of hard work." She correctly gauged that in my heart of hearts I didn't really want to be a handyman. But what she hadn't put into the equation was my even greater determination to never again lug that chemical toilet, or burn my fingers on a candle, or any number of other trials regularly demanded by our primeval way of life.

With her reluctant acquiescence, I would attempt a variety of ill-fated schemes—like my hot water heater that consisted of a hose snaking over the roof. My plans didn't exactly receive a rap-

turous welcome. "But we've only just put the place back together after your last idea," she protested. "I don't want to sleep
under God knows how many tons of water. Those beams are rid-
dled with woodworm; it'll come crashing down on us in the middle of the night. Especially if you've had a hand in it."

As if guided by divine providence—or, as Helen suggested,
some darker force—I found a handyman manual in English at a
secondhand store by the coast. It might as well have been in
some Eskimo dialect for all the good it did me. Its authors
wrongly assumed that the reader already possessed some handyman skills. In that respect it was like one of those cookbooks that
say "add ingredients to a pastry base" but don't tell you what a
pastry base is, or how to make one. Also, I wasn't helped by my
tendency to skim, because I find anything technical so dull that
my eyes glaze over. The results were predictably disastrous. For
example, my hot water system gave us water that was scalding
for thirty seconds and then instantly became freezing again.
Altogether the book turned out to be less of a handyman bible
than a juju manual that I opened at my peril.

Another natural tendency was to look for shortcuts. If a
screwdriver was called for, I would try to make do with the
kitchen knife that happened to be right there. I would only
bother to get up and look for the screwdriver when I'd mangled
the thread of the screw so badly that *nothing* could turn it.
Another problem I had was that the celestial powers were on
Helen's side. Over the year they made it quite clear that my attempts at handiwork were in defiance of divine law. I would start
off in the rational belief that if I followed a logical procedure,
then success would follow. By the end it was clear, beyond a
shadow of doubt, that there was something like a voodoo curse
on the project. Sometimes it got quite eerie. For instance, even
if I lined up a shelf and marked it off with pencil, it would still
hang crooked. Concrete mix always hardened before I got it to

where I wanted it. No matter which way I hit it, the nail never went in straight, and glue never stuck to anything except my fingers.

Nevertheless, a haphazard "progress" on the house continued in the background of all our experiences on the farm. Whatever adventure we went out to encounter, we always came home to the clutter of one unfinished project or another. In the background, too, was the continuing conflict between the inept but determined handyman and the naturalist unhappily acceding to his schemes. But it was more than a disagreement about plumbing or piles of bricks in the yard—we were at odds over our respective views of the future. When I got out my tools, Helen took it as a signal that I wasn't happy with things the way they were. I guess she felt I wasn't just dissatisfied with the farm, but with her. Thus each "improvement" in the house brought with it a new deterioration in our relationship. The more the building came together, the more we seemed to fall apart.

I could sense that we were both beginning to feel that there *ought* to be something more between us; because two people who owned a property together *should* feel that way, and because it had been unnerving when some of our neighbors gasped the first time we told them we weren't married. Neither of us was about to commit our hearts because we *ought* to. At the outset, we both said we were coming to look for ourselves. Instead we seemed to be spending more time looking at each other. Suddenly the big question in life had become "Who did I *really* want to grow old with?" Without intending to, I couldn't help wondering if that person might be right there in front of me after all.

7

Fiesta

Even though there was a cesspool to build, baby vegetables to tend, and arguments to fight, we did get off the farm from time to time to enjoy ourselves. Unless we were going to eat nothing but nuts and figs, we would have to come to terms with the culture of our surrounding area. There was a whole new world around us to explore. And despite everything, we were still just a couple of kids in our twenties—we liked to party.

That the Spanish also liked to party was something we'd already discovered back on the Costa Blanca. In fact, on our first night in Spain we were kept up until five in the morning by loud music. This was too much even by our standards. To begin with,

I tried smothering my head with my pillow to stop the noise, but even a band playing in your bedroom is preferable to suffocation. Finally, I got up and went outside to see where the inconsiderate revelers were. Unbelievably, the noise was even louder outside. It seemed to fill the night. I paced up and down the deserted street but could only see darkened houses. It was impossible to sleep so I took the car and angrily drove in search of these thoughtless, noisy people. Everywhere seemed abandoned, but then it *was* very late—or very early—depending on how you looked at it. As I followed the coast road toward town, I was astonished to notice the racket grew yet louder, something I had at first thought impossible. There appeared to be some sort of outdoor disco taking place in the middle of the night. I determined that if I couldn't shut them up, I would certainly call the town hall to complain.

Finally, I tracked the source of the offending noise down to a particular square. As it came within sight, I was in for a shock. To my disbelief the entire town was there, from young children to old-timers. It transpired that the town hall had organized the event. Since Helen and I were the only people within a fifteen-mile radius who weren't taking part, I could instantly see that complaining would be futile. I went home and waited impatiently for a silence that finally arrived with the dawn. This was my first experience of the great Spanish *fiesta*.

There are so many fiestas in Spain that it seems the colored lights and bunting have barely come down from one when preparations start for the next. When we were exploring the country looking for a farm at a giveaway price, we encountered many different celebrations. More than once we came across a "Moors and Christians" festival with elaborate medieval costumes and mock battles, complete with explosions loud enough to wake the dead. Religious holidays were often accompanied by parades, and every new area seemed to have its own variety of local festivals to add to national and regional days. If we'd mapped out our journey carefully, we could have crossed Spain without alighting anywhere that wasn't enjoying a day off. Mind you, it was hardly necessary to travel to reap the benefits of this festive culture. Sometimes different sections of our own first town, or even individual streets, had their own patron saint day or other excuse to break out the vino and fireworks and turn up the music. Looking at a diary of local holidays, it was a miracle any work got done at all.

That's not to say all fiestas rated the same. For instance, the Fallas festival in the Valencia province was so significant that it spawned a series of lesser street parties throughout the year— allegedly to raise funds for the big event itself. During Fallas week in the Costa Blanca coastal town where we first stayed, each neighborhood produced giant cartoon figures out of wire and plaster that could reach three or four stories high. Perhaps to contrast with the piety of religious festivals, these were usu- ally caricatures of corrupt political figures with a strong satirical and at times pornographic content. That year a giant represen- tation of the mayor fornicating with a developer blocked the street to traffic for several days. To the unsuspecting, it could be quite a shock to turn a corner and come face to face with one of these things. On the last night, a panel of judges ranked the car- icatures according to how outrageous they were, and then they were burned, starting with the dullest and ending in the small hours of the night with the most scandalous. You have to admire a culture relaxed enough to so casually put the torch to months of planning and work.

Fortunately, when we moved to our farm, we were too far from any local fiestas to have our sleep disturbed. The closest was in the small village of Santa Maria, a couple of miles down the road toward the nearest town. Santa Maria consisted of one general store, one bar, a couple of dozen stone houses, and acre after acre of big modern pig sheds. If the pigs ever got hold of a copy of *Animal Farm,* the vastly outnumbered human residents would be in trouble. This unexpected and highly isolated flowering of pig farming was apparently due to one of the villagers having a cousin in the government department responsible for livestock subsidies. If you've ever smelled just one pig farm, you can guess how pungent an entire village of them was. It was substantial enough that when the wind was in the wrong direction, we could smell Santa Maria as far out as our place. We always rolled up the windows of the car when we drove through, even if doing so produced a temperature of a hundred and ten degrees.

So we were less than enthusiastic when we got invited to the local fiesta. But we knew the time had come to step beyond the comforting surrounds of our valley. We were running out of basic supplies and knew that sooner or later we'd have to face up to the idiosyncrasies of the wider area and mix with the natives. Being so far off the tourist trail, we were oddities without even trying. In turn we found the mysterious culture around us both fascinating and intimidating. Our neighbors were extremely friendly but they were forced to live with us. Should anyone else take serious offense at our presence, they wouldn't have far to go to find wilderness suitable for dumping our bodies. Or so our thinking went during the paranoia of our first few weeks.

So our decision to party with the pig farmers was also a political one. Especially as we'd been invited by Vicente, the village storekeeper. We'd heard that he was such an influence in the area that it wouldn't pay to upset him. The village was too small to have an official mayor but he was the next best thing. Since he owned the only store for miles around, he knew everyone. His counter was the source of all news and gossip, so a kind word there could make you as popular as a lottery winner and a cruel one could send you into the isolation of a leper. Luckily for us, he decided it was his privilege to call himself friend to the only

foreigners eccentric enough to live in this remote farming community. As a source of gossip, our foibles were too good to pass
up. It would be misleading to imply by all this that he was in any
way a menacing figure. On the contrary, he had a baby face and
childish laugh, both of which belied his fifty years of age.
Perhaps, if you were looking for a fault, you could say that his
status had gone to his head a little. If a conversation broke out
anywhere in his store, within moments he would be at the center of it, loudly asserting his opinion.

Every time we visited him, he insisted on marching us up and
down his shelves, like a president reviewing the troops with a
couple of visiting dignitaries. He wanted to make sure we were
aware of the latest addition to his stock—even if it was only a
food supplement for pigs. In time we would primarily go to his
store to collect our mail, preferring to drive a littler farther and
shop for food in town, where there was a better selection of
products for humans. Vicente was not offended—most of his
customers did the same—but it was comforting to know that if
there was something we couldn't find at the town market, then
he'd get it for us. It's been said that you can buy anything in the
world in Harrods, the London department store. Well, Vicente's
store may have been a dusty affair with nothing much on show
besides a few cans of tuna and peas, but if you needed a semi-
conductor or a camel train, he'd have them there by the end of
the week. It took a versatile man like him to run a rural store offering everything from a gasoline pump to a metered telephone
for public use. If you were ever short of money, he'd even ex-
tend credit without fuss.

This cheerful and helpful pillar of local society was the clear
choice to be chairman of the village fiesta committee. All agreed
that he did a marvelous job, although there was some quiet
mumbling about the profit he must have made supplying the
food, wine, decorations, and fireworks. All three hundred yards

of the only street through the village were so festooned with decorations, it was hard to distinguish the buildings beneath them. Speakers were set up to broadcast flamenco music throughout the vicinity, interrupted only by the sound of Vicente himself announcing the winner of this or that agricultural competition. At the center of these noises and lights, which would have rivaled many a circus, was a somber collection of black-clad, elderly peasants. This tiny crowd stood around his makeshift bar and tried to yell to each other over the din. When he announced our arrival to the surrounding countryside over the microphone, we were set upon by the entire gathering. Helen did her best to engage in conversation on farming issues ranging from pigs to pork. Meanwhile, I got a little too drunk on sangria, a potent Spanish variety of punch that goes down like fruit juice only to come back up again as battery acid a few hours later.

The most positive upshot of the evening was meeting a delivery driver who had a problem with his computer. The fact that he even owned one was itself good news. Helen was able to fix the problem and the man drove out to our place the next day to pay the token sum she'd asked for. The real gain from this visit was his infatuation with our canary, which was once again aggravating my hangover. "What a wonderful voice," he said. "I have a canary but it doesn't sing."

"This one sings all the time," I told him. "You don't know Diego who lives across the valley, do you?"

"No."

"In that case, how would you like to swap?" An hour later the deliveryman returned with his bird, which was a little fatter and greener than ours, but differed primarily in that it was mute. I had to pray that Diego would never notice the switch. The man was delighted with the swap but felt he was getting by far the better deal. So he also insisted on paying us something for our feathered singing virtuoso, although I'd gladly have paid *him* to take it away.

When the deliveryman gave us more for the canary than Helen had asked for her computer skills, she naturally wondered if she'd undervalued her services. Our dwindling reserve—and the fact we had yet to sell a single almond, olive, caper, or fig—meant that mastering local bartering techniques was as important as learning to prune the trees or stumble around in the dark. The prices of most things in our area were negotiable but we were far too polite and well brought up to argue over money. Having been raised in England, we automatically paid whatever price we were given. Our behavior not only brought us ridicule from our neighbors but even threw off the salespeople themselves. They weren't used to getting what they asked for. Ironically, it was the surprised reaction of the usually poker-faced market traders that blew their cover. Pretty soon we would haggle over the price of a pea.

I'd always associated bartering with dubious characters, and it's not easy breaking long-held attitudes. So at first we drove around the outskirts, desperately searching for a superstore. I'd never had to engage in a battle of wits with the checkout girl at Safeway. But all we managed to find were a mechanic, a ceramic tile warehouse, and a cemetery. The town was pretty small and only had an indoor market facing the shady square. This sold sausages, cheeses, and whatever was locally grown and in season. Once a week the square would fill with stalls offering clothing and leather goods. Some of the stallholders were gypsies or Africans who had made the short ferry crossing from Morocco to our nearby port of Almería.

Since mixing with the natives was clearly going to be on their terms, we needed a friendly one to coach us. We knew we were in luck when Emilio, the doyen of all things Andalusian, hobbled forward to assume the role. For an upstanding senior citizen, he sure knew a lot of low-down tricks. His dusty suits and gentlemanly bearing gave just the right cover. Especially when he played up the limp and feigned deafness. We, on the other hand, looked like a couple of young tourists, and stallholders continued to rub their hands together with glee at our approach. It was only his protection that kept the clothes on our backs. One market day, he went off to church to say confession. After hearing some of his tips on how to swindle stallholders, we figured he'd be gone a long time. Helen had spotted a small rug she wanted to put in front of the fireplace and thought we should put his advice into practice. "Barter for a rug? Can't we try it out on half a pound of oranges first?" I suggested cautiously.

"It can't be too expensive," she asserted. "Let's toss to see who does it." Losing the toss, I determined to bury my cultural reservations and apply every strategy old Emilio had given me. First of all, we surreptitiously transferred the bulk of the money out of my wallet and into Helen's purse. She lingered to watch from a distance as I approached the stall as casually as possible and began to look at a few items. Following my training, I ignored the fine rug in question so thoroughly you'd think there was a gaping hole in the stall just at that point. After only a moment or two, I asked how much a couple of other items were, and as the stallholder gave his response my eyes finally lighted on the rug with a lack of enthusiasm bordering on disgust.

"And how much for this?" I said. I'd pointed briefly at it and then moved on with my eye, trying to appear inattentive to his answer.

"Ten thousand pesetas," he said with finality. As I had been briefed to do, I acted as if the absurdity of his answer alone merited my engaging him on the issue.

"Ten thousand?" I said with a forced chuckle. "No, I asked you how much for this rug *here*."

"You're right to laugh," he said. "Normally it would be fifteen thousand but I'll let you have it for ten to make way for new stock."

"You must be joking," I said, struggling to recall Emilio's script. "I've seen the same rug for five thousand in Lorca." Somehow, it wasn't as convincing coming from me. The man suddenly appeared to be choking. As he struggled to control the fit, he wagged his finger at me. It was some moments before he'd recovered and was able to speak.

"Five thousand? It cost me nine thousand just to buy it myself," he said.

"You were tricked," I said, trying to keep my waning confidence out of my voice.

"No, no," he said and tutted with amusement at my foolishness. "Look at the quality. This was handwoven in the Sierra Nevadas."

"If I was interested in it, I wouldn't pay more than six," I said tentatively.

"For six you can have this one," he replied and held up a thin white towel. It was time to fall back on Emilio's ultimate weapon. He'd assured me it worked every time. I opened my wallet, picked through the paltry amount left there, and then shook my head.

"I've only got seven in here and I need a thousand to get home. You see, my elderly mother's sick and needs a rug like this to keep her feet off the floor."

"There's a bank up the street," the man snapped. "Do I look like a charity?" He crossed his arms and gave me a look that was both injured and annoyed. I told him my final offer was seven thousand. When he scoffed at this, I played the final gambit and walked away. He called me back. "Go on then," he said. "Take it for seven thousand five hundred. I hope you're happy with yourself, because my family has to eat as well, you know." He rolled up the rug and grumpily handed it to me.

Helen congratulated me when she heard I'd got an old pro to knock twenty-five percent off his original price. I'd been worried that he'd seen me coming a mile off, but it seemed that Emilio's pep talks had done the trick. Having acted out so many emotions, from amusement and shock to horror and outrage, I was drained. Helen said I deserved an Oscar—or at least an ice cream. When we got to the square to sit for a choc-ice and a well-earned rest, I noticed a woman with an identical rug.

"How much did you pay for yours?" I asked.

"Three thousand," she said. My rapidly melting ice cream stopped inches from my mouth. As I considered this startling information, a sizeable chunk broke off and splattered on the ground.

"That's a very good price," said Helen. She shot me a reproving glance.

"Not especially," said the woman. She pulled back the threads on our rug and showed us a little tag that read "made in China." "He only pays a thousand for them himself," she said. It would take a few more pep talks and a little practice in front of the mirror before I was confident to take on the street market again.

Besides Emilio, the other master of negotiation was of course Vicente, the consummate storekeeper. We were so remote that even a trip to his store would have been a day trip without transport. But when we first moved in, we needed to return the rental car we'd been abusing on dirt tracks and buy a cheap second-hand one of our own. Since even in England car dealers were notoriously sly, I was filled with trepidation at the thought of what they'd be like here. After the farm, this was to be our biggest purchase, and I was determined that this time I wouldn't get lumbered with something from the Stone Age that only had power on sunny days. Survival in the wider world would be irrelevant if we couldn't get there.

Fortunately, Vicente had already taken us under his wing, and when he heard via the grapevine that we wanted a car, he drove straight out to our farm in his pickup. "All the local car salesmen are robbers," he said, "but they all owe me so I'll get you a good deal." We'd heard that some went so far as to touch up write-offs and sell them off at a huge markup to foreigners who were too baffled by the language barrier, the paperwork, and the mechanical issues to quibble. In other words, foreigners like us. Vicente promised to be our savior.

He greeted the main car dealer in our area as if he was a long-lost pal. He inquired how his family had enjoyed the gift of melons from his store the previous month. Then he asked him in confidence to find us a good cheap car as a personal favor to him. It seemed almost too easy. I winked at Helen confidently— but prematurely. Twenty minutes later, Vicente and the dealer were yelling threats at each other with questions of parentage and accusations of thievery. Shouting at each other, then storming away, again and again, like two roosters in a ring. Helen grabbed my arm. She wanted to forget the car and go home. But Vicente grabbed my other arm, pulling me toward the car dealer while he yelled something that seemed to be about how poor I was.

Finally a deal was struck on the Spanish version of the Fiat 500, one of those old European cars that are little bigger than a motorized shopping cart. Given the bumpy dirt tracks we had to drive, something closer to a tank would've been more suitable. But by this time I was just relieved to sign the papers and get out of there before it came to blows. It seemed unlikely that the two red-faced men would ever talk to each other again. We were embarrassed to be the cause of such an altercation. However, as soon as we assented to their tentative agreement they were sud-

denly best pals once more. It had all been part of the necessary
ritual—but no joke. I've never paid less for a car, and to my
amazement it turned out to be reliable. The only snag was that
we got tossed around like two dice in a tumbler every time we
drove the tiny thing in or out of our valley.

We didn't really have too much to do with Vicente again until
Easter. Spring arrived as early as mid-February with the return
of a warmth that lasted through the night. The valley was a fairy-
tale setting with its thousands of almond trees covered in white
or pink blossoms. One afternoon, as we sat with Emilio on our
patio, he told us that the blossoms were the real reason there
were almonds in southern Spain. Apparently a Moorish prince
had introduced the trees to remind his homesick northern bride
of snowfall. Beneath this beautiful canopy, a carpet of grass and
yellow flowers began to grow, and flocks of migrating birds
passed through on their way north from Africa. The farm was at
its best and there was nothing pressing to do except admire the
breathtaking scenery. Peace reigned at El Águila.

Vicente had asked us for feedback on the Santa Maria fiesta
and, with crossed fingers, we told him we enjoyed it very much.
But there are no secrets in such a small community, and he
somehow came to hear that we'd actually been less than impressed. Rather than taking offense, he decided to redouble his
efforts to show off the local culture. "You must come with me to
the Holy Week parades in town," he said. "Until you've seen
such a spectacle, you haven't lived."

I doubted it would rise to his sales pitch but we owed him,
and besides, we were still determined to fit in with the local culture. The main town was divided into three societies; each
charged with representing stages of Christ's trial and crucifixion.
The result was three parades—on Wednesday, Thursday, and
Good Friday. Streets and balconies throughout the town were
covered in banners and anybody who could blow, pluck, or bang

things together was enlisted into a marching band. Humor might have been the main goal in Valencian fiestas, with their irreverent three-story caricatures, but down here you laughed at the parade at your peril. This rural and backward part of the country was deeply religious and Easter was *the* fiesta of the year. Few had forgotten that in the civil war of 1936, the locals had fought in defense of the Catholic Church against the northern city liberals of Barcelona and Valencia. Bear in mind that some of the old-timers, like Emilio, could remember 1936 better than they remembered what happened yesterday. So if you made unfavorable comparisons with fiestas in Valencia you were likely to get elected to spend Good Friday lugging a six-foot cross around town dressed in a toga.

Consequently, we found ourselves feigning as much piety as we could when we went with Vicente to watch the first evening parade on Wednesday. We joined a large crowd in the main square, where band after band was forming up before setting off one after the other to tour the town. I'd heard there was some sort of competition between them, but judging must have been difficult because all the bands looked and sounded exactly the same. They all seemed to have more trumpets and drums than anything else, and every tune they were practicing would've been melancholy had it not been for the fact that half the band was either out of time or out of tune, and sometimes both. When the last group had marched off on its tour, the crowd began to disperse. In the distance it was now possible to hear a general din of overlapping trumpets, drums, and clashing symbols.

Dusk was beginning to fall and Vicente told us the main parade would start in about an hour. In the meantime he took us to see the religious effigies. There were more churches and chapels in this one small town than there are casinos in Las Vegas, but the big church in the central square was the showpiece. The ceiling was covered in gold leaf and fluffy baroque renditions of heaven. A little farther down the wall, purgatory was detailed graphically enough to put you off the place as a vacation destination. Lower still were depictions of hell itself. These put Hannibal Lecter's twisted imagination in the shade and should have earned the painter a referral to a mental institution. It was from this church that the statues of saints were lifted by teams of men and carried through the streets. Until that time, a slow procession of straight-faced townsfolk made its way around the aisles to pause at each effigy. Helen raised her eyebrows at me. This wasn't what had sprung to mind when we were invited to a "fiesta." When we reached the statue of the Virgin Mary, Vicente touched my arm and pointed. "Tradition says that if you make a prayer as the Virgin passes, it'll be answered," he said gravely. I tried to appear impressed but out of the corner of my eye I could see Helen trembling in an effort not to laugh. Whatever tickled her must have been contagious. I only managed to maintain the required respectful expression by focusing hard for a few moments on a representation of a demon who was doing something anatomically impossible to one of his victims.

Finally we left the church and joined the growing tide of people making its way toward the starting point for the procession. Many of the men wore long, priestly robes. The women had their hair pinned up and had on colorful gowns inspired by gypsy flamenco. There were dozens of altar boys and girls in their First Communion whites. "For most people, these are their best clothes," said Vicente proudly. "Many are made especially for this week and worn only now."

By this time I'd already decided that the whole thing was just a little too pious and way too sober for my tastes. I felt I'd done enough "fitting in with the natives" for one day. I quietly conferred with Helen but she was keen to see it through. She claimed I was in need of a more spiritual outlook, and besides, we couldn't offend Vicente. Under my breath I urged her to reconsider and she finally agreed to make some excuse and leave, but only when it was politic to do so. While we were waiting for that moment to come, my attention was naturally distracted by the young women, many of whom looked like the beautiful painted dancers that grace music boxes, only much more appealing in the flesh. They must have been quite far off because I suddenly realized I'd been ogling my slightly goofy-looking neighbors. "Hey, look," I said. "It's Maria's daughters, Simona and Theresa." I waved to the girls and they waved back. Helen squinted off in the wrong direction.

"I must've left my damn glasses back at the church," she said. "There's no point in me looking for them—I can't see. Will you go back?" I quickly returned to the church, which was now eerily empty. Even the effigies had been removed. I'd only been there a moment when the door creaked open behind me and Simona and Theresa came in.

"We saw you wave and then leave in a hurry. Is everything all right?" said Simona.

"I didn't mean for you to follow," I said. "I only came to look for Helen's glasses."

"Maybe we can help," said Theresa. The only place we'd paused was in front of the Virgin. The Madonna had been taken away and the empty pedestal on which it stood was closed off in its miniature shrine behind a sturdy gate. Something shiny glistened in the folds of the material covering the pedestal.

"I think I see them, but I can't quite reach through the gate and it's too high to climb," I said.

"We can give you a leg up," said Simona.

"But how do I get back over once I'm on the other side?" I

could imagine how well it would go down if the entire town trouped back to find me standing on the sacred Virgin's pedestal. They'd throw me in the dungeons and toss away the key.

"You can probably reach the pedestal from the top of the gate if you lean over," said Simona. "I'll get a chair and hold your legs so you don't fall." We found a chair and I launched myself from it to straddle the top of the gate. Then Simona got on the chair and grabbed my trousers around the ankles.

"Okay, here I go," I said, and began to dangle over the other side. The blood rushed to my head and I could feel my trousers slipping from my waist. It was only a matter of time before she'd loose her grip or I'd lose my trousers. Now there was a real danger of getting stuck in the Virgin's shrine in only my underwear. My fingers desperately stretched to reach the cloth covering the pedestal. "Shit! They're not here," I said. It was only a fragment of decorative glass I'd seen. "Pull me up." While Simona yanked my trousers, I gripped my way up the bars and then jumped down to the other side again. With my trousers now halfway to my ankles, I landed poorly and toppled over. The girls, flushing with embarrassment and giggling at my predicament, each took an arm and lifted me up. Just then the door creaked open again and there stood Helen, wearing her glasses and glaring at us in horror. Vicente appeared at her shoulder. As I pulled up my trousers he hurried to my side to help.

"You'll have to negotiate this one on your own," he whispered to me. On the way back to the parade he was the only one to break the uncomfortable silence. "Her glasses were in her pocket all along," he announced, smiling weakly. We made it back in plenty of time for the festivities, and the girls took off with unnecessary urgency to get to their places. Before long it was clear that the entire town was either in the parade or watching it. It took awhile for everyone to find their positions. "Nobody minds the delay," Vicente said. "Everyone here has one or two loved ones taking part." Helen glowered at me threaten-ingly. The *penitentes* looked like the Ku Klux Klan ready for a lynching, but they weren't half as intimidating as Helen when she was jealous. I wondered if my only hope was to join the pro-cession as a flagellant. Finally the religious effigies were lifted up on their platforms. Apparently it was a great honor to be one of the bearers. It was also a great honor to be one of the maids in attendance of the Virgin and an honor to accompany one of the priests. In fact, we were told it was an honor to be in the pa-rade at all, and later we learned it was even an honor to watch it go by.

Candles were lit and at last there was movement at the front of the procession. However, like a long train, it took some time for this movement to relay all the way down the line. It didn't help that the ancient priest at the front was only capable of a slow shuffle. As the statue of the Virgin went by, the crowd made the sign of the cross and each said his or her individual prayers. It went by so slowly that they could've said prayers for their entire family tree dating back to Adam and Eve before it passed. The last group was a collection of bewildered young children chaperoned by a teenage boy and girl. By the time they'd gone by, I was glad it was over and sensed our opportu-nity to leave. "Well, marvelous," I said, looking at Vicente hap-pily. "Anyone fancy a drink?" Vicente looked appalled.

"Oh, you can't go now," he said. "You must see them go by the market street; all of them reflected in the windows. It's a deeply moving experience." As far as I could tell, it was barely moving at all. I looked at Helen for help but she refused to meet my eye. "At this time of year we remember the holy sacrifice," Vicente continued. "The parade is an expression of penance by the whole town." Now *that* I could believe.

"Penance, did you say?" said Helen. "Some of us need that." She gave me one of her most scathing looks.

"If we hurry, we'll catch them," said Vicente. "You've never seen such a marvelous sight." I had a feeling that I had indeed just seen the marvelous sight he was referring to.

"Ahm, I'd like to, but I think we have to get back," I began.

"Nonsense." Helen cut in. "We're in no hurry at all." Having completely reneged on our deal to make an early escape, she marched off with Vicente, leaving me to tag along sheepishly behind. I had a sinking feeling that I was in for a long night of atonement for my alleged sins. We pushed through the crowd that grew thicker in the narrow arteries of the town's old streets. We arrived at the market street in plenty of time to see the old priest at the front tottering along unsteadily as if on the way to his own grave. Once again we had to watch the entire procession crawl by. Every now and then Vicente would turn smiling toward us and nod enthusiastically. A slow ripple of prayer passed through the crowd as the Virgin floated by. Under close surveillance, I made a point of looking away uninterestedly as Simona and Theresa passed. Nobody moved until the last of the young children had gone by several minutes later. It was gridlock on the sidewalk. Then suddenly there was no standing still as the crowd pressed on and carried us with it. Vicente's keenness got him separated up ahead. He turned and shouted: "To the fountain!" I contemplated dying, or slipping away, but Helen kept me locked in her angry tracker beam. In any case, we were now trapped in the clutches of the crowd.

I was pleased when Vicente rejoined us at the fountain because the other member in our group still wasn't talking to me. By now the old priest was leaning heavily on his mace. As the Virgin went by, I prayed the procession would end soon. Meanwhile, anarchy had broken out among the young children, who were snatching each other's flowers and running amok. The two teenagers left to supervise them were in a world of their own. They strolled along side by side, occasionally brushing shoulders or glancing at each other flirtatiously. I figured that by now I'd surely endured enough of this to absolve me *and* Genghis Khan. So I took Helen's hand and again tried to escape, but she snatched it away and the masses dragged us along once more. Hours later we ended up in the main square where the parade, its candles burned down to stubs, finally dispersed.

"Fantastic, eh?" said Vicente.

"Very penitential," I said in a flat voice. "I really felt I was on the march to Calgary." Helen kicked my shin.

"You must come back for the parades tomorrow and Friday," he said.

"We'd be delighted," said Helen. This time I kicked her in the shin. We went home and locked ourselves in the house for the next two days, pretending to be ill. Truthfully, she didn't want to go again either, and I felt that my health really would be in danger if we ran into the sisters another time. Despite my protestations of innocence, I spent the first night expelled to the sofa with a bemused Bobby. Given the smells he emanated, she knew this was close to a death sentence. On the Saturday before Easter, Diego came by to see if we were okay.

"Just a cold," I lied.

"Have some brandy," he suggested. He just happened to have some with him, from which he took a swig as a precaution. Then he suddenly cocked his head and looked perplexed. "The canary isn't singing," he said. He cupped his hand to his ear and set off through the house as if in a trance. We followed behind, united once more in panic. When he came across the cage, he stared at the deliveryman's bird with bewilderment. "I don't understand it," he said. " It *always* sang before. It was my best bird."

"Perhaps it's under the weather too," I suggested.

"It *is* looking greener than usual," said Helen.

"This is so strange," Diego said. He started whistling but the bird refused to join in. Diego was more than puzzled, he was shaken. It was as if he'd found olives growing on an almond tree. He took out an unlit cigarette and poked the canary with it through the bars of the cage. All it did was flutter to a different perch.

"Perhaps it's gone off singing," said Helen. "Birds change, you know . . . like people." Diego scratched his chin. Then he did a double take.

"Wait a minute," he exclaimed. "This is a female. I gave you a male. It can't have changed *that* much." I had to think quickly.

"I see what's happened now," I said. "This must be the one we got to keep him company."

"You didn't need to buy one." He looked offended. "I'd have given you another if I'd known you wanted two."

"We didn't want to put you out," I said. I realized this line didn't sound too plausible considering the number of things we'd persuaded him to help us with around the farm.

"So what happened to the one I gave you?"

"Introducing the female must have been too much for him," I said. "Right after that, he died."

"Died?"

"Dropped off his perch, just like that." I clicked my fingers. *"Madre mía."*

"Must have had a weak heart."

"I'll get you another one—one that sings," Diego said. "Then maybe this one will sing too."

"No, you mustn't trouble yourself," I said, mortified by the prospect of *two* singing canaries.

"It's no trouble at all. I'll bring it this afternoon."

"No, really," I pleaded. "We don't *want* a singing bird." Diego looked horrified. I struggled for words. "You see, we were so upset to lose the first one, we couldn't bear to have another that sings just yet." It was a close thing but in the end I think we got away with the canary swap. At least he never mentioned the bird again.

"Was I convincing?" I asked when he'd gone.

"I'd forgotten what a good liar you are," said Helen. "And to think I'd almost started to believe your story about why you had your trousers down in front of those girls." For some reason I spent that night on the sofa too.

8

Growing Pains

In the spring we at last got notification that someone was coming to talk to us about our application for electricity. I couldn't contain my excitement and contacted our electrician to insist that he put wires and switches into the simple circuit he'd drawn and that I'd painstakingly chiseled out of the walls. Manolo cautioned that optimism was premature, but I figured he was just dragging his feet. We were proposing to pay him so little that it would hardly be worth the wear and tear on his car from our dirt track. Eventually I nagged him so much that he did the work just to get me off his back. Two weeks after he'd finished, the man from the electric company came to see us. "I've got bad news," he said. "The nearest transformer is too far away."

"Don't tell me we can't have electricity," I said, head in hands.

"You can have it," he said, "but we'll need to put up another transformer to reach the valley." I peeped at him cautiously through my fingers.

"Give us the bad news," I said. "How much would it cost?"

"It'll come to about ten times what this house is worth," he answered, glancing around. I slid off my chair and sat on the floor, rocking back and forth. "Perhaps your neighbors would share the cost with you?" he suggested. "They'd all be able to connect."

"All of them together haven't got that kind of money," said Helen. I just moaned.

For two days I was inconsolable. The central pillar of my plan to modernize the farm had collapsed. I admit I was no agricultural expert but, unlike Helen, I didn't feel our crops were coming along very well. The young almonds were so small and the emerging vegetables so stumpy and inedible looking. To my mind, not only was the Titanic going down, but I'd just found out there was no lifeboat. I didn't know what to do so I drank a crate of beer and moped around. Meanwhile, life without an electricity connection seemed harder than ever—not just because we didn't have one, but because we *couldn't* have one.

We now had a butane-powered refrigerator, but it stank and as the bottle emptied it became temperamental. In that heat it only took a few hours for food to turn into something furry and dangerous. It wasn't nice to open the refrigerator door with a growling stomach, only to have your lunch growl back at you. The entire plumbing for the whole house remained one outside tap that didn't work if it was cloudy. And after all this time I was still emptying the chemical toilet every day without the protection of a gas mask. The only light was a single dim bulb attached to an extension cord that weaved a tangled trail through the house—and was the cause of several trips and falls. I can't tell you how disorienting it was to suddenly find yourself sailing through the air just as the room vanished into blackness. Being teased by Manolo's ridiculous new switches and plugs just made the torment worse.

It's not that I wasn't happy to live rough for a short time. What crushed me was the realization that a short time was already turning into a long time. And without electricity the place would *always* be a shack; not a nice modern home, or one that we could borrow on, or sell if worse came to worst. It made me particularly uncomfortable that my safety net now had a gaping hole in it. Persuading Helen to sell off seemed unlikely anyway, and I didn't have a clue what I would do even if we did sell. I'd been relying on Plan B and didn't even have a Plan C. The only thing that was clear was that I wasn't going to be able to fix the place up and make a profit on it that year, or possibly ever. In fact, at that point I felt we would *never* be able to sell it, even if we wanted to. It seemed I might be destined to pass away my days growing almonds and end up like old Emilio or his cousin Pepe, only with less know-how. Helen was correspondingly delighted with developments and kept telling me to look on the bright side. Unfortunately, one nine-watt bulb doesn't make for too many bright sides.

Eventually the beer ran out and I pulled myself together. Helen had always wanted to keep the house as it was and live off the land. If we couldn't do things my way, there was no choice for the foreseeable future but to try hers. Overnight we reversed roles. She was the one putting forward schemes—about what to plant and which animals to rear—and I was the one digging in to resist every suggestion. I'd come here to ask the fates what stars

I should follow in my life, what mountains I should climb. The answer the fates seemed to be giving me was that I could forget stars and mountains—I was going to be a poor peasant.

My spirits soon received another blow with the arrival of our things from England. Apparently, getting rid of us was not enough for Helen's mother. Gripes about the boxes we'd left behind were peppered throughout every letter we'd received from Rita. Finally she'd arranged for it all to be sent out. The growing feeling that I was now trapped at this remote farm was suddenly heightened by the arrival of everything I owned in the world. We awoke early one morning to see a truck driving away from the farm and a small mound of boxes in the middle of the threshing circle.

The boxes comprised all those things we'd deliberately left behind because we knew they would be useless in sunny Spain: umbrellas, gloves, scarves. Manual labor had by now reduced many of my clothes to threads, but five wool sweaters, some thermal underwear, and a ski jacket weren't going to do me much good. Neither would I need my smart job-interview suit, which in any case had become moth-eaten and as full of holes as my résumé. There were two boxes of books that must have cost more to ship than to buy new. The low point of the unpacking was the discovery of Helen's old vacuum cleaner. It was a short, round thing on wheels that we'd nicknamed R2D2. Not only would it be no match for the dust of the *campo,* but if we'd somehow been able to connect it to our solar setup, it would have drained the battery in the time it took to flip the switch.

Basically it was just more things to find space for. We'd gone from sharing one room to having an entire farmhouse with acres of land. Yet we were still running out of places to put things. There must be some universal law to the effect that junk will expand to fit the space available. The lack of a garbage collection service in this area of wilderness was partly to blame. Organic things went into our compost pile, but the rest proved harder to get rid of. The non-smelly stuff tended to get stockpiled in unused outbuildings. Helen's response was to try recycling; boxes became bedside tables, old cereal packets became fire lighters, and cans showed up thinly disguised as pencil or toothbrush holders. She even turned my thermal underwear into a set of matching washcloths and hand towels. I couldn't get into our pantry for all the glass jars and bottles she'd put aside "in case of emergency." It was hard to imagine what sort of emergency would require so many jars. Or even what kind of emergency would befall two people who lived on a farm and didn't have running water or electricity in the first place. Anything short of Armageddon was likely to pass us by.

When we first moved in, we used to take all our garbage to the municipal dump eight miles away. Not even Dante's broad imagination could have come up with such a place. The heat, flies, and stench defy literary description. The authorities weren't prepared for individual customers and expected you to drive right into the midst of a giant rotting pile to unload. I tried to think of what could be worse, and the only thing that came to mind was swimming in sewage. If we were going to be here for the long haul, we realized we'd have to devise a less hellish plan.

Our next tactic was to discreetly dump our garbage at bins in town. This was something the rightful users of the bins weren't too happy about. Consequently, we decided to come back after dark, when they'd gone to bed. Before long we found ourselves furtively cruising around town in the thick of night with a carload of garbage. I don't know what we would've said if the police had pulled us over and then noticed our cargo—not difficult since it was usually piled up to the roof and stank like a public rest room. I wondered what paragraph in the criminal code covered dumping garbage in someone else's bin in the middle of the night.

It was while committing this clandestine felony that we discovered we weren't the only ones cruising the bins. Furniture and other household items were put out by the road for collection on a Thursday. Most of it was broken or covered in stains commensurate with a mass murder. But occasionally there were things in pretty good condition, especially in the better neighborhoods. Some people did the rounds, and anything decent would be gone before the trash collectors got there. Items of furniture I'd seen by the side of the road at night often showed up in secondhand stores with a hefty price tag the next day. The fact that we became tempted said a lot about our dwindling finances and the slippery slope we were now on. Finally, we couldn't resist a table we saw by the road with a wobbly leg that even I could fix. Having tasted the fruits of this temptation, we found ourselves out scouting again the following Thursday evening. We'd done one circuit when I suddenly pulled the car off the road.

"What are we doing with our lives?" I said.

"Whatever do you mean?" said Helen.

"Well, look at us," I said. "We've both got good degrees and here we are cruising in the dark in Timbuktu, either trying to dump garbage . . . or *looking* for garbage to take home."

"But we're doing something environmentally friendly by recycling," she said.

"Isn't the fact that we're confined to solar power environmentally friendly enough?" I said. "We're already professional peasants by day. Do we really have to be ragpickers by night?"

We didn't actively scavenge for discarded furniture again, but I have to admit it was hard to keep my eyes on the road while driving around town on a Thursday evening. When you're as

broke as we were rapidly becoming, you can't be as picky as
you'd like. We went home and I determined I'd ask the neighbors what they did with their trash. I wondered what advice
they'd give as I'd seen the younger Diego simply toss things out
of his window as he drove along, and Maria's yard was littered
with broken items. Emilio didn't buy anything and so didn't produce any garbage. Diego senior seemed like the man to ask.
"Burn it," he said, "but be careful you don't set fire to the *campo.*"

It was a little depressing, now that we couldn't have electricity, that my home improvements were confined to building
something to burn trash in. The incinerator was only my second
challenge with bricks. The first was the cesspool, which had
ended in humiliation when Emilio pointed out that I'd been laying the concrete blocks the wrong way up. It's pretty bad when a
ninety-year-old almond grower who lives in a house made of
rocks and straw knows more about modern building techniques
than you do. My incinerator was a square of leftover concrete
blocks, carefully laid the right way up. Heeding the elder Diego's
warning, I chose a patch of barren ground where there was little
adjacent foliage to catch fire.

One later modification was made after an exploding aerosol
can nearly blew my head off. I had to place a wire mesh over the
open top of the incinerator to stop larger projectiles from starting a forest fire or bringing down a passing airplane. Burning
days continued to sound like the Fourth of July, but now the
biggest danger was that the wind would change direction and
cause the house to smell like the municipal dump for the rest of
the week.

Helen saw the guiding hand of destiny in my failed bid to live
like a twenty-first-century man. She used a carrot-and-stick
combination to get my help with her vision of the place. "Come
on, Shaun. Be positive!" she would cry as I staggered past with

singed eyebrows and reeking of garbage. Our days of kissing each other till we were numb were long over. Now it was becoming a question of who would make the excuse and be the quickest to blow out the candle and turn away. Only her bad temper still elicited the same old responses. No matter how many times I kissed her I couldn't awake Sleeping Beauty. And no matter how many times she kissed me, I was still just a frog. But we both knew that as long as we were stuck out here together, we needed to make a go of our relationship. Each of our foibles were now so familiar to the other as to be both annoying and comforting at the same time. Yet all the old attractions that originally brought us together were still there somewhere too. She was so assured of her own appeal and believed she should get her way so strongly that she had me convinced on several occasions.

Nevertheless, I found myself taking solitary walks to one of my favorite spots on our land, far from the house. Where our last field met the bottom of the hills there was a dip where the trees made a dense orchard and the grasses were always lush. Climbing the hill a little ways above this peaceful hideaway, I'd found a large rock that was comfortable to sit on and offered a view across the valley that was different from the one we were used to at the house. From this slight elevation I could see an abandoned farm that was becoming a ruin, away in the distance. Even the seemingly impregnable solid stone walls were crumbling. "The Rodriguez farm," Diego once explained. "Nobody likes to talk about that." They hadn't made it through one of the periodic droughts that hit the area. Drought or no drought, I took it as a harbinger of things to come.

Sitting on my own, staring out at the otherwise unchanging Spanish countryside, time occasionally seemed to dissolve away. I was aware that one day, not too long ago, men had all been fighting tigers and throwing spears. A bit later on, the planet would plunge into the sun, taking us into oblivion with it. In the timeless valley, all these points in history seemed to converge into a single moment. The illusion quickly vanished to be followed by an urge to go to the nearest bar and get hopelessly drunk.

I decided to take my woes to Emilio and walked up to his farm. We sat on tree stumps in his yard under the shade of his tall pines and sipped a milky nut drink called *horchata*. I didn't know where to begin, so I just up and told him I was having trouble figuring out where I fitted in with the whole space-time continuum thing. It took the dictionary and several trys, and even then I'm not sure either of us knew what I was saying. "One thing I will tell you about time," he said finally. "Time is *not* money." On our farm that was certainly proving true.

He may not have gotten my full meaning but he intuitively understood the problem. "You're a young man, Shaun. I would gladly trade places with you any day. Look at me." He tapped his bad leg with his walking stick. "Nothing works anymore. But you have your whole life ahead of you. Life is too short to worry." He grinned wryly. "Unfortunately, by the time we figure that out, it's usually too late."

"Thanks for the encouragement," I said.

"What do you think you're missing?" he asked with a smile. "This might not be paradise, but it's where you are. That's how life is, whoever you're with, and whatever you do, only a fool would refuse to be happy."

So I did my best to look at our situation optimistically. There might have been no road, mail, telephone, television, lights, power, water, sewage, or trash collection, but one service we did have was fresh bread delivered daily to our door. It was some consolation, I suppose. I could never figure out how the baker made any profit sending a truck out on a circuit of remote farms, to sell loaves costing fifty cents each. It turned out the driver was a nephew of the baker. My theory was that his uncle sent him on this lengthy errand to get him out of the way. For although he was personable, he was so dim you could monitor his thought processes through his slowly changing expressions. It was wise to have the exact change ready unless you wanted to stand around for a few minutes while he lost count on his fingers. Having said that, he did at least have two words of English and the guts to use them. He would always pull up honking his horn, his brow would wrinkle, his eyes search the heavens, and then he would stutter "he-llo." His other word was "good-bye." The successful excreting of these words would be followed by a sheepish look until we showed our appreciation.

The other daily ritual involving the bread man was trying to contain Bobby. The puppy used to bark at strangers but pretty soon changed his tune and became friendly. Yet dogs seem to be genetically predisposed to resent people who regularly deliver. In the absence of a mailman, Bobby had it in for the baker. The honking horn sent him into a frenzy of snarling and growling that was disrespectful for one so young and bold for one so small. The driver made a tactical error by running away, which only prompted the dog to chase as if it now had justification. It was quite a sight to see a grown man fleeing in terror from a puppy a foot and a half long. I found it hard to take the stern approach demanded by his pleas as he climbed an olive tree. Eventually the driver grew so shaky about visiting us that he stayed in the truck and passed the bread through the window.

Despite the excellent bread service, I still found the counting of blessings required a blind eye and a dull head. As I toiled away, unsure if I would ever see civilization again, I really struggled to find something to lift my morale. Helen was always going on about the spiritual benefits of living in a remote corner of Spain, but despite Emilio's advice I needed something more solid to feel good about. I wracked my brains to think of some *tangible* advantage to living here that I could point to. It was hard to point in any direction without pointing to an almond tree, and I concluded that this was the only commodity we were really spoiled for. With four hundred trees we had almonds up the gazoo.

Needless to say, this abundance of trees also gave us an enviable supply of wood for romantic log fires. Since on winter nights our supposedly warm climate did a good impersonation of the arctic, this heat was essential. Of course it wasn't as easy as turning up a thermostat. The snag was that you had to go out and cut it yourself. I would soon learn that I had been blessed with a plenitude of one of the most solid and difficult-to-cut woods on the planet. I was conscious that Maria was watching from afar when I made my first effort to break up the remains of a tree trunk that had been felled long ago. The axe stuck on my second blow and I ended up careering around the yard, dragging the tree trunk with me as I tried to get it out again. After two more attempts with the same outcome, I decided to go in and try again later when no one was around. Finally we concurred that owning several hundred of these rock-hard trees was a good enough excuse to buy a chain saw—even if it was one of the last major purchases we could afford.

Our new chainsaw made so much noise, an armored division could have rolled into the valley without me noticing. So I suppose I shouldn't have been shocked when I looked up and saw Emilio's cousin standing right over me. It annoyed me to have to turn the machine off because it had taken a good half hour to get it started in the first place. Pepe gave me a toothless grin and asked how much the saw had cost me. "I know a man who wants his small orange grove cleared," he said. "Whoever clears it can have the wood for free. What do you say we do the work together and split the wood fifty-fifty?" Since both of us already had a lifetime's supply of wood, this proposition didn't fill me with zeal. However, orange is a soft wood that cuts and burns easily and so it's useful for a small fire or for getting bigger almond logs going, which are as hard to ignite as they are to cut. When life seems too short for almond wood, having a little orange around wouldn't hurt. Let's face it, you take whatever offers you get when you're stranded miles from the nearest toilet or functioning light switch, with a girlfriend whose burning ambition in life is to grow vegetables. As for Pepe, he just couldn't resist anything that was free. He persuaded me to go, and the next day the two of us set off in my car for a farm near Santa Maria. My first reaction was horror at the size of the overgrown grove.

"We'll never get that done today," I protested. "It's nearly a quarter of an acre." He was so deaf I had to say it twice.

"With your machine it'll cut like paper," he finally replied. "You cut and I'll clear. When we're done we'll borrow Diego's trailer."

"Let's do half," I said. When I'd said it again, he wagged his elderly finger at me and shook his head.

"But we've already made a deal," he said. "We can't go back on our word. The farmer wants to replant the field with a new variety tomorrow." I tried to remember what deal *we'd* made or when we'd given *our* word.

"As it's you Pepe, I'll do my best. But if we don't finish by sundown, you'll have to get someone else tomorrow."

"Eh? Don't worry, we'll split the work fifty-fifty," he said. Three things should have occurred to me at once. First of all, Pepe didn't have a saw or any other tool with him and, secondly, he was a bit elderly for heavy exertion. Thirdly, I recalled that his daughter and granddaughters did all the work at his farm while he sat around and rolled cigarettes. So not surprisingly I both cut the wood and loaded it on and off the trailer. Pepe dragged the odd branch along and under the din of the saw he would pat the growing pile of logs and smile at me. Cutting the field and loading the wood took all day. When I'd finished I was barely able to move and bent double like an eighty-year-old, while Pepe looked as sprightly and unruffled as a healthy young man.

Maria and her daughters were surprised to see me when I dropped him off at their farmhouse. He clearly hadn't told them what we were up to. When he acted as if he'd done me a favor, they swatted him away under a barrage of reprimands. To make up for their grandfather's behavior, the girls offered to cook me a meal and massage my damaged back. Tempted as I was, I knew that Helen was waiting for me. If she ever found out I'd had a rubdown from Simona or Theresa, I'd probably be expelled to the sofa for good. So I declined graciously and hobbled away.

Back home I collapsed exhausted in a chair and surveyed my own massive pile of orange wood, which I needed like the Saudis need more oil. We still didn't have a toilet, but the firewood situation had gone from abundance to surfeit. Most of it would still be there years later, and the only purpose it served was providing a home for several generations of lizards and scorpions. Helen was delighted with this "emergency supply." In her view, it was yet another blessing and exactly the kind of thing that should make me feel optimistic.

Pepe aside, there was no question our neighbors gave us much more than they received. This was a constant embarrassment to us because we were so unestablished on our farm that we had little to give back. Emilio was always plying us with grapes and plums from his garden. Diego senior gave us pork and potatoes, and Maria made goat cheese and brought us milk. God knows how we'd have survived that far without them. Real trouble only began when they started trying to give us live farm animals. Our neighbors were determined that we should diversify, as they had done, to overcome the financial limitations of the almond market. Diego junior tried several times to give us chicks for the fine chicken pens installed by the previous owners of our farm.

These offers always resulted in an unsightly quarrel between Helen and myself that had Diego retreating as fast as he could. I had always assumed that we would draw the line at raising animals. We had enough trouble trying to cultivate things that couldn't run away or bite you, and that didn't leave droppings all over the place. Besides, where would we put all these chickens and goats if we ever went back to London? I could just imagine my mom's expression if I showed up with a clucking and braying truckload and tried to release them into her backyard. Helen replied that the animals would probably be easier to sell than the house. She argued that since we couldn't have electricity to modernize and then either borrow on or sell the house, the *only* option was to farm more intensively. If we were going to get by, we'd need to be more self-sufficient and also have something else to sell, like eggs or cheese. I hadn't yet developed a counter-argument but that didn't stop me. I slammed my hand on the table and declared I wasn't going to become a goatherd. Since we couldn't reason with each other, we just shouted about everything: have animals, don't have animals; who kept who awake with their snoring; and which end of the toothpaste tube it was wrong to squeeze.

One day, Diego drunkenly intervened in our dispute by bringing around an old chicken whose laying days were over. He held the live chicken upside down by its claws. "Have this for dinner," he said. "The fresh taste will convince you to start keeping poultry." Before I could do anything about it, he'd released the bird into our enclosed yard. "I'll be back tomorrow to see how you enjoyed it," he said. Helen fell on the frightened chicken with squeals of delight and promptly named it Betty. We both watched the bird with fascination as it pecked its way around the yard. Then Bobby showed up and gave chase for a while, nose to the ground and wagging his tail.

"Haven't we got any grain we can give her?" Helen said, picking up the dog. "Poor Betty looks starving."

"Don't forget we're supposed to eat the damn thing," I said.

"Well, we should fatten her up then," she said indignantly. She spent most of the afternoon talking to the bird in a babyish voice while I continued to tackle the cesspool. A silence fell over us as evening approached. We waited and waited until eventually my stomach started rumbling.

"It's going to be getting dark soon," I said. "Who's going to do the dirty deed?"

"Why can't we let her live out her days in peace?" said Helen. "She's had a long life of service. It's only right she should be allowed to retire."

"This is a chicken you're talking about," I said. "Come on— you're the one who wants to go into poultry farming."

"I can't do it," she protested.

"Well, I never said I wanted it. I only like the preprepared bits that come wrapped in plastic at the supermarket."

"We'll have to tackle this together," she said. We went out and stood in the enclosure while Betty pecked around at our feet. "How are we going to do it then?" she said, looking pale.

"I think you're supposed to slit their throats or break their necks or something." I might as well have been talking to myself because Helen was leaning on the fence looking sick. We went back inside. "This is absurd," I said. "We eat chicken all the time. If we're farmers and we can't do this, we're pathetic."

"You'll have to do it for me, Shaun, please." I went out and confronted Betty face-to-face.

"Look, you're a chicken and I'm a human," I reasoned with

her. "Humans eat chickens and that's all there is to it." I tried to grab the bird but she wasn't cooperating and I lacked the nerve for a decisive lunge. I needed another approach. There was a hefty stick nearby that we used to prop the gate open. I decided a swift blow to the head would be the best thing. Several times I lined the stick up but lost my courage. What finally pushed me over the edge was the thought of telling the neighbors we'd adopted the chicken as a pet.

The first strike missed. The second was far too half-hearted and only injured the bird. The third hit the body and it was now squawking and darting about the pen. I'd turned into a desperate man as I chased it around. Since the bird was badly injured, I knew there was no going back. I had to finish the job. In the end it was a bloody massacre. For several minutes I stood trembling over what was left. When I'd gathered myself together I went inside for something alcoholic.

"Murderer!" yelled Helen. I could see she'd been crying.

"I've done the hard part," I said bitterly. "Now you can pluck it and prepare it." We ended up cremating Betty's uneaten remains in the incinerator, after a small ceremony of remembrance. Although I was remorseful for my bloody act, I sensed victory in our dispute over animal farming.

"Absolutely delicious," I told Diego the next day, "but we've decided we're not going to acquire any chickens for the time being."

Even so, we couldn't escape farm animals just because we didn't yet have any of our own. The last chicken feather had barely been cleared from our yard when Maria asked us to help the vet with her donkey. She had to be out with her flock, and both daughters were picking broccoli on another farm that day. It went without saying that Pepe would be no use. I couldn't imagine what use we could be either until we showed up to find the vet rolling around on the ground in the corral.

"The bastard kicked me in the knee," he said. "You'll have to hold him while I take a blood sample." The donkey had disappeared into its stable where it was watching us with suspicion from the shade. I hoped that Helen was thinking about how bad the corral smelled. I know I was. It was home to the donkey by day, the goats by night, and thousands of insects day *and* night. The ground was a sludge of droppings and the air was thick with flies. Some rural idyll.

When we were within three feet of the donkey, it suddenly bolted right between us and raced around the corral like it'd been stung by a bee. Each time it stopped we crept up on it again. It would taunt us by waiting until we were poised to lunge, and then race off. Before long we'd dived and slipped so many times that we were as covered in muck as the vet. I think he was getting ready to throw a syringe at the donkey like a dart when Pepe showed up. With a wink he casually tossed a pile of carrots into the corral and shuffled off. The donkey stood and ate with such concentration that the vet could've amputated without it noticing.

Helen reached out toward me in what I mistook for a gesture of affection. "Hold still!" she snapped and picked a goat flea off my shoulder. The week's events led her to agree that we should find some way other than husbandry to make ends meet.

Determined to consolidate this decision before she could change her mind, I set about destroying the animal section of the farm—or "renovating" it, as I diplomatically called the procedure. The unsightly chicken pens came down and the enclosed yard became an internal courtyard complete with flowerpots. There's nothing like a good cleanup to turn up long-abandoned relics and old tools. Many of these tools of the almond grower were handmade from materials available on our land. We found a mortar and pestle hewn from almond, a yoke, and baskets woven from the grass that grew on our fields. There were clues

to poverty as well as quaint self-sufficiency, such as a pair of sandals cut from car tires. We turned some of these things into ornaments. Others, like the sandals, were condemned to the
incinerator as unwelcome reminders that even the experts
found it hard to earn any money here.

Then one day, with a little help from Diego, I finished the
cesspool and gratefully buried the evidence of my sloppy handiwork under a couple of feet of soil. We'd bought a regular ceramic toilet, but it had been sitting in pieces to one side of the
bathroom for weeks. At last I was able to join all these elements
together. The chemical toilet was ceremoniously retired to stor-
age in an old goat pen. The only drawback was that the new toilet wasn't yet connected to the water supply, which still ended at
the tap by the back door. So the toilet's tank was going to have to
be filled each time by buckets. We topped it up and were at last
ready for our inaugural flush. With plastic champagne glasses in
hand, Helen pulled the lever for the first time. After a few more
glasses of cheap Spanish bubbly, we both found that we needed
to make use of the new facility. Unfortunately, we'd forgotten to
refill the tank, so we ended up running outside and heading in
opposite directions to nearby trees.

To make up for our failure with animals, Helen put all her
hopes into our plants. The whole self-sufficiency issue was at
stake. Was I right in beginning to think we'd screwed up, or was
she right to believe we could really make a go of it? She pointed
out that Emilio managed to live without animals other than his
two mangy dogs. But then he had a lot more land than we did.
Furthermore, he ate a squirrel's diet. Nevertheless, her dream
of feeding ourselves didn't seem completely preposterous. After
all, our land did provide a surprising bounty. Apart from several
hundred almond trees, we had dozens of olives, several figs, and

a couple of pomegranates. Capers and prickly pears had been planted for cultivation by the previous owners, and thyme was everywhere.

However, despite this abundance of food, there wasn't much we could eat. There was no use telling me these crops had powered Emilio into his ninetieth year. In my view, a normal person can only consume so many almonds. The same goes for capers—although goats seem to have a limitless appetite for them. We put all the olives we thought we could eat into jars with spices. The rest we gave to the local cooperative in return for olive oil and some cash. As for the prickly pears and pomegranates—they were so full of seeds it was like eating grit. Furthermore, the cacti on which the pears grew were coated in fine needles that got into our skin like glass fibers. We had to knock the pears off with a stick, and roll them on the ground to remove the needles before they were safe to pick up and peel. That's a lot of effort for a mouthful of grit.

Of course, no one grew absolutely everything that they ate themselves. Among the poorer farmers there was a whole economy based on barter rather than cash. If we couldn't yet grow or buy what we needed, perhaps we could trade for it. The trouble was that everyone already had what we could offer them. No one would swap the fruits of their labor in return for our almonds, anymore than they'd swap for our rocks. Emilio tried to help by showing us how to graft a plum or apricot on to an almond tree. In his dotage he was going around gradually turning all his own commercial almonds into fruit trees. Under his supervision, we grafted a couple of trees near the house but even this meager contribution gave us nothing that wasn't already abundant locally. We needed to offer something that others *didn't* have.

At last Helen saw her chance to come into her own. It was in her vegetable patch that we would stand out from the crowd.

There was a lot riding on that well-dug and lovingly tended field. Nature's abundance in spring had given us the delusion that even we could grow things ourselves. So we had great expectations for the encyclopedic variety of vegetables we'd planted when we moved in. Helen always had my full cooperation on this. I may not have been as keen as she was on self-sufficiency, but I was even less keen on going hungry. The first problem had been Bobby, who insisted on helping by digging everything up. Then when some green shoots began to appear, Maria stopped by and her goats took their toll. In the end, the whole patch had to be fenced with an unsightly circle of wire from the recently dismantled chicken pens. It began to look more like Auschwitz than a verdant pasture.

The locals all grew the same limited combination of crops and then horrified Helen by spraying them mercilessly with pesticide. We were going to teach them a lesson by having a wide variety of crops that would not be touched by toxic sprays. She let them know she was looking at the big picture. The future lay with her style of organic farming, she insisted. Once again, we dreamed of being on the cutting edge.

Instead we had to endure a humbling "I told you so" from our neighbors as only the standard range of broccoli and runner beans withstood the soil and powerful sun. Even these were inedible stumps after the bugs had been at them. The cruel irony was how cheap vegetables were in the market. So far we'd devoted months of work, moved tons of manure, and used gallons of precious water—all for about a dollar's worth of vegetables. I had flunked economics, but even I could see this was not free enterprise at its intended best.

The conclusion that we weren't cut out to be farmers, in any form, seemed obvious to me. I thought even Helen would see the light now. After all, she'd dreamed of orchards brimming with enough fruit and vegetables to put Vicente's store to shame. But she seemed content to blame this "minor setback" on me and concentrate in the short term on keeping Bobby away from the next round of emerging stalks. There was still the almond crop to look forward to, and that was the main thing. We had to hope that, on our farm at least, money really did grow on trees. Her faith in Mother Nature was such that she was sure we'd get it right the next time. The good earth would provide—eventually. She had this capacity to sit cross-legged on the patio and meditate for hours. Then she would emerge from her trance spouting words of optimism.

My personal inclination was to panic. We might well be able to turn our nuts into cash, if we could hold out that long. But it was now clear to me that we weren't going to make it to the almond crop. Sitting around daydreaming didn't seem like an option anymore. Necessity was forcing me to become a man of action. I had to admit it: I'd even failed as a dropout. Back in England, if I'd been able to see into the future, I wouldn't have recognized the life I was now leading or imagined the changes it was causing in me. At times it had seemed as though laziness was the only thing Helen and I really had in common, but so far this wasn't turning out to be the best basis for a joint business venture. Both our dreams for El Águila had been shattered. It was no life of leisure and no rural bliss either. We probably couldn't sell the farm and come out on top, and we couldn't feed ourselves. We quickly needed to find a new source of income before the cash dried up completely.

My immediate reaction was to borrow Diego's handheld pesticide sprayer. It was too late for our first batch of vegetables but black flies was starting to threaten the olives, which were, after all, a cash crop. One of our other projects to fend for ourselves was just getting started—a realistically small orchard consisting of a grapefruit, an orange, and a lemon tree. I was determined that no bugs were going to destroy these tender young plants. And they didn't—I did. Unfortunately, I sprayed so much that I killed not just the bugs but also the fruit trees. It seemed that God was telling me I couldn't win.

9

Expats

Helen knew better than to give me lectures on nature for a while. But that didn't stop her trying it out on people too far away to know about our debacles. She was already in too deep with her mother to admit defeat. So she proceeded to dig herself even deeper by sending Rita letters about how wonderfully it was all going. Yet no matter how she described our picturesque scene of rural tranquility, Rita still said it stank.

What baffled me was Helen's sudden enthusiasm to communicate with a woman she'd spent the last ten years trying to avoid. Her mother wound her up so badly when we lived together that it had taken the first few months in Spain for her to calm down and stop complaining about it. Finally, time and distance must have been enough to induce amnesia. Helen harped on about Mother Nature so much I guess it became hard to ignore her own mother. The big role that family played in the lives of our neighbors also served to prick the conscience. Family seemed to be an integral part of a life spent close to the land—the kind of life she wanted. Most locals had several generations of relatives around them. We only had Bobby.

This barrage of heartfelt correspondence must have been as much a surprise for Rita as it was for me. She kept telling her mother that the natural beauties of our surroundings had touched her spirit. Apparently, living here was on a par with going to Mecca or cuddling the Pope. On the one hand, I felt these epistles could soften the hardest of hearts. But on the other hand, the arrival of such a letter during the bustle of a busy morning in urban England might lead the reader to conclude that Helen had finally lost her mind. Since Rita thought we were lunatics to be here in the first place, this interpretation seemed most likely.

One detail Helen deliberately left out of her glowing accounts was the fact we'd spent practically all the money we came out with. We probably wouldn't have lasted this long if the farm had cost anything to run. Thankfully, there were no taxes to pay, no rent, no mortgage, no heating bills, and no water costs. In fact, there were no bills at all. Even what little electricity we had was free. All we had to do was feed ourselves. We weren't doing too well at that, but if it looked like we were really going to starve, there were always almonds and prickly pears to eat. Nevertheless, the cash was getting so low that we had no choice but to mention selling off at a loss, or returning to England to jump back into the rat race for a while. I could picture myself, crammed penniless into an Underground train at rush hour, lamenting our failure to get any return on all the time and money we'd invested here.

In an act of hopeless defiance by Helen, and reckless abandon by me, we went out and bought three items we didn't really need. Down to our last couple of hundred bucks, we now couldn't afford to relocate to England even if we wanted to. The first of these items came from Manolo the electrician. I was wary that he might be jinxed and that anything we bought from him was destined never to work. But he seemed sincerely remorseful when he heard that we'd failed to get connected. He had a suggestion to make things a little better. The suggestion involved giving him even more money, this time for a device to turn 12-volt solar power into a standard European 240-volt supply. In this form, electricity from our panel would work through the circuitry he'd installed. With this new device we were able to turn lights on at the switches, just like ordinary people, and tripping over the extension cord became a thing of the past. We told ourselves it was a good investment, because if we had to sell quickly, it at least created an illusion of modernity.

The converter didn't give us any *more* electricity, so it really was an illusion. In fact, a certain amount of power was lost because of it. Consequently, we could still only have one light on at a time, unless we were planning a very early night. Living with a solar panel really teaches you to respect that electricity is something expendable, like a log pile or a candle. Of course, this was always true in the past, but back when we lived with company power I, at least, had the false impression that there was an endless supply of the stuff. I didn't stop to think that to maintain this delusion, the utility companies were stripping the planet bare and choking up the atmosphere. Even Helen, who had always griped against the electricity generators, never showed any inclination to cut back on her own consumption when we lived in

England. But making our own electricity was a whole new ball game. If we accidentally dozed off for a while with the light on, we'd wake up to find we had no light and no water either. This tends to hone your energy consciousness.

So even with our plugs up and running, there were very few appliances undemanding enough to insert in them. However, we knew from Diego's house that it was possible to run a small television set on a minimum of solar electricity. A portable television was the second of the three items that just about bankrupted us. This outlay rewarded us with two channels in Spanish and one in some bizarre mountain dialect that not even our neighbors could understand. Finally, from a secondhand store, we also acquired a satellite dish. Expenditure on troop morale, we agreed, was legitimate in our hour of despair. We might die of starvation but we weren't going down in poor spirits.

We'd been told the dish was still angled correctly to pick up a signal. Certainly it was well off target by the time it'd bumped over our dirt track and been hammered to the wall. I spent hours hanging precariously from the side of the house, moving it an eighth of an inch at a time in either direction. Meanwhile, Helen sat in front of the television watching fuzz and listening to static. I was starting to feel sure we'd been ripped off when she finally screamed out excitedly: "I see dim shapes in the fog!" A few more adjustments and we had sound and then finally a picture.

We could only have it on for a little while, so it didn't pay to get too involved in anything with a plot. Many a time we'd just be getting to the denouement when the whole house would black out. Sadly, neither our budget nor our electricity supply would stretch to a cable box. Consequently, we could only pick up the channels beamed via outer space for free. On our set these consisted of twenty channels in German, CNN, and the Cartoon Network. Once you'd seen the news and lost the plot in a German soap opera, there wasn't much for two adults to watch anyway. The nearest thing to drama in English was *The Flintstones*.

Nevertheless, it was refreshing to hear almost anything in our own language after such a long time. We'd become so immersed in our local society that the world beyond seemed hardly to exist. Besides the greetings of the bread deliveryman, the only local who had any English was Bobby—and all he had was "sit" and "shake hands." For months we could only count on unimpeded conversation with each other, and after a fight we couldn't even count on that. One advantage of having no other English speakers around was that Helen and I could use our native tongue to talk privately in a public place. When we went to cafés, we got in the habit of commenting freely and loudly on the food or other customers, safe in the knowledge that no one could understand us. For instance, on one occasion I remarked how miserable the man at the next table looked. "No wonder, when you look at his wife," said Helen.

"She is rather unappealing, isn't she?"

"If I ever end up looking like that, please handcuff me to a gym instructor." At this point the woman got up quickly and fled the café in tears. The man glowered at us.

"Now look what you've done!" he said in perfect British. We felt so guilty that when we spoke English in public, we did it sotto voce ever after.

Usually we had to drive all the way down to the coast to run across any foreigners. In July and August there were thousands there of every nationality, but in the off-season only a few retirees and a handful of businessmen remained. The first year-round resident we ran into was a coquettish Scottish woman called Brenda, whose husband was a sales rep in the swimming pool business. She flirted outrageously with me but was so past her prime that Helen decided it would be picky to object. In fact, she did so much to conceal her age it was difficult to see her at all. Hats and scarves hid a lot, while inches of makeup covered the rest. If all of that failed, there was usually enough jewelry to dazzle your eyes. When we greeted her she always proffered a cheek, but I learned to blow a kiss and not make actual contact. This is because the first time I met her I got my lips stuck and came away with a mouthful of creams and potions.

There were so few native English speakers that they all knew each other and formed a close-knit community. It was an unlikely grouping that cut across social classes and personality types. Back in their home countries, most of them would have preferred to shoot themselves rather than speak to each other. However, the basic human need to interact with others in fluent language was overpowering—as we discovered for ourselves. Having bumped into Brenda, we were soon introduced to everyone else in this motley circle. Our youth turned out to be our main attraction and we began to feel like fresh blood at a gathering of geriatric vampires. The main problem for most of these people was boredom. What do you do in a foreign resort in the off-season if you're retired? The easy answer was to drink. For many it was literally an intoxicating lifestyle. In a group already full of bizarre escapees, this resort to the bottle only evoked greater eccentricities.

Becoming involved with this expatriate community was to prove a lifeline when we were near to drowning. Many expats felt they were too old to learn a new language and consequently struggled with simple things like shopping or dealing with the town hall. Others were frail and couldn't drive anymore or do heavy lifting. The arrival of two fit young people capable of communicating both with them and with the natives was a godsend. No one expected us to run around doing errands all day for nothing, so the godsend cut both ways. It was quite a long drive from our place to the resort, but we'd at last found a way to get by until the nut harvest. As the financial pressure lifted a little, one benefit was that we could afford to appreciate each other once again; or at the very least amicably agree to disagree.

I thought the high-rise of the coastal resorts would be comfortingly familiar after months in the wilderness. But we'd been living in our remote stone house with our rustic neighbors for such a long time that the coastal development now seemed almost surreal. After my first ever prolonged absence from modern city living, the urban environment suddenly felt disappointingly impersonal. It was so visibly shaped by money and so far removed from nature that I started to wonder whether Helen had been on to something all along. In the country, it was impossible not to see that nature is the bedrock of everything on the planet—indeed, it *is* the planet. In the city, "nature" is no more than an exotic tourist destination or the subject of a rather dull television documentary. After our first visit with Brenda, even I found it reassuring to head off the road at our dirt track and leave modernity behind.

The initial shock of seeing something once so familiar with a totally new perspective soon wore off. Then, for me at least, it was back to an appreciation of the comforts of "civilization." Helen's desire to overthrow it all was too mind-boggling in its scope for me to embrace. This was the world we'd created, and it seemed to me we were stuck with it. The best anyone could hope for was to find a private piece of the past, as we had done at El Águila. On the occasional days we spent working down by the sea, we didn't so much commute between areas as between eras. I was already confused about whether I was American or English, but now I was starting to wonder what century I belonged in.

Our first customers at the resort were a middle-aged gay painter and his writer partner who had fled to Spain for privacy.

The partner spent most of the time passed out with drink. Helen and I decided he was trying to develop a new style of writing that would be called "stream of unconsciousness." They'd heard we'd put up our own satellite dish and wanted one for themselves. It was ironic that something we thought might be our last extravagant expenditure actually led to the paycheck that saved us. We went through the fog and static routine again for them, and thereafter the painter, Brian, used to send me to Alicante to buy his supplies. The first time I made a delivery he was out, but I found a worrying note fixed to the gate that read: "Please enter via my back passage." I never commented on it.

The real money came with bigger jobs such as decorating or renovation. Naturally, those who'd heard about my handiwork weren't going to let me loose on their own home. Usually my job was to hire someone without my disabilities. The consensus was that the locals, while admirably tolerant of foreigners, had a tendency to treat them like old fools when it came to pricing. Of course, my bartering wasn't up to much either. I did explain this, but some people feared unbridled Spanish profiteering more than they feared my incompetence—at least I meant well. If a new kitchen was required, I'd shop around and get it done for them by professionals for a reasonable price. They'd give me something for my trouble and the plumbers, carpenters, and builders would also hand me a small percentage of their takings in gratitude for being given the work. We never made a great deal of money but we were surviving.

The first major job was for the distinguished Sir John and his wife, Lady Cynthia. They had a nice villa by the sea, but noisy tourist crowds in summer enraged him to the point of criminal behavior. As he was a retired judge with a reputation to maintain, that simply wouldn't do. He felt that most Britons could be defined as either yobs or snobs, and proudly put himself in the latter category. Fortunately, this elderly gent had enough money to buy a second home—an old house in the hills—to escape to in July and August. The house was on the edge of a small village that was unremarkable except for a well-tended civil war memorial and a little church with a blue tiled dome. As it was known that we lived even deeper into the wilderness, he mistakenly concluded that we must be experts on all things rural. By our standards, the house was already the height of luxury, but by his it was in need of renovation. We would find that getting anything up to John's standards was tricky. As it was, we only got the job because he didn't trust the locals, or "foreigners" as he called them, to run things properly. "The Spanish couldn't run a bath," was his catchphrase.

Although John and Cynthia had lived in Spain for nearly a decade, they weren't going to let anything Spanish contaminate their lives. The decor inside their coastal villa had clearly been transplanted direct from Buckinghamshire. The London *Times* was read every morning and tea taken every afternoon. John couldn't tell you when the local fiesta took place, but if you wanted the latest cricket score, he was your man. To a fellow English speaker he was a perfect old-world gentleman. However, if a Spaniard came to his door, he just shut it in their face as if no one was there. "Whatever would I want to learn Spanish for?" he would say with contempt.

The Spanish got off lightly compared with Germans. He was like that Japanese soldier who was lost in the jungle; the one who thought World War II was still going on years after its end. As far as John was concerned the war was far from over. The judge was determined that no Kraut was going to better his parking place by the port or his table reservation at the tennis club. He wasn't the only one. The English, Americans, and Australians teamed up, but the Germans, Dutch, and French all kept to their own cliques. In John's view, it only went to prove that a modern Englishman had more in common with Americans and Australians than with Europeans, and that the whole European Union was a big mistake. "Just look at how badly things are done here in Spain," he said.

"So why don't you go back to England?" I asked him.

"Wretched place has gone to the dogs too," he mumbled. John's view of the world had been set in an English private school in the 1940s. Since then Britain had gone from an empire over which the sun never set, to a small island over which it never seemed to rise. A certain disgruntlement was only to be expected.

Cynthia grumbled far less than her eminent husband, but was equally uninterested in the culture of their adopted country. When people tried to speak Spanish to her she looked horrified, as if they'd made an improper suggestion. Unfortunately, she was another of those who'd succumbed to drink in a big way. A little gin and tonic set the morning up nicely, and lunch was always preceded by a cocktail and accompanied by at least one bottle of wine. You could get drunk just watching her put it away. It was only the break for siesta that kept her upright when she resumed drinking in the evening. A certain dulling of the memory was bound to follow. What she said was often what she'd said five minutes earlier. But in terms of her amiability it wasn't a problem, because she also forgot how many drinks she'd had and was always brightly ready for another.

The two of them made a peculiar sight in a Spanish hillside village. His posture was so upright it looked as if someone was poking a gun in his back. She wore long floral dresses whatever the weather and had a hairstyle that stood up rigidly, as though made of cardboard. You knew if she was about to come around the corner because you could smell the vast amount of perfume she wore to cover her drinking. She was the only person I knew who was never bothered by mosquitoes. After doing a couple of odd jobs for them, they unexpectedly invited us on a day trip to the Sierra Nevada mountains. We were torn between horror and fascination. In the end we accepted because I was eager to get the work they were hinting at.

We met them at their villa one chilly dawn. The question of whose car we were going in wasn't even raised. I was prepared to take them in our motorized shopping cart because I knew I could get through the day sober, but Cynthia, who looked like the bride of Dracula before her first drink, briskly ushered us to the backseat of their Jaguar. I wasn't about to complain, because if I was going to die, at least it would be in style. Their car was the most luxurious place I'd been in a long time. The three-hour drive to Granada flew by and soon we were climbing toward a resort called Sol y Nieve. A day spent at the historic Alhambra would have suited me fine, because although we'd been in Spain for months, we had yet to do much sightseeing. I wanted to behave like an ordinary tourist for a change instead of an almond grower taking a day off. However, John had his heart set on a spot of skiing. It was really odd to get out of the car in the Spanish sun and crunch over snow. But at least I'd found a use for my wool sweater and winter jacket. The first port of call was a bar for a bite to eat and a quick round of drinks. "I'll have a gin with a twist of lemon, please," said John in English.

"*Qué?*" said the waiter.

"Gin and lemon," the retired judge said louder, as if there must be something wrong with the waiter's hearing. The Spaniard shrugged. "Gin . . . with lemon. It's quite simple."

"*No entiendo, señor.*"

"Look, you imbecile. Gino witho lemono, got it?" I hastily ordered for all of us. Then it was on to the ski rental store and from there to the slopes. I wasn't much of a skier, so I was in no hurry. Basically, I didn't like standing in long lines for the privilege of launching myself down some precipitous escarpment. In my opinion, snow and ice were slippery enough without putting on skis. Sure enough, I spent most of the day flying down the mountain on my stomach with my legs and skis tangled up behind me. Before long the wind and sunburn had turned my face into a bright red beacon, which at least gave the skiers who could steer a warning to get out of my way. At intervals John or Helen went sailing by with some remark about what a lovely day it was. Then at last the sun dipped below the peaks and I felt I could move on to the après-ski with honor. When I got to the bar, I could see that Cynthia had been there some time—all day as it turned out. "Fancy meeting you all the way up here," she slurred. "What a coincidence."

"Actually, we drove up together this morning, Cynthia."

"Did we? How lovely. Will you be skiing?"

"I've been on the slopes all afternoon, but if you look outside you'll see the sun's going down."

"Jolly good. Fancy meeting you here though." When I sat with her, the staff looked at me with pity.

It all proved worthwhile because between ginos with lemonos, John asked us to renovate their village house while they took a spring tour of relatives in England. When they returned in five weeks they expected to see a new bathroom and kitchen, ready in plenty of time to escape the summer crush at the coast. "Can't trust the Spanish to do it right," the former judge said, "so I'm depending on you, old boy. These foreign builders never do anything with respect for the law. It wouldn't do for a man of my standing to have his house connected with any sort of illegality." The financial arrangements were simple enough. He'd got a quote from a professional builder that I rashly denounced then and there as a rip-off, and vowed that we could beat it. John was more interested in the fact we weren't Spanish and duly gave us the amount of the original quote. He said we could keep the difference as our payment for managing the project. I assured him we would use only the highest quality workmen and supervise them closely at all times. We managed to keep up the confident smiles until we'd seen them off at the airport. Then we turned to each other with mirrored expressions of fear.

Five weeks should have been ample time to do one bathroom and one kitchen. What we didn't know was that it could easily take five weeks just to get someone to drive up to the village to look. Everyone seemed to be too busy, especially when we told them how much we wanted to spend. They said they'd come and look at it *mañana*. The dictionary says this word means "tomorrow," but anyone who's been to Spain knows the meaning is closer to "in this lifetime, if you're lucky." We couldn't even rouse anyone from the village itself. As far as they were concerned, if the British snobs didn't like their house, they could move. With the exception of a small gathering of children, the locals determinedly ignored the whole operation from start to finish.

The village was too far off the beaten track to have municipal sewage, so Helen and I made a start by getting a tractor in to make a hole for the new enlarged cesspool John wanted. We also tore out everything in the old kitchen and bathroom. That was our expertise exhausted. A week had already passed when I finally sought advice from Vicente the storekeeper. "I know just the people to help you," he said. "There are two brothers in Santa Maria on unemployment payments who do building work on the side for cash." I knew John wanted everything legal, but at this point I didn't care if they were two serial killers on the run from the police. So far we'd only managed to destroy things. We needed someone who could put them back together again.

Vicente sent José and his brother Juan around to our place the next day. I was instantly troubled. "Juan, I see you only have one arm," I said, trying to sound indifferent. He smiled at me with an empty look in his eye and a spot of dribble on his chin. It turned out his brother did all the talking for both of them.

"He's an idiot," said José, twirling his finger against his head. "But he does the work of two men." This statement was only true, we discovered, in that José made him do his work as well. There was an innocent look about Juan, but José's expression was dark and cunning.

"I don't think this is a good idea," said Helen.

"But they cost next to nothing and we're broke," I said. "If we use them, we'll have enough to live on for months."

"If we use them, Sir John won't let us live long enough to spend it."

"He doesn't ever need to know," I said. "Anyway, we shouldn't allow their appearance to prejudice us. They might be excellent builders."

"Yeah, and I might be the Queen." I eventually persuaded her that there was now little choice in the matter, so we drove them out to the village house. José had spotted Helen's skepticism and responded "no problem" to everything on the long list of jobs we reeled off. The only thing that threw them was the inclusion of a siphon in the new sewage pipe to the cesspool. John had insisted on one because they stop nasty smells filtering back up the pipes. I only had a limited understanding of what was required, and the language barrier added to my difficulty in explaining. In the end I stood by the new pit, with an audience of local children, and resorted to my old standby—a combination of pantomime and sign language—to convey the journey waste would take on its way there from the toilet. It was a bit like the blue-parrot fiasco, only more sordid. Juan got the giggles and ended up getting pushed into the hole by his irritated brother.

Helen still wanted to call it off before it was too late, but José clinched the deal when he said he knew a source of cheap materials. His cousin had a derelict farm and we could buy bricks and roof beams for the cesspool at half price. He would even deliver the materials himself. Helen later regarded the pile of chipped and dirty bricks with disgust. "You told John you'd hire the best professionals and use only the finest materials," she said accusingly.

"These are for a *cesspool!*" I said.

"Don't forget he's a retired judge," she said. "If we screw this up, he'll have us cleaning cesspools with our toothbrushes down at the local prison."

Over the coming weeks we went out a couple of times a day to check on their progress. We usually found José asleep under a tree while Juan struggled to drag a sink or box of tiles on his own. "Just napping," José would say. "The work is so hard I need to rest sometimes." I tried to impress on him the urgency of the deadline. With two weeks left they'd barely got started. "We need to get everything prepared first," he said.

With a week left they got the upstairs bathroom finished, and I started to believe we'd get away with it. Besides a new sink and toilet, there were tiles where before there had been a cork floor and a bath where there had been a shower tray. It actually looked pretty smart. There was only one problem. When you turned on the cold water tap you got hot water and vice versa. "No problem," said José, and out came the tiles again. To my amazement, the kitchen was also finished with three days left. The pipe run didn't follow the most logical route but you couldn't tell once it was covered with plaster and tiles. We agreed to meet up after the weekend to tidy up and settle the bill.

That Monday morning I was nervous about John's return the following day but also pleased that we'd finished the job to a surprisingly good standard and well below the anticipated cost. As we drove up to the house, Bobby stuck his droopy jowls out the window and assumed a disapproving look worthy of John himself. Then he started barking and I nearly stopped breathing. There were three beat-up old cars parked out front and half a dozen grubby children running wild in the yard. Washing was hanging on the line. "Oh my God, we've got squatters," said Helen. Then I spotted José at the upstairs balcony.

"Good morning," he called out cheerfully. "I thought I'd bring my family up for the weekend!" The place was strewn with beer bottles and litter. I was furious. "Don't worry about it," he said. "The women will have it clean in no time." He paused and looked guiltily at his feet. "There is something you should see though."

"Here we go," said Helen. While his kids played with Bobby, José led us into the kitchen. It all appeared fine at first glance and then I looked up and saw the crack and the dangerous sag in the ceiling.

"It's the bathroom upstairs," said José. "The weight of the new tiles and the bath are too much for the beams."

"What have you done?" I said in a choked voice.

"Me?" He shrugged. "Nothing. The kids were dirty so they had a bath, that's all."

"No, you bastard, I mean what have you done to Sir John's house?" I pointed to the ceiling, poised to collapse on our heads. "You said you knew what you were doing!" He looked offended.

"I did everything you told me," he said. "You asked for a bath and tiles and that's what I gave you."

"Oh, I get it," I said. "Silly me. I thought I was paying for a builder. Normally that means someone who knows about building."

"There's no need to be like that," he said. "You got exactly what you asked for."

"Forgive me for being upset," I said. "It's just I thought your work might last more than two days."

"Enjoy your last hours of freedom," said Helen, "because

when the judge gets back and sees this, he'll throw the book at you." I believe she was talking to me but José thought it was him. It was the first time I'd seen him look concerned about anything.

"Just relax," he said, thinking more quickly than he was accustomed to. "We can stick two beams under there and that should hold it. In fact, I can pick them up right now from my cousin." He was gone in a moment and his family tidied up their things and left. Helen and I paced up and down, convinced we'd never see him again. Sensing the depth of our agitation, Bobby hovered by the door with his tail between his legs. But an hour later José and Juan showed up with two slightly weathered beams. For some reason, one of the beams was painted black and the other was white. The rest of the day and much of the night were spent knocking them into place and repairing the damage. By the time they'd finished and repainted, it looked as good as it had originally except there were two new beams and the slightest dip where the collapse had taken place. Nevertheless, it was as good as we were going to get, so we paid them and said our farewells.

As they were getting in their truck, I noticed Bobby disappear over a mound and reappear a moment later with a bit of plastic pipe, which he proceeded to chew. I walked to the top of the mound and in the moonlight saw a massive pile of rubble and other waste. "Hey!" I shouted after them. "You haven't cleared up."

"The house is tidy," José shouted back. "What more do you want?" With that he started the engine and drove off. Helen came over with a flashlight and we surveyed the ruins.

"They deliberately hid this," she said bitterly.

"What are we going to do? His Almightiness is due back first thing in the morning and we'll never get a truck out here in the middle of the night." In unison we slowly turned our heads to our little Fiat 500. The car could only manage a few bags of shopping before the exhaust started to drag on the ground. This was going to take several trips. We did our best to haul it out of there without disturbing the other villagers, who were asleep within their shuttered houses. Dawn arrived and then the hour of their return. We'd just put the final load of building waste into our car when Bobby's barking announced their arrival. I staggered out to greet them as Helen quickly raked over the spot José had used as a dump.

"Hello, old boy," said John, petting Bobby. "Everything all right?"

"Yes, just thought we'd come up here to greet you," I said, trying to hide my exhaustion and fear.

"Can't wait to have a look at the place," said Cynthia. I closed my eyes with dread as they went in and inspected the work. A few minutes later they reemerged.

"Jolly good show," said the retired judge. "Splendid job. Just goes to prove there's no substitute for quality."

"And all legal," said Cynthia.

At this point Helen emerged from behind the mound. "I was looking at the garden," she said tiredly. When I saw her I realized we looked like we'd crawled out of a bomb site. We said good-bye, grabbed hold of Bobby, and made a hurried departure in our overloaded car.

Later on we called in on Vicente to let him know how the work had gone. "You're lucky you've finished," he said. "There are robbers about in the area stealing building materials."

"Really?" I said.

"Last week they stole bricks from a site on the other side of Santa Maria," he said, "and yesterday two beams were taken from a farm near town. One of the beams was black and the other was white."

10

Alien Invasion

We were pleased to find our small group of English speak-ers down by the coast, but it was equally gratifying to get away from them again when we made the long journey home. For six months we remained the only foreigners in our remote area. When we heard that an American woman had moved in just beyond our valley, we were a little peeved at losing our pio-neering status. Ironically, it was our own arrival that had in-spired a local farmer to seek a foreign buyer for his building. No Spaniard had wanted the abandoned farmhouse. We had alerted him to the fact that there were people from distant places who didn't know any better.

Vicente the storekeeper reported that some of the locals were now worried we were the vanguard of an invasion. After all, the foreign population had about doubled. They were happy to welcome the occasional eccentric, but not hordes of us. They didn't entirely believe me when I said that none of the foreigners I knew were in a hurry to move somewhere with no electricity or running water, near a village of pig farms, on the edge of a wilderness. Nevertheless, that didn't stop me from having a nightmare that Sir John had moved in next door.

Some said the new American was a witch who lived alone and spoke to no one. Others that she was a lesbian who had short hair and dressed like a man. The flurry of unkind gossip made us wonder what they'd said about us when we first moved in. But these reports from Vicente's store only made us more curious to see her for ourselves. In particular I wanted to know what kind of person I might be able to persuade to buy out here. And she'd certainly be a convenient customer for our services.

Her house was set in an open plain that sloped gently down toward our local town about five miles away. It was a typical rural farmhouse except that it hadn't been whitewashed. The natural stone colors were camouflage in the tans of the landscape. A twisted olive tree stood right in front. We knew the woman was in because we saw the door close as we pulled up. The windows were open and a light breeze ruffled the curtains. I called out *"hola!,"* the customary greeting in Spain, but there was no answer. Helen went around the back and shouted but there was still no reply. We waited awhile, in case she was on the toilet or otherwise indisposed. The sun glinted off glass far across the plain. A bird doodled in the sky. We listened to the hum of traffic on a nearby road. Then, when enough time had passed for even the most agonizingly constipated person, we tried calling *"hola!"* again. There was still no response from the house. "Do you think she's all right?" I said in a lowered voice. "Perhaps she's deaf."

"I saw a curtain twitch the first time you shouted," said Helen. "She knows we're here—she's just ignoring us." I wondered if she'd already heard about the work we did for expats. If so, then I suppose hiding was understandable. Nevertheless, I felt a little offended.

"Maybe the gossip wasn't too harsh after all," I said as we left.

Over the coming days we listened for news down at the coast in case any of the other expats had heard of her. They hadn't. It seemed the woman was living like a hermit. Locals said that workmen from outside the area had been at her house, but that was the last we heard for weeks. Then one day Vicente came tearing up to our farm in his pickup.

"Come quickly," he said. "The American woman has gone mad."

"Are you sure she hasn't been mad all along?" I said.

"She's hopping around her yard and calling out in English," he said. "I think she needs help but her neighbors can't understand her."

"I'm not sure I can give the kind of help she needs," I said as Helen and I jumped in his truck. Ten minutes later we finally saw the object of all this mystery. She must have been in her sixties and her graying hair was cut short. She had bare feet and wore a pair of overalls. At this moment she was not her usual withdrawn self. She was dancing around in the open and screaming her lungs out.

"Are you English? Thank God!" she said. "I've been telling these people I'm dying but nobody's doing anything."

"What's the matter?" said Helen.

"I've been stung in the foot by a scorpion," she replied. "Please get me to a hospital. It may already be too late." I translated for Vicente and the small group that had gathered to watch the spectacle. Their roar of laughter was a little cruel.

"There aren't any deadly scorpions in Spain," said Vicente. "All they'll give you is a nasty sting like a bee." She was not pre-pared to believe him, of course, so we took her into town to the hospital where she was given an anti-venom injection to ease the pain. The woman, whose name was Myrtle, was convinced we'd saved her life.

When we took her home that evening, we learned that she was originally from Nebraska. Since I'd visited my mother's side of the family in neighboring Kansas on many occasions, we were able to grumble together about the Midwest. As a young woman she'd fled there to go to New York as soon as she was old enough, just as my mother had fled to Chicago. In recent years Myrtle had lived in Paris, where she'd worked as a guide. She and her American lover were planning to get a quiet place in Spain and live off their pensions. But at the eleventh hour he'd abandoned her and gone home. Having lost touch with her fam-ily back in the States, she decided to stay on in Europe and press ahead with her retirement plan regardless. She wasn't used to living on her own and had become a little paranoid. "These peo-ple keep coming to my door, jabbering away unintelligibly, and pushing fruit and vegetables at me," she told us. "I don't want to buy anything from them but they practically force the stuff on me—it's terrifying. Now I hide when I hear them coming." That explained why she'd run when we called out *"hola."*

"I think you'll find those are welcoming gifts," I said. "It's a neighborhood custom."

"Oh dear." She looked distressed. "I thought they were after my money." Myrtle was useless at reading other people and pretty hard to read herself. Her apparent aloofness turned out to be lack of confidence, and her frightening behavior was born out of fear. In a nutshell, she was as dumbfounded by the locals as they were by her. Misunderstandings were bound to follow. Even Helen didn't know how to take it when, in a fluster induced by having guests, Myrtle put salt instead of sugar in her coffee.

Although her house was small, it was very pretty, with lovely views across the plain to the town—which looked like a scale model from there. I'd already nosed around and found out that the farmer, *Señor* Mendoza, sold the abandoned house for ten thousand dollars. This was considered a windfall because the modest building had no electricity and came with only one small field. "I think the place was a bargain at twenty-five thousand dollars," said Myrtle. I nearly spilled my coffee.

"Twenty-five?" I said. "That's not what the farmer told us he sold it for."

"What farmer?" said Myrtle. "I bought it off an Englishman in Murcia called Ron. I'd seen an ad in the English language paper. He used to be a priest you know, but gave up the cloth for love."

"If this is the same Ron from Murcia that we know, then he told us he used to be in the marines. He must make up a new life history to suit every occasion."

"Oh dear. I did have my suspicions. I thought he was a little overfamiliar for an ex-priest, if you know what I mean."

"You could've bought a little farm in an isolated part of Nebraska for the amount of money he charged you," I said.

"Yes, but then I'd have a little farm in an isolated part of Nebraska. I hate Nebraska."

"Good point," I agreed. "Nebraska is a place to leave, not a place to go."

"Still, you've got a lovely home here," said Helen, trying to soften the blow. "All the plumbing looks new and I noticed you have a solar-powered water pump too."

"I won't tell you what it all cost," said Myrtle. "That Ron really cleaned me out. After I'd bought the house, he told me I'd need first this and then that. Honestly, if I'd known, I wouldn't have bought it in the first place. But by then what could I do? So I gave him even more money to get it fixed up for me. To start with, he was here every day trying to sell me something new. I thought at least he was my friend, but since the money ran out I've never seen him again. Men—I just don't understand them."

"I know what you mean," said Helen and gave her a hug. Naturally I felt a little excluded and silently vowed to make myself as understandable as possible in the future. After her ex-lover and Ron, Myrtle certainly had reason to look at any male with a jaundiced eye. Between the two of them they'd managed to leave her almost penniless in Europe's equivalent of the outback.

On the plus side, her house was beautiful. The place was so tastefully decorated it could have come straight out of a magazine. Glazed pots stuffed with dried flowers sat in little alcoves and beautiful Persian rugs lay across polished tiles. The furniture was dark wood and leather in the traditional Castilian style. Although there was no electricity, she had old-fashioned oil lamps dotted around. It could have been a well-to-do house from the turn of the century. Turn of the *nineteenth* century, that is.

And she wasn't totally alone. As we'd sat with our drinks, a scruffy one-eyed dog had strolled in through the open door. I was poised to scare it off when it casually flopped panting at Myrtle's feet. As she talked she scratched behind the dog's ears. When we toured the small house, we came across a different mangy creature in each room. Altogether I counted two dogs and three cats. The cats should have made easy prey for the dogs because one of them limped and the other two looked like they were recovering from malnutrition. However, one of the dogs had an eye missing and the other was so old it took him ten minutes just to stand up.

"I take them in," said Myrtle. "I can't help it." The really weird part was how they'd found her. My guess was that word had got out among the locals that the strange American was taking in unwanted animals. She was convinced they made their own way there thanks to some natural sixth sense.

In the little field beside the house there was a goat with a gray beard like an old man, and an equally ancient horse, which she called Silver even though it was black. "Let me show you the scorpion that stung me," she said. She went to a rock in the yard and tipped it over. I expected to see a dead scorpion, but a very agile one scampered out. I tried to kill it. "Stop! Stop please!" she shrieked as I stomped it with my shoe.

"Why do men have to be so violent?" Helen added.

"But it's a scorpion. It stung you," I protested, still determined to be as understandable as any man could be.

"That's not its fault," said Myrtle. "Poor thing—it's only protecting itself." Fortunately, I suppose, I failed to harm the scorpion. Its armor was so tough it would take a jackhammer and a can of pesticide just to give it a headache. With her love of animals and happy acceptance of gas lighting, I knew Myrtle was bound to become firm friends with Helen, who at last had someone she could complain to about me.

We both felt sorry for Myrtle and angry with Ron for exploiting her. We agreed we'd do what we could to help her adjust to life in the *campo*—and not charge for our services. Even though her house was much closer to the road and town than ours was, it was still out in the sticks. I thought she must feel terribly isolated, especially in the silence of the night. Even with each other's company, and surrounded by caring neighbors, we got lonely as the sky reddened and the wind fell still in the grasses. If I went outside on my own on a cloudy night it was so dark and quiet that I had to feel my pulse to make sure I hadn't died.

What she lacked in life, I felt, was some way to be in contact with other people. I offered Vicente to help buy her a car. "But I can't drive," she said helplessly. It seems that back in Nebraska in the forties and fifties the boys had done all the driving. And having spent her adult life in New York and Paris she'd never needed a car.

"Do you *walk* to town?" I said in astonishment.

"No, I have a bicycle. I glide down, and push it back up when I've bought my groceries." I found it incredible that someone her age couldn't drive and promptly offered to teach her. I knew what it was like to feel stranded in the middle of nowhere. "That's very kind of you," she said, "but I must warn you I don't have very good coordination. I don't think I can do it."

"Nonsense," I replied. "Anyone can drive." Almost anyone, as it turned out. We started off with a quick lesson on the dirt tracks of the *campo*. There was no traffic except the odd wild hare and it didn't really matter if you strayed off the marked route. The only real difference between the track and the surrounding countryside was pre-existing tire marks. Myrtle unintentionally opened up a few new tracks of her own that I hoped wouldn't result in the bread deliveryman getting hopelessly lost or send a drunken Diego veering off into a field on his way home. Especially as her course weaved dangerously close to several almond and olive trees that seemed to attract her like magnets. I kept grabbing the wheel and slamming my foot to the floor in an instinctive braking action. To show her where we lived, I got her to aim the car at the low hills surrounding our valley. We got to the summit all right, except for setting off a landslide as we strayed a bit close to the edge. Going down the other side proved a bigger problem. As the car picked up speed,

Myrtle lost control. We nearly took a shortcut straight over the edge. "Brake!" I yelled. She hit the accelerator.

"Oh, I give up," she said and let go of the wheel. She sat there with her arms crossed as the car sped down the hill, with me climbing over her to steer from the passenger seat. Pepe had witnessed the whole thing and asked me later if this was what it would be like if the place was overrun with foreigners. Not even the wild hares would be safe. After nearly being driven over a cliff, I didn't feel too safe myself. I tried explaining that not all foreigners drove like Myrtle. But the only other foreigners the locals knew were Helen and me. They'd already adopted us as surrogate Spaniards and, as Pepe put it:

"I mean no offense, but you and Helena, you're *unusual*."

As for Myrtle, some of her paranoia was starting to wear off on the natives. You can imagine how a small farming community in Nebraska would react to the arrival of a foreigner who didn't speak any English and hid every time someone went to say hello. For her part, she felt like a lone pioneer left stranded among the Indians. Only from our vantage point in the middle could we see that it was more like a foal had been put in a field of calves; both sides friendly, both curious—but neither daring to get too close.

Not even the bread deliveryman saw her. She left his money outside on top of a barrel to save them both from trying to converse. This measure seemed a bit extreme given that there were only two words that they both knew anyway. Occasionally she forgot to pick up the stick of bread, and I noticed it became rubbery after one day and hard as a baseball bat after two. Even foxes wouldn't touch it. I began to wonder what eating it was doing to us.

They say bad luck comes in threes and, unfortunately, this proved true in Myrtle's experience with men. It seemed one resident was making a determined effort to get through to her after all. "This man keeps coming here and pestering me," she complained. "I think I know what he's after. Just because I'm a woman living alone doesn't mean I'm desperate. José Pedrera's his name. Shaun, will you please go and have words with him? I'm really worried what he might try to do out here in this remote spot. The brute!"

I wanted to smooth out Myrtle's misunderstandings with the locals, but I was a little apprehensive about confronting this "brute." How would I phrase things without sounding like I thought he was a molester and potential rapist? For all I knew he liked a good fight too. I limbered up before setting off alone to confront him. His house was in a cluster of half a dozen dwellings grouped near a spring. A number of people watched with hostile suspicion as I got out of my car. "Can you tell me where José Pedrera lives?" I said. A child pointed to a yard where two sturdy middle-aged men sat. I took a deep breath and approached them with determination. They both stood up defensively. "Which one of you is José Pedrera?" I said. The biggest one answered.

"He's in the house," he said. Three against one, I thought. "Here he comes now." An old woman emerged, followed slowly by an arthritic and toothless man not a day under eighty. As he tottered feebly toward the men, one of them said: "Papa, you've got a visitor."

"There must be some mistake," I said. "The man I'm looking for has been visiting the American woman."

"That'll be him, all right," said the old woman.

"I'm just being sociable," said José Pedrera. He looked worriedly at her.

"I'll give you sociable," she said and started hitting him with a wooden spoon. As José Pedrera cowered under the blows, his sons laughed and told me that he had a reputation in the area for being lecherous. "I don't know why he bothers," said the woman. "He hasn't had an erection since nineteen eighty-two."

Although I felt Myrtle had exaggerated the danger somewhat, she was once again grateful to me for saving her. As we got to know her better, we came to realize that she was holding back about something else that troubled her greatly. "What's the matter?" said Helen. "You can tell me anything. If it's private, I can send Shaun away."

"It's not that," said Myrtle. "I'm worried you'll think I'm crazy."

"I promise that whatever you say I won't think you're crazy," I said. She chewed her lip and considered deeply before speaking.

"I think aliens from outer space are landing near here," she said.

"I take it back," I mumbled.

"Shut up, Shaun," said Helen. She comforted Myrtle, who had burst into tears.

"Oh, come on," I said. "You've been living alone too long. I did advise you to get in touch with your family. Can't you see your paranoia has got out of hand?"

"I knew you wouldn't believe me," she said. "But I've seen them landing with my own eyes. Every Friday night they come."

"It must be a helicopter or something," I said.

"No, it isn't," she said. "See for yourselves. They wait until one in the morning when they think everyone's asleep, but I've seen them."

"Do you think anyone else would be able to see them?" said Helen. "Or is it just you?"

"Delicately phrased," I muttered.

"I think we should come and check it out for ourselves," said Helen.

"I'm not sitting around in the middle of the night waiting for aliens to land in Myrtle's backyard! Besides, if you were going to invade the planet, don't you think you'd start in Washington or someplace like that? Can't be a very intelligent life-form."

"Don't be so smart," said Helen. "How do you know what aliens want? Perhaps this is the ideal spot because it's so isolated." When we got home, she persuaded me to humor Myrtle by going to investigate her story.

"She's become so paranoid, she probably thinks these aliens have come for *her*," I said.

"Well, the first step to helping her is to discount the possibility that aliens really are landing."

"And we actually have to *look* for them in order to do that?" But I knew when my peace was threatened. When Friday night came around we went over to Myrtle's after dinner. I couldn't tell if she was nervous because of the aliens or because her sanity was in the balance. Just before one o'clock we strolled out front. The lights of the town shimmered in the distance but otherwise it was a dark night. Crickets scratched away and the scent of a nearby jasmine bush filled the air. "Shall we give them until half past then?" I said.

"Wait," said Myrtle. "Here they come." For a moment Helen and I stood in stunned silence. A constant stream of green spheres cascaded out of the sky over the far edge of the plain. I couldn't believe what I was seeing.

"This is incredible," I said. I was transfixed.

"It goes on until four or five," she said.

"Figures," said Helen. "That's about when everyone goes home."

"What do you mean?" I asked.

"Look where it's coming from," said Helen. "It's that night-club on the way out of town. Those are lasers—it's quite common these days." Suddenly it was obvious she was right.

"Yes, I knew it was that," I said, quickly trying to recover my poise, but greatly relieved I wouldn't be wrestling with aliens that night.

"I've been an idiot," said a distraught Myrtle.

"Look on the bright side," I said. "At least it wasn't a figment of your imagination. For a while there I thought you'd—" Helen glared at me. "Never mind."

Having regained confidence in her own sanity, Myrtle decided it was safe to get back behind the wheel of my car. So despite our first near-death experience I was pressed into service again. After a few tries where she passed trees without my feeling she intended to knock them down, I foolishly decided she was ready for the open road.

Driving in our area could be harrowing even for someone with experience, because the rules were a little different. For instance, red traffic lights were merely considered a warning to look out for crossing traffic. It was quite common to watch a man drink an entire bottle of wine on his own with lunch and then stagger behind the wheel of a truck. Meanwhile, the habitual use of horns was guaranteed to jolt a person of Myrtle's nervous disposition. Despite her growing confidence across the open terrain, I knew we were in for a difficult ride when she set off so slowly that tractors were overtaking us. Even when she'd climbed to thirty miles an hour, she was still in first gear and it sounded like the engine was about to shear off.

"Please shift up," I pleaded with her.

"All right, all right! I can only concentrate on one thing at a time." I winced as the car was plunged straight into fourth without any assistance from the clutch pedal. An impatient line of vehicles was honking away behind us, but with the gear change Myrtle began to pick up momentum. The car started to weave as it gained speed. Pretty soon it was clear I was strapped into a runaway vehicle.

"Try easing off the accelerator," I suggested. I tried to keep panic out of my voice. "In fact, there's a junction up ahead. You'd better brake. Er, Myrtle, the brake pedal? Brake!" Apparently I still wasn't making myself understandable enough. We went sailing across the intersection to the sound of skidding tires and more horns. "I can see you pick up local habits quite easily," I said as I disembedded my fingers from the dashboard.

In hindsight, taking her into the historic part of town was a mistake. I figured our tiny European car could manage in those narrow streets and that conditions would encourage her to stick to crawling speed. But unleashing her erratic driving into a stream of other tiny European vehicles created a chaotic scene reminiscent of bumper cars at the fairground.

One benefit of teaching her to drive was a temporary reawakening of my spiritual side. I thought I didn't need religion, but by bringing me closer to the Almighty she frequently gave me doubts. After an hour out I was just starting to think she was doing better when the car began to swerve. She was flaying at the air and not even looking at the road. A sidewalk café emptied as pedestrians fled inside. "What are you doing?" I said.

"There's a wasp in here. Help!"

"Pull over to the curb!" She stopped the car rather abruptly in the middle of the lane. After the usual horns and rude gestures, the following cars went around. Then in the mirror I saw a police motorbike pull up behind us. We had all the windows down and were batting at the wasp with a magazine. The bearded policeman peered in quizzically.

"It's a wasp," Myrtle said in English. "*Una vespa, una vespa.*" She pointed to the backseat. The man looked even more puzzled and a little suspicious.

"No," I said. "A *Vespa* is a moped. Are you trying to get us locked up? A wasp is an *avispa!*" I succeeded in explaining it all to the officer, who put away his Breathalyzer and was kind enough to let us proceed as long as I did the driving. After that I felt there were plenty of other things I could help her with that were less hazardous, and found her a local instructor who could speak English.

Since moving to the *campo*, a new love had come into her life—her horse. Silver had quite happily lived to a ripe old age champing local grasses with an occasional mix of alfalfa and oats. When Myrtle came along all that changed. At her request we spent days on a fruitless search for hay. It seemed there was no hay to be had south of the French border.

"Why don't you tether him up on the farmer's land so he can eat the grasses?" I said.

"That grass is too dry," she said. "Besides, I'm not tethering him. I want him to be free." So she kept him locked into the small, bare field at the back of her house. The horse spent all day staring longingly over the fence at the grass. Three times a day she went out with a bowl and hand fed him sliced apples, carrots, and muesli. You could almost see the confusion in the poor creature's eyes. Finally Vicente came up with a supplier of hay in the city of Almería. As it was imported it was going to be expensive and she would also have to pay for its delivery. Her pension was a pittance in American terms but fortunately went a long way here. In any case, she didn't care what the cost was. She'd have sold herself to José Pedrera if it meant getting hay for that horse.

We drove her down to Almería to translate her demands for the supplier. The city was hot and dusty and full of Moroccans newly arrived off the ferry from Africa. The dealer himself was a short, Arab-looking man who sat on a low stool in the entrance of a giant warehouse near the port. He gave us mint tea while we looked at his supplies. Myrtle was very particular about getting hay that was neither too dry nor too damp. I thought she was being too picky but the trader took her perfectly seriously and they soon struck up a rapport. He too was a lover of horses, who owned a couple of thoroughbreds. At last a deal was reached and he said he would bring her order of hay and straw himself.

The next day we laid out crates and a large plastic sheet on which to store the delivery. With uncommon punctuality a truck bumped and lurched up the track to her house. The trader was in high spirits as he directed his worker to unload. "Where's the horse?" he said enthusiastically. "I must see it." I translated for Myrtle and, herself all smiles, she eagerly led him around to the field. "But where's the horse?" he said.

"That's it," I told him.

"That? That *thing?*"

"It's a bit old and scruffy," I agreed with him.

"You don't want hay for that," he said. "You want a vet to put it out of its misery."

"Shhh." I put my finger to my lips and whispered: "She loves the creature." He looked at me, puzzled.

"I was expecting a fine thoroughbred stallion," he said. "This is practically a mule!" He turned and marched off. Within moments the empty truck was bouncing back down the track.

"What did he say?" said Myrtle.

"He was just expressing admiration for your fine horse," I lied. At first she smiled happily until she saw Helen's expression and became suspicious. With much ceremony we broke into the first bale, crammed some into a net, and dangled it in front of the old horse. Silver sniffed the hay cautiously and then walked away. Myrtle began to chase him around the field. She stood in front of him and chewed some of the hay herself, rubbing her stomach and saying "yum, yum." It was no use. Silver just draped his old head over the fence and gazed at the grass beyond.

Myrtle got off to a shaky start with the locals again when she got in a farrier to shoe the animal. In a farming community, where donkeys and horses still acted as beasts of burden, the farrier was in constant demand and too busy to waste his time. After referring to Silver as "dog food" he pointed out that the creature didn't go anywhere to need shoes anyway. I begged him to consider how much the animal meant to her. "Remember how strange everyone used to think I was for taking Bobby in the car with me everywhere and letting him sit in the front seat?" I said.

"What do you mean *used* to think?" he replied with a grin. "Oh, to be the pet of an Englishman!" He looked at Myrtle again and this time smiled—she had been accepted. Now he seemed to thoroughly enjoy himself, chuckling and shaking his head as he put a pristine pair of shoes on the bewildered old horse. When several months went by and no more Myrtles appeared, the natives relaxed. It was clear there was to be no invasion. We had a new friend, and Myrtle—and her eccentricities—were absorbed into the peaceful equilibrium of our rural outpost.

11

Kids These Days

While we waited for almonds to ripen, we'd do just about anything to get by. Apart from assisting expats, the other work that came naturally to us was tutoring in English. All we had to do was say things like "the cat sat on the mat" for an hour and people paid us. Even I could manage that. Since sober Englishmen were in short supply in our area, we had people lining up their schoolchildren outside our door. For some reason it was the kids who needed help the least that got extra lessons paid for by their parents. Helen said some of them spoke better English than I did. Once their parents had left they only wanted to grill us on various slang words and the coolest ways to swear.

This tutoring work came to us through Antonio, a young schoolteacher we'd met in the town. He liked most things English and loved anything American. We wondered if this had something to do with the fact that he'd never been to either country. He was introduced to our language through a dated tape course for travelers and was now teaching it to elementary schoolchildren. He could say phrases like "can you show me the way to the embassy" or "I have lost my luggage" almost as well as Prince Charles. However, he'd learned everything else in his vocabulary from books, and the rest of his pronunciation was so bad it often led to embarrassing misunderstandings. He couldn't say the letter "h" and—to my discomfort—the closest he could get to Shaun was "June." It was clear when we first visited him at work that he needed help. He was giving a test when we walked in. "You 'ave farty minutes to fill the shit of paper," he told the young class. Worryingly, they all understood him.

Besides bringing us our language customers, Antonio was roughly our age and we quickly became good friends. Like many young locals, he said he wanted nothing more than to get out of such a remote and backward area. But his family and his girl-friend, a dark Latin beauty called Clara, had other ideas. So for the last few years he'd sought his escape in the bottom of a beer glass. Unfortunately, hangovers were starting to hurt more and go on for longer. And he was getting tired of not remembering what he'd done the night before that caused Clara to be in such a bad mood with him. When we met him, he had just pledged to reform. Unfortunately, it's hard to avoid alcohol in a country where cheap wine is a bedrock of the culture. One glass he could handle. Two were fine and a good place to stop. But if he had three glasses, you could see a change in his eye and after that there was no getting him home until the last bar closed at dawn.

Before Antonio came along, we'd been immersed in an older

Spain. By the time the noisy nightclub he frequented was opening its doors, everyone in the *campo* was fast asleep with only
the call of the *búho* to break the deathly silence. Antonio ate
cornflakes for breakfast and heated things up in a microwave.
My neighbors ate a salty porridge called *migas* and cooked in
earth ovens alongside their houses. He had modern American
music blasting from his town-center apartment, but in the country you were more likely to hear a sad flamenco song emanating
from some passing shepherd. While some kids in town did
drugs, in our neck of the woods people bred pigeons for kicks.

"Spain 'as changed belly muck in the last twenty-five years,"
he told us. There seemed little doubt traditional Spain was on
the retreat. Even in our limited time we'd seen stone cottages
abandoned and their uneconomic olive trees left to die of ne-
glect. Overgrown ruins littered the foothills like relics of a lost
civilization, while just up the road in the desert a futuristic landscape of shimmering plastic greenhouses seemed to expand almost daily. It was as if a giant had come down and wrapped the
desert in Saran Wrap. Big corporations were using machines to
cultivate tomatoes and other export crops there—which was
probably just as well since we'd proved that some people, even
with a farm, couldn't grow their own. Meanwhile, the old quarter of town became buried deeper and deeper in a maze of
bland and anonymous high-rise apartments as people fled the
countryside.

This battle between the forces of modernity and tradition was
also being fought out on our farm by Helen and me. But on a
day-to-day basis our lifestyle was closer to that of the peasants—
despite all my efforts. Our car was often indistinguishable from
a mound of dirt, and sometimes the same could be said for us.
When Antonio invited us to eat with his family we cleaned the
car, but by the time we reached a paved road it was covered in
dirt again. We also washed our least tattered clothes for the oc-

casion. Perhaps I didn't put enough effort into hand washing, but I could neither get the stain out of the collar nor get the soap out of the shirt. Once they'd dried in the sun and wind, our clothes were as stiff as cardboard. We didn't have sufficient power for an electric iron so we didn't even own one. The result was that we looked wrinkled and starched at the same time. I was hoping that Antonio's family would put our strange appearance down to our foreignness rather than personal eccentricity. It was amazing how many things we could escape blame for by saying that was the way things were done back home. If one of us let off wind at supper, we could turn grimaces into understanding smiles by claiming that in England or America it was a customary and flattering expression of pleasure after a great meal.

We made our first cultural gaffe of the day by showing up at one in the afternoon. In fairness, we'd been told to come at one, but in a land where tomorrow means next week and next week means next month, "one" means no sooner than two-thirty. Mother was just getting started in the kitchen and other members of the family were yet to arrive. We went out on the back patio to find Clara sunbathing topless. She grabbed her drink and got up to talk to us. I have to confess I found it difficult not to be distracted. Let me use a cultural excuse again. England is a cold country where people are wrapped up even in summer. It would be a real shock to go out and suddenly see everyone walking around downtown, dressed only in the bottom half of their underwear. Yet this was precisely what it was like in many Spanish resorts in summer. You get used to it pretty quickly but even so, a fine young bosom thrust in your face is hard to ignore. As Clara spoke to me, I nodded politely and was pleased with myself that I managed to keep my eyes firmly fixed on hers. I thought I was giving the appearance that my mind was focused where my eyes were. The only problem was that when she'd pause, expecting a reply, I didn't have a clue what she'd said.

Fortunately, she covered up when Antonio's short and weathered grandparents arrived. They couldn't have been a bigger contrast—he in his traditional cloth cap and she in a long black dress like someone in mourning. Antonio got back from work and the gathering split on gender lines. I confessed to the guys that topless sunbathing was still fairly new to me. They laughed knowingly and told me it was new to them too. Under the dictator Franco, women were arrested for wearing a bikini. It had taken a long time for a backlash of liberalism to filter down to this former heartland of the *Generalísimo*.

It was usual on occasions like this for the men to sit on the porch and drink beer while the women gossiped in the kitchen. But that afternoon a paella was being cooked. A paella is a huge platter of rice, usually mixed with shellfish and chicken. In their family it had a status similar to that of the barbecue in Anglo-American society, in that it was the one dish customarily made by the man of the house. It was quite normal to eat outside in Spain but, like a barbecue, a good paella was also cooked outside. "The kitchen is the women's parts and the garden is the men's parts," explained Antonio. His father made a major show of heating up lots of ingredients already laboriously prepared by his wife. He was so pleased with this achievement that he did everything but take a bow at the end.

Antonio and Clara had plans to take us to a bullfight and then a nightclub. "You must see 'ow young peoples live," he said. "It's not good stuck in the country with the pissants." Since I'd become a country bumpkin, I started to notice how different town life was—even in our local town, which was no metropolis. It even smelled different from the *campo*. This wasn't just a matter of car fumes versus animal fumes. In town the sheer number of strong aromas was remarkable. There were perfumes worn by men and women alike, and the mixed potions of the pharmacies spilled out through open doors. Frying olive oil and garlic emanated from numerous street cafés and mingled with the odor of strong, bitter coffee. There were detergents evaporating off the little gray tiles of the sidewalk and the smell of trash bins cooked in the sun.

We were strolling around after lunch when I felt a desperate need for the toilet. However, the only public toilets in town were in the covered market and that was closed. It was a situation that worked well for bars, because in order to use their toilet you were expected to have a drink, and so the cycle went on. Antonio's solution, to limit both intake and outlay, was to order one small black coffee and four straws. But first he insisted that I hold on until we'd walked halfway across town to what was apparently the one bar that didn't seem like it was in a dusty little town on the edge of a large desert. He wanted to show us the "in" crowd—or, more precisely, the crowd that wanted "out." I guessed my bladder could just about make it, but then I didn't know how far away it would be. The place was full of young men in tight trousers and open shirts, and young women in short skirts and low-cut blouses. Everyone looked terribly cool in their sunglasses. In cloudy England only blind people wore sunglasses. Only the dirty nails, sun-bronzed faces, and rough Andalusian dialect gave the game away—that and the tractor in the parking lot. But the bar itself was a haze of perfume, cigarette smoke, and young love. I broke the spell a bit by bursting in and tearing across the room toward the toilets at full speed.

Once we'd sipped the coffee, and convinced Antonio that we were impressed with his bar, we headed for the bullring. There the ambiance was totally different. Young and old had gathered to watch the killing of the bull. It was a bizarre and uncomfortable mix of family occasion combined with ritual slaughter. We all found the atmosphere so tense that before we went in we had to stop at another bar for one coffee and four visits to the toilet. The bullfight was no tourist spectacle here, but a vibrant sporting event with the kind of following that rodeo gets in certain small towns in Texas. Antonio explained that those who fought on this provincial circuit were often older has-beens, or young men hoping to one day make their way to Madrid and the big time. Against this opposition it was not unheard of for the bull to win. But apparently there was little chance of that happening on this occasion. "The matador today is one of the best—you 'ave lick," he said.

"I think you're trying to say "luck." I *have* luck," I said.

"Yes, June, you are white. The word is lurk, you are lurky."

Inside the circular stadium we rented cushions to sit on and listened to a brass band doing a warm-up routine. The band would burst suddenly and unexpectedly into life at various times during the evening's fight. When the place was full, an announcer invited "brave young men" from the audience to come into the ring with a couple of bull calves that were being trained. As we were sitting in the front row, the last thing I wanted was any kind of audience participation. Two skinny young bulls—or "balls" as Antonio called them—were let in to the ring. They had no horns to speak of and looked more playful than menacing. After inspecting them for a while, and consulting with Clara, Antonio decided it was safe to climb over the barrier along with about a dozen others. I was practically the only male in his twenties still sitting down. I found myself identifying with an older generation, and only wished I had a few gray hairs to make me less conspicuous.

"Go on then, June," said Helen. "What are you waiting for?" I reluctantly followed the others over the wooden barrier and jumped down into the sandy bullring. I wondered if there was a clause in my medical insurance exempting coverage for acts of reckless stupidity. Helen threw me a red scarf.

"Thanks a lot," I said. "You're a real pal." The bulls weren't much bigger than Great Danes, but I figured I'd hang around behind everyone else just in case. As the cluster of guys moved, I moved with them so there were always at least two or three people between me and those stubby horns. Meanwhile, the young bulls were starting to get the idea. They scampered around chasing their teasers. To the crowd it was the comic relief for the evening. One or two people were knocked over without harm and each time the crowd cheered. Antonio turned out to be quite a clown. He entertained the audience by doing a silly dance in front of one animal and then diving behind a barrier at the last minute. By contrast, I did nothing but stand around twiddling the scarf and feeling self-conscious. Then I looked up at a bull and our eyes met across the crowded arena. Before I had a chance to panic, the animal was after me. As I sprinted for the barrier I heard Helen excitedly screaming "Go on! Go on!" but I wasn't sure if she was cheering for me or the bull.

When the games were over, the ring was raked and the band played a somber tune. Back in the safety of the stands, I felt pleased with myself. I had trod in Hemingway's footsteps—even if I was fleeing in the opposite direction at the time. I was busy knocking the sand out of my shoes and thinking I'd never look at a cow in the same way again when suddenly the crowd roared. A bull the size of a bus thundered out of the tunnel and strutted defiantly around the ring. Now here was a seriously dangerous animal. Surely its opponent would have to be a man of great skill and bravery.

The trumpets played a fanfare and out stepped the matador and three assistants. The bull stared at them with a look of affronted honor. To see the bullfighters, it was hard to blame him.

To be honest, their trousers were too short and as tight as a ballet dancer's. On top they had waistcoats that were also too small and covered in glitzy sequins. On their heads they wore what looked remarkably like those Mickey Mouse hats. As if all that was not enough to enrage any self-respecting bull, the three assistants began to prance about the ring waving pink capes. Pretty soon the macho bull was pawing the sand in readiness to charge. But every time he raced up to them, they did a pirouette with their pink capes and he went sailing by. The main fighter was marked out by a red cape. Each time he took center stage, the assistants fled behind the barriers and the trumpets laid on a fanfare. Here at last was a real contest. Tons of masculine muscle and raw animal strength—versus one very brave guy dressed like a mincing ballet dancer in a Mickey Mouse hat.

After we'd seen the bullfighters perform their moves for about ten minutes, things began to turn nasty. First of all, Helen started shouting for the bull and then she loudly booed the matador. The people sitting behind us yelled at her to sit down and shut up. She was having none of it and cupped her hands to scream more effectively at him. On one occasion, she managed to distract him and he narrowly avoided having a horn rammed up his backside. "She wishes good lick to the balls," said Antonio, shaking his head. Part of me was embarrassed by her behavior but part of me was proud of her for standing up for what she believed in. The demise of the bull was indeed quite sickening. It turned out Nureyev had a sword hidden in his cape. The creature was finally dispatched and its tail cut off and presented to the matador as a memento. He did a lap of honor with the tail held aloft. I felt he paused a little longer in front of our section of the stand. When it was all over, the audience launched their seat cushions into the ring. Most of them did anyway. One or two sent theirs sailing in our direction.

❀   ❀   ❀

The sky had darkened while the bullfight ended, but there were still several hours to go before the nightclub opened. Antonio insisted that we couldn't go home until we'd tasted the nightlife of modern Spanish youth. Apparently, nothing got started until well after midnight. To pass the time, we got some filled rolls called *bocadillos,* and slowly sipped one beer after another. Despite the food and the slow rate of intake, Antonio crossed his threshold. Before long he was loudly advocating an all-night drinking binge. The mischievous little demon was in his eye.

About one o'clock we ended up at the nightclub with the green lasers where Myrtle had thought aliens were launching their invasion of the planet. By this time I was already tired and would've been happy to go home. Helen felt the same because we hadn't been home since morning and it was several hours past our usual bedtime. When there's nothing to do after sunset except sit around a single dim bulb, you don't tend to stay up very long. Let's face it, we'd become a couple of old almond growers. Besides, if you weren't the disgruntled offspring of a farmer or market trader, the disco was not exceptional. There was a beat like a pneumatic hammer, drinks were extortionately expensive, and you had to scream directly into someone's ear to have any hope of being heard. Large groups of men leaned on the walls, drooling over smaller groups of women on the dance floor. A mass of thrusting pelvises flashed in and out of darkness as they were swept by colored lights. There was enough smoking going on to give the effect of dry ice. Not all of it was cigarette smoke.

"You can get anything 'ere," yelled Antonio proudly. He didn't take drugs but felt their presence was a sign of cosmopolitanism.

"I'll have some Coke," Helen shouted.

"She means to drink," I clarified at the top of my voice. We gave up shouting because it was making us hoarse. The noise level wasn't conducive to the meeting of minds—only the meeting of bodies. There was plenty of that going on in the darkened corners of the room.

That such a place existed in our little rural town with its churches and traditions was a shock. I guess, like Antonio, a lot of the local youth were trying to compensate for what their conservative elders put them through. If I'd been forced to dress in a cassock and take part in the Holy Week parades every year since I could walk, I'd probably be in here most weekends too. In the dark it was possible to imagine we were anywhere. But if someone were to suddenly pull the plug on the music and turn on the lights, we would've seen a room full of farmers' kids standing around awkwardly, trying not to look like peasants.

We had a couple of dances to make the journey seem worthwhile, but by then we were eager to get out of there. The gaps between Antonio's trips to the bar were shortening and Clara was already fed up with his slurred speech and drunken stomping on her toes. We took a vote that was won three to one by those who wanted to leave. Antonio said that if we didn't know how to have fun then we could all go, but he was staying. This seemed fine to us but Clara begged me to stay too and keep an eye on him. One last attempt was made to persuade him to leave and then the girls deserted me with the task of keeping him out of trouble.

I leaned against the bar and watched Antonio stagger around the dance floor. Amid that noise and all those moving bodies, the way he managed to make himself so conspicuously visible and audible was quite a feat. I decided the best way to get through a situation like this was to be inebriated myself. The rum might be expensive but at least the servings were generous. Soon the primitive beat seemed less disagreeable. Now that Helen had gone, it was safe for me to observe a fairly pretty woman who was an exceptionally good dancer. Okay, maybe she was exceptionally pretty and only a fairly good dancer. As the rum went down, and everything grew a little fuzzy around the edges, all the women in the room seemed to become better looking.

Scanning the dance floor, my eye was drawn to a couple of slightly blurred beauties dancing together in the farthest corner of the crowded floor. I did a double take and realized I was again ogling my neighbors, Simona and Theresa. They appeared relatively unsophisticated in their plain and unfashionable dresses, no doubt crafted by their own hands from discards of their mother's. At the time, I felt the look gave them a charm and innocent beauty that was disconcertingly sexy when set in motion to music. In the poor light it was easy to overlook their other defects. As they deftly sidestepped a couple of guys who were trying to get their attention, Simona seemed to look my way. I gave her my best smile and waved across the room.

Despite her crossed-eyes, she managed to see me and before long the girls and I were dancing together. Even when I'm sober I dance like Mr. Bean, but, by this point the rum was taking effect and I looked more like I was having some sort of attack. They didn't seem to mind. In fact, each appeared to be nudging the other out of the way—one minute smiling at me and the next glowering at each other. Despite my drunken condition, I was still aware on some level that I'd been left there to keep Antonio out of any questionable entanglements. What I was realizing was that given enough booze, I was in just as much danger. Luckily the girls excused themselves and went off to the bathroom together, gesticulating aggressively as they conferred. Quickly I located Antonio and dragged him through the crowd to the door—before we both ended up in trouble.

"You promised Clara," I said in answer to his bemused look. Fortunately, Antonio only needed autopilot to find the way back to his house, where we'd all agreed to spend the night. Having consumed enough alcohol myself to sedate a rhinoceros, I don't recall much about the journey home. I just remember Antonio's slurred protest that he was only trying to impress me with the way youthful Spain moved to an international beat. For some reason, he was ashamed of the Spain we knew, with the simple poverty of its rural life and values unchanged for thousands of years. "We 'ave progress," he kept repeating.

The next morning my brain was swimming in rum and, although the music had stopped, the pneumatic hammer was still going. Imprinted on my closed eyelids was a frantic scene of entranced bodies writhing in the flicker of a strobe light. Did I really own a farm? Perhaps the whole experience had just been a drunken fantasy and I was actually still in England, or maybe America. I opened my eyes onto an unfamiliar scene. Bright light poured in through a set of curtains I didn't recognize. The sounds of a town starting its day filtered in from outside. Helen was there, wiping sleep from her eyes and clearly disoriented herself. "Whose house are we in?" she said sleepily.

"Who the hell knows?" I said. "I don't even know what country I'm in." That morning I was more sympathetic to Helen's desire to live a primitive life. Again I wondered if she could've been right all along. Did anyone know where all this "progress" was taking us? We went home and I sat recovering in the shade of a wrinkled old olive tree, with Bobby snoring gently at my feet. There were goat bells on a distant hill and wildflowers sprinkled throughout the tall dry grasses around me. Lying back peacefully in the fresh breeze, I thought to myself, "now surely *this* is progress." Maybe we should stick it out after all.

12

Rustic Authenticity

A good summer in England is one that coincides with a weekend. Other years there doesn't seem to be a summer at all. Maybe the rain's a little warmer, but that's it. Moving from there to Spain was like crawling out from under a stone. In our first year we didn't see a cloud in the sky between April and October. To start with, it seemed cool within those thick walls, compared with the soaring temperatures outside. Then by the middle of June there was nowhere to hide from the heat. A general sleepiness descended on the *campo* and even the breeze dragged its feet indifferently. A shimmering haze played tricks with our eyes and the screech of the cicadas became frenzied.

Meanwhile, the sun glared off the shiny leaves of olive trees, and even the grasses that had gone yellow and crisp underfoot made us squint. We gave up sunbathing on the patio because it was too much like being cremated.

Down by the coast, hordes of tourists had taken over and everything was in full swing. By contrast, the countryside had gone into hibernation. It might have been nothing like summer in England, but strangely it had a few things in common with an English winter—all the crops stopped growing, fields lay fallow, and the people disappeared into their homes. In that heat my unrelenting desire to do things to the house began to relent a little. I'm not referring to a change of heart. I might have wavered after a night out with Antonio but that was soon forgotten, along with those vows never to touch another drop as long as I lived. No, it was just that I couldn't get much renovating done lying naked on top of the bed waiting for the slightest of breezes to blow over me. There wasn't much farming we could do either. Only our figs gave us a summer crop, and one in the autumn too. Unless you're suffering from constipation, it's unwise to eat too many figs in one sitting. So we sensibly laid them out to dry for later use—and promptly lost most of them to flies and wasps. Even our expat social scene had gone dead. The loneliness of the winter off-season had ended for coastal dwellers. Many of the usual crowd were either entertaining visitors or away in England.

One expat had to make a hasty and permanent departure after falling foul of an aggressive local family. By all accounts, the Mendozas didn't become an aggressive family until they found out that Ron from Murcia had pocketed twice as much as they did from the sale of their run-down house. A little profiteering is an accepted part of life in Spain, but there are still limits and degrees of subtlety to be respected. Moving to a foreign land allows a person to reinvent his past with no one who knows the real truth there to contradict it. As usual, Ron took full advantage of this perk of living abroad. However, telling the Mendozas he was a secret agent in retirement failed to deter them from daubing his house with graffiti and letting the air out of the tires of his Land Rover. Even before this incident, he'd been finding the burden of his reputation hard to carry. Among the expats he'd become known as "Ron the Con." Locals began to refuse him service in bars and turn their backs on him in the streets. Finally it got to be too much for him and he fled to Australia—at least that's where he told everyone he was going. Knowing him, he probably only moved fifty miles up the coast, informing his new acquaintances that he'd just escaped from Red China.

With his exit there was temporarily a void in the "remote-hovel" sector of the local real estate market, which we tried to fill. We certainly hoped it would become another source of income. But the reason I was particularly keen to master this area of the property business was so I'd be able to dispose of our place when the time came. Besides a few crotchety old locals who feared being overrun by outsiders, everyone we met seemed to have a dilapidated farmhouse in the family that they'd happily sell to any foreigner who wanted it. For the most part, those who grew up in the impoverished *campo* shared Antonio's preference for modern urban living. On the other hand, foreigners from the big northern cities had a romanticized view of Mediterranean country life. Blinded by the sun and in vacation mode, they had been easy prey for Ron's sales patter. His whole pitch focused on what he called the "rustic authenticity" of the tumbledown farmhouse. Ron had the ability to show a pile of rubble in the middle of nowhere and get people gaggling to give him thirty or forty thousand dollars for it. He knew that these inflated prices would appear reasonable to anyone used to the high cost of housing in England. And an hour's drive from the sea seemed like a short excursion when you'd been lying on a beach for a week.

It was only when people came back for their first vacation in their new "chalet" that they discovered they'd paid well over the going rate for a remote shack. Sunbathing at home was out of the question unless you wanted to get eaten alive by flies, and popping out to the beach was suddenly a day trip. There was a good chance of getting up in the morning to find a goat in your kitchen, eating its way through everything including the table-cloth—and that's if you were one of the lucky ones who had a kitchen. The valleys of the interior were littered with cursing ex-clients of Ron.

Helen and I vowed that we wouldn't exploit the reckless or profiteer off the backs of locals. Like proper estate agents, we'd merely take a percentage from the seller. Most of our other income-generating schemes were suffering a drought. With the expats disbanded and school out for the summer, there wasn't much else to do except chase flies and sweat a lot. Despite all that had happened to us, we didn't realize we'd be as bad at real estate as we were at everything else. In truth, my heart was never in the job. Trying to keep my integrity while following in Ron's footsteps proved to be as hard as keeping vegetarian principles in the meat trade.

Our first victims could not have been easier prey. They were a nice old couple who were polite and uncomplaining. They had money ready for a quick sale and were desperate to buy a country house away from the tourist crowds. With two such eager customers, I was tempted to lead them straight to our place but Helen slapped me down. She sternly reminded me that I couldn't sell it to anyone until the day she was ready to put her signature on the sales agreement. I was also aware that if that day ever came, the place would be worth a lot more if I could finish modernizing it. Through word of mouth at Vicente's store, we'd accumulated a list of twenty other properties, most of which were less than half an hour from the sea. The rest could pass for half an hour away, if I floored the accelerator and didn't stop for traffic lights.

The day we picked up our first clients, there was an air of expectation in the village. The fear that Myrtle's arrival had generated in some locals was conveniently forgotten. The others knew that foreigners were prepared to pay crazy prices. It was widely felt that this would be someone's lucky day and all talk in the village bar was about how each would spend his windfall. We collected an unsuspecting Mr. and Mrs. Craddock from their hotel. They told us immediately that they only had a couple of days' vacation left and were eager to pick a place that afternoon. It was hard not to pity them. "Do you mind living without electricity?" I said. I'd already violated Ron's first rule, which was not to mention the lack of electricity unless they'd noticed for themselves.

"Will we miss it much in this terrific climate?" asked Mrs. Craddock. The appropriate words caught in my throat and instead I heard myself denouncing life without electricity. I concluded that it was only suitable for young people actively seeking a challenge. "We'd better stick to the ones with electricity then," she said. That quickly narrowed it down to five.

Nevertheless, we spent several hours tearing up and down dirt roads. Unfortunately, the nearest we had to air-conditioning was rolling down the windows. So when we and our clients emerged from our tiny car, we all looked like we'd just crossed the Sahara on foot. The houses that were for sale were easily recognized, as they were the ones that were freshly whitewashed. Often the front door and window shutters were painted in a contrasting bright color, like deep blue or green. Mr. and Mrs. Craddock thought we had an excellent selection. The first place would have suited them. "It's no good for you," I said. "It was finished without planning permission. A Spaniard might get away with it but you wouldn't want to risk it, would you?"

"Oh dear, no," said Mr. Craddock. The next place was also to their liking.

"Yes, but this really is the middle of nowhere," I said. "It'd take you nearly an hour just to pop out for some milk. That wouldn't do." Mr. and Mrs. Craddock shrugged and got back in the car. The next house dated from the time of the civil war and was built like a fortress. The ironwork was beautiful and there was a stunning inner courtyard covered in bougainvillea and geraniums. I could see their eyes light up and then turn almost warily to me. "Sorry," I said. "That main wall is starting to buckle. See the crack that's been painted over? If that goes, you've had it." The following place would have done too but I felt duty bound to point out the rot in the roof beams. They sheepishly got back in the car.

Finally, we came to the last viewing. The house backed against a mountain that was dotted with olive trees. Spread out in front were small hills cascading down toward a view of the sea in the distance. An orchard of fruit trees surrounded a well similar to our own. Inside, there were dusty pictures of saints on the walls and a crucifix over the mantelpiece, but otherwise it showed all the signs of a long desertion. Mr. and Mrs. Craddock walked around in an enamoured daze. After a while, they sneaked off to the front terrace to talk conspiratorially with each other. When Helen and I went out to join them, Mr. Craddock turned to me with a look of determination. "We'll take it," he said.

"I suppose you noticed there's no toilet?" I said.

"We'll have one put in," he said firmly.

"And you smelled the plaster in there? That's damp, you know."

"We don't care," he said. "We want it."

"Those things will take you way over the budget limit you mentioned to me earlier," I said. "You don't really want it."

"Yes, we do! We'll save up if we have to. We want to buy it and that's that," he said with a forceful nod. His wife backed him up.

"It's the nicest place we've ever seen," she said. I sighed.

"Look," I said. "This place is jointly owned by three brothers. All three of them need to sign for the sale to be legal."

"It could be done," said Mr. Craddock.

"Theoretically," I said. "But one of them lives in Latin America. He went there after a family feud years ago and hasn't been heard from since."

Mr. and Mrs. Craddock returned to their hotel looking totally dejected. "What came over you?" Helen hissed angrily. "The pope would've done a better sales job than that."

"I couldn't let them fall into the trap," I said. "Look what happened to us."

"But I *like* living in our farmhouse," she said in an injured tone.

"It has its good moments," I conceded, "but it would be too much work for people as elderly as they are. Every time I saw Mrs. Craddock, I kept thinking of my mother. It was clear they didn't understand the difficulties involved. Somewhere there's a lovely house for them that has all the modern conveniences and doesn't need rebuilding. That's what they really want."

"You can be so patronizing at times," she said. "You really are dreadful."

News of our failure didn't go down well in the village. When Helen recounted what had happened, no one spoke to me for a week. I told myself I'd failed to be ruthless because they were old. I'd felt sorry for them. The trouble is, I proceeded to feel sorry for a set of clients with young children. Then I was sorry for those without children who were just getting started in life. In the end we sold one house, to a German builder who spent

the entire viewing unsuccessfully trying to entice us into a mé-
nage à trois. We figured he deserved everything he got.

It transpired that Helen was much better than I was at exagger-
ating the qualities of a property. In her letters to her mother she
had gone out of her way to deny that we were suffering any dis-
comforts as a result of living in a remote location. She went so far
as to say that our place was perfectly livable and that it possessed
conveniences equal to those of any modern home. This economy
with the truth was all very well until her elder brother, sister-in-
law, and their two kids decided to show up that summer for a look
around. They didn't consult with us about when they were coming,
but just informed us when to expect them. Folks back home assumed that, as we were living in Spain, we must surely spend all
our time sitting by a pool with a cocktail in hand. It was the kind of
image that enticed me out there in the first place and one that
Helen had done nothing to dispel in her letters home.

Convincing her brother, Simon, and his wife, Margaret, to see
the merits of our life would not be easy, even if her picture of
the place was true. They were urban people who tried not to go
outdoors if they could avoid it. The thought of getting their
hands dirty or rubbing shoulders with peasants would horrify
them. Simon was tolerable to be with but his wife was a snappy
creature who behaved as though she belonged to royalty. Helen
hated her snobbery but strangely expressed this by struggling to
rival it. They'd start off sounding fairly normal but gradually
each would escalate their tone of voice and their airs until it became like a tea party at Buckingham Palace.

Helen went into a panic when she heard they were dropping
by during their vacation farther up the coast. We had less than a
week to make our dusty pile into a paragon of chic upper-class
civilization. It would've been easier to launch a rocket to the
moon. As chief promoter of home improvements, this was my

chance to strut around feeling vindicated. And I took full advantage of it. She'd spent so long dragging her feet over modernizing that I was tempted to sit back and let her sweat. Personally, I didn't care what her family thought, but Helen bribed me with promises. If I helped her pull this off, I'd be sitting with my feet up for a month while she waited on me. "Wouldn't it be easier to rent somewhere else and pretend it's ours?" I said.

"It's no use," said Helen, looking hollow eyed. "I've already told them where we live."

"Can't we say one of us is sick and call the whole thing off?" I suggested.

"If we do that, my family will take it as confirmation that we live in an unhealthy environment. I'd never hear the end of it. Besides, they'd probably still come."

So as the remaining days sped by we swept, dusted, and washed everything in sight. Fresh paint was applied where necessary, and I scrambled to finally connect the toilet to our water supply. It's amazing what a bit of incentive can do. When we'd finished, we thought the farm looked wonderful. Compared to a few days earlier it did. However, compared to an ordinary house it still looked like a peasant hovel. It was a sorry mix of traditional handicrafts and the feeble efforts of a modern would-be handyman. Most of my additions were far more rickety than the stuff that was a hundred years old. There wasn't a lot we could do to beautify our trash incinerator and its blackened debris. The internal courtyard was cluttered with spare roof tiles, chicken wire, and rusty farm tools we'd salvaged during my "renovation" of the former animal quarters. We stacked all these in a shed and closed the door. Our guests were only staying one night. We figured we'd be able to prevent them from nosing around in that time.

In our preparations we made one major mistake. We cleared a large patch of prickly pear cactus near the house, which we'd noticed was a breeding ground for all sorts of bugs. Having been evicted, the bugs came looking for shelter at our place. Even worse were the snakes. In among the cacti were half a dozen or so black snakes. They were only about six inches long—more like worms really—but we knew Margaret would go berserk if she saw one. Although they disappeared as the cacti fell, Bobby made it his business to find them and bring them up to the house to show us. By this point he'd shaken them to death, but that was little consolation as their smell made burning rubber seem like perfume. We knew wild creatures would be an issue for our city guests, but there wasn't much we could do about them. Lizards, earwigs, giant ants, and massive spiders frequently showed up around the house. I did try spraying with insecticide but as usual went too far and nearly exterminated us as well. In order to breathe, we had to throw open all the windows for two days—by which time the bugs had returned.

The day they were due to arrive we raced around adding the finishing touches. We were putting the kids in a spare room with the blow-up bed, parents in our room, and we were going to make do with the sofa. Bobby and his various smells were expelled to the yard. In each of their rooms we put out a bowl and a jug of water. We hoped this would distract from the lack of sinks and taps anywhere else in the house. We bought fresh goat meat to cook in a delicious recipe we'd tasted at Maria's house. Even Bobby had a haircut and a bath. Curtains were hung on makeshift bamboo poles. Ornaments were placed just so, and furniture positioned in front of cracks and over holes.

There was nothing left to do except wait. Heat shimmered in the valley. A small twister scattered dust as it blew through. The hills loomed over the scene like a tidal wave about to break. We waited and waited. At last we saw a car edging along the dirt track in our direction. I wondered if their slow approach was due to caution or reluctance. I half expected them to turn around at any moment and make off at full speed. Finally they crawled to a halt in our drive. When they got out of the car, I felt underdressed in my T-shirt and shorts. Simon had socks on under his long trousers and Margaret looked like she was going for an evening at the theater in an ankle-length dress and high heels. "I wasn't sure we were on the right track," said Simon. "In fact, I wasn't sure we were on a track at all."

"You couldn't have picked a more out-of-the-way place, could you, darlings?" Margaret said, dusting off her dress.

"Anyway, I'm sorry we're late." Simon shook my hand. "We got stopped by paramilitary policemen. I don't know what we'd done wrong."

"They just throw up a road block and stop people randomly," I explained. "You go for months without getting pulled over and then it happens three times in the same day."

"Barbaric, if you ask me," said Margaret. "It's the sort of behavior you'd expect in a banana republic."

"They had machine guns and everything," said their twelve-year-old son, William. His eight-year-old sister, Beatrice, was busy swatting at a fly. When a second and third fly arrived, she ran screaming into the house.

"Good idea," I said. "Shall we go in?" Simon looked at the log that acted as a support beam over the door and hesitated. I nodded reassurance and he stepped quickly under it. Our first reaction to the terra-cotta tiled floor and beamed ceiling had been one of delight. Margaret scanned the place with barely concealed contempt.

"Your rocks are showing," she said.

"Pardon?" said Helen.

"Under the paint, darling," she continued. "The rocks that presumably hold the place up."

"It's exactly the same as a stone cottage back home," said Helen.

"Of course it is, darling."

"Anyone for a cold drink?" I said. I hoped this would cool our frazzled travelers and at the same time demonstrate that we at least had refrigeration. On our way through to the kitchen I showed them where the bathroom was. The cement floor in there was my pride and joy. Getting it laid had been an epic struggle for me. By their reaction I could see that to them it was just a cement floor. I felt hurt when I realized our magnificent light switches were likewise unremarkable to our guests. They didn't seem to notice them at all. Surely they'd appreciate our toilet, even if the new inlet to the cistern was a bit of old hose? I saw an arrogant smile form at the corner of Margaret's mouth and became as determined as Helen that we wouldn't be looked down on.

Unfortunately, Beatrice had inherited her mother's personality without yet developing the cushioning of adult tact. "Yuck, it's disgusting," she said when she saw the kitchen. A plastic sink rested between two stacks of bricks. It had no taps and no drain. Between the refrigerator and stove stood a butane bottle that those appliances shared. In the middle of the room was the table we'd rescued from the roadside. Fresh thyme and mint from our land, as well as bottled spices, lined the top of the stone fireplace. We sat on our wobbly bamboo chairs and did as best as we could to make sophisticated conversation after six months of living in isolation.

Simon handed his sister a promisingly large present. She unwrapped it with glee but her face soon dropped. It was an electric coffee percolator. Without needing to check the side of the box, we knew that even working flat-out, our solar panel would barely be able to illuminate the little light that said it was plugged in. Actually switching it on would produce smoke from our converter before any steam hit the coffee granules. "How lovely," said Helen, trying to smile.

"Well, do you fancy a cup of coffee then?" said Simon. "I could murder for one after that journey."

"It's too hot for coffee," I said quickly. "Let's have something cold." I passed out the drinks before anyone had time to protest. Helen put our battery cassette player on to create the sound effects of a powered-up house. In truth, we'd stumbled around in the dark for two nights to store up electricity for their visit. But even with a fully charged battery it was easy to run out. If the lights and water pump were to go, it would be hard to sustain the pretense that ours was like any normal house.

The only one yet to make a comment was William. He had headphones on and his face buried in a Game Boy. When his drink was placed in front of him, he lifted one headphone. "Can I watch TV?" he said.

"Well, er, wouldn't you rather do something else?" said Helen.

"You do have a television, don't you?" said Margaret.

"Of course we do!" said Helen.

"How'd you like to watch Cartoon Network?" I offered hopefully.

"No, that's crap," said William. "I want to see MTV."

"I know," said Helen. "Let's all go for a walk."

"I'll stay here and watch TV," said William.

"No. Lets *all* go," said Helen, through gritted teeth. William and Beatrice came along with bowed heads and grumpily scuffed the ground with their feet. I was sympathetic because I could recall how difficult I once found it to go a whole day without TV. Since then we'd survived a period of several months deprived of television. But in the past I'd always craved a regular fix of the news. After our enforced abstinence I managed to kick the habit. Now the news seemed no more important to me than a soap opera, and I'd missed so many episodes I didn't care anymore. When we did get glimpses of a bulletin, it seemed that very little had really changed in the world anyway. In the world where we lived, nothing had changed at all.

Helen's idea of a walk should have been a masterstroke. If the house failed to impress, despite its charm, then surely our massive spread would succeed. Simon and Margaret's garden was just big enough to park a car. We had over ten acres of trees in our backyard. The oppressive heat had begun to fade as evening drew on, and a beautiful crested bird happened to land near the patio just as we set out. Among the leaves of the trees were baby almonds or clusters of caviar-sized olives. "Our land goes all the way to that hill over there," said Helen, drawing their attention away from our trash incinerator. "If you look through the gap there, can you see the medieval Moroccan fort?" I felt sure we were at last winning, yet no one showed the appropriate awe. The kids swatted flies and regarded everything with wrinkled-up noses. Margaret hobbled along the uneven ground in her high heels, her attention fixed on each step. Unfortunately, in the summer the grasses produced round seedpods covered with prickly spikes, like miniature limpet mines. Every few yards someone would cry out in pain and then remove one from their ankle.

As Simon and Helen caught up on family affairs, I drew the short straw and accompanied Margaret. "You're not into religion, are you, Shaun?" she said.

"What?"

"I mean this John the Baptist lifestyle," she said. "You're both looking rather wild." She made me realize how much we must have changed since we'd left England. With our deep tans and scruffy clothes, we'd started to look and think like a couple of Apaches. Let's face it, a year ago we wouldn't have considered a toilet a status symbol.

At the edge of our land we saw Emilio inspecting his trees, and he came over to say hello. I could tell that the sight of this

bristly old man horrified Margaret, and her children demonstrated their feelings by hiding behind her. Emilio was his usual
friendly self, but only made them more edgy by jabbering away
in Spanish and trying to kiss them. I interpreted his greetings
and then told him that they'd replied in a similar vein. In fact,
Margaret had said "tell this dirty creature that if he doesn't stop
trying to kiss me I'll sock him where it hurts." Meanwhile,
Bobby had started mounting Emilio's dogs one after the other,
regardless of their sex. Helen and I decided to cut short the walk
and head for home.

When we got back we were in for a shock. I could hear voices
from the lounge, so I rushed in to find the television had been
left on and William's Game Boy was plugged in and recharging
next to it. I dreaded to think how much of the night's electricity
had been used up, as we'd been gone over an hour. Simon came
in and saw me unplugging the TV and the game. "You're looking
off-color," he said. "Are you all right?" I told him I was just
cleaning behind the cabinet. I couldn't admit that something so
minor had thrown us into crisis. When Helen and I had a moment alone, I explained what had happened.

"We'll have to switch off the water pump," I said, "or the
lights will go off halfway through the evening."

"What about the toilet?" she said.

"We'll just have to fill the cistern by bucket each time someone's been in there."

"That'll really impress Margaret."

"It'll be dark soon," I said. "I can sneak out to the well and do
it without anyone noticing. We just have to be vigilant about
who's gone to the toilet and also make sure no lights are left on
unnecessarily."

"Let's try to keep everyone together then," she said. "I'll suggest a card game."

When darkness fell, we sat in the lounge and Helen growled at William and Beatrice every time one of them asked to have the TV on. We tried to sit under one light without appearing stingy. "I like it cozy," Helen explained. It was my behavior that attracted attention. You'd think we had criminals staying with us the way I got up and checked whenever someone left the room. I turned off lights after people and, if they went to the toilet, I raced out to the well and hauled up a bucket of water to refill the tank. Since we generated our own electricity, we'd forgotten what it was like to leave lights on and not care about the waste. Similarly, we used water very sparingly, and much of what we did use got recycled to mop the floor or water plants. While everyone else gradually cooled off in the night air, I was rushing about getting covered in a sheen of sweat.

After one swift trip into the dark to the well and back, Simon looked at me and said: "Are you *sure* you're all right? You're looking a bit flushed now."

"Yes, quite sure," I said breathlessly. My excuses for leaving the room were getting less and less plausible. "I'm just popping out to check the vegetable patch," I said.

"In the dark?" said Margaret.

"There's a local proverb that says shoots come up more quickly during a full moon," I said. "I'll just nip out and check." Meanwhile, we began making trips to the kitchen to start the dinner. We struggled to get everything ready by candlelight. "Can't you stop serving them drinks?" I said. "One more trip to the toilet and I'm going to collapse."

"It's what we'll do if they ask for coffee after dinner that worries me," said Helen. "We can't snub their gift."

"We'll just have to make chugging noises while we prepare instant coffee on the stove."

"Quick! The lounge door opened." I managed to get the light

on, but we didn't have time to put the candles out. It was Margaret.

"Why the candles?" she said.

"We thought it would be romantic," said Helen.

"If you want to soften the light, then you should put up lamp shades," said Margaret. "I suppose you keep your lights uncovered because they're so dim."

"We prefer low-watt bulbs," I said. "Better ambience."

"Yes, well, I just came out to ask for more water."

"You used the whole jug?" I said.

"Why ever not?" she said. "If you will live in the desert . . ."

"Fine," I said dejectedly. "I'll just go to the tap."

"Why are you going that way?"

"Thought I'd have a quick look at the stars first," I said.

We came close to catastrophe when Beatrice ran shrieking into the lounge. "There's a snake on my bed!" she cried. Luckily I got there first, removed the creature, and smacked Bobby on the nose as a warning not to do it again.

"What was it?" said Simon.

"Just a piece of string that the dog had been chewing," I said.

"It was a snake," said Beatrice.

"Now darling, don't be silly," said Margaret. Beatrice didn't argue, but she sat there scowling with her arms crossed. Finally, we served dinner, which included goat meat for the main course and goat cheese with figs for dessert.

"What is it?" said Beatrice. "Snake meat?"

"Fresh kid," said Helen, staring threateningly at her. Even in the light and without pressure, Helen and I were not the best of cooks. In this case, the meat was overcooked and so tough we had to wrestle it across the plate just to spear it with a fork. Then it took so long to chew that it caused jaw ache. The presence of a gecko on the ceiling with the legs of some insect stuffed in its mouth didn't help to whet the appetite. Only William went "wow!" as he watched it hunt a moth right over our heads. Poor Beatrice never took her terrified eyes off it either.

The only consolation when disaster struck was the timing. Margaret was the first to say "what's that foul smell?" I saw Bobby standing proudly over another snake a couple of feet behind her chair. Beatrice's eyes had picked it out too. She began to point when—bang—the light went out and we were plunged into total darkness. I heard several screams as I fumbled around the table, located Bobby, and ejected both him and his toy. It's a good thing Helen and I were used to groping around like a couple of blind people. She found matches and lit a candle. In its small circle of light we could see that Beatrice had climbed onto William's lap. Simon had stabbed himself in the face with his fork but wasn't badly injured, and Margaret had turned to stone—with a fixed expression of openmouthed shock. When she recovered enough to speak, she informed Simon that they were leaving. "We can't stay here," she said. "You're living like primitives."

"You've got to admire the rustic authenticity," I said, trying to salvage something.

"Admire it, hell! Come on, Simon, let's go."

"Just one word of advice," I said. "It's almost impossible to navigate the dirt tracks in the dark. Some of them go for miles into the interior. Are you sure you wouldn't rather stay the night? You could get lost forever."

"Now there's an idea," Helen said rather viciously.

"So we're trapped here?" said Margaret. Beatrice started crying.

"It's not so bad with a few candles," I said. "Think of it as an adventure." They decided that staying till dawn was perhaps the quickest way out of the nightmare. By now the dinner was not only chewy and cold but also an unappetizing gray color in the dim light. We skipped straight to dessert. Surprisingly, it was the children who complained the least. Now that there was a power outage, they could accept that TV was out of the question. They seemed to take my advice about adventure at face value and showed signs of enjoying themselves. The grown-ups had a harder time. While we were trained to duck at the right places, they banged their heads, walked straight into walls, fell down steps, and burned their fingers on matches. We all ended up outside. At last, under the amazing canopy of stars and in the calm of total silence, Helen's family conceded that we had something special here. As they said good night, Simon turned to me and seemed to struggle for words.

"Very authentic," he said at last.

The morning got off to a bad start. I can't cope with pandemonium before my first cup of coffee. Before I was properly awake, Simon poked his head around the corner to inquire about a shower. He saw my look and said "never mind." A minute later he came running back in. William was in agony and needed a doctor. We all went to see, and sure enough he was rolling around, clutching his stomach in considerable pain.

"It could be a hernia," I suggested.

"Or his appendix," said Helen.

"It's those figs you encouraged him to eat, I'm sure of it," said Margaret.

"He only had *one*," I protested.

"This dreadful place has poisoned him," she continued. "I knew we shouldn't have come."

There was no use calling an ambulance to the house. We'd all have died of old age before they found us. So we bundled William into their car and they followed our trail of dust as we sped toward the road. By the time we reached the hospital in town, Margaret had worked herself into hysteria. "That fig has done this. It's your wretched fruit. If anything happens I'll sue you—family or not." Ignoring her, we took him into the emergency room. A doctor and a team of nurses set upon him straightaway, asking questions, prodding, and taking blood. Before long, the doctor returned looking grave.

"Is he going to make it?" said Margaret. "Tell me what's wrong."

"We've looked at every possibility," said the doctor in good English, "and we've concluded it can only be one thing. The boy is constipated."

"You mean . . . ?"

"Yes. He just needs to have a movement. The build up of gas can give very bad pain. The problem is caused by his diet. It's obviously been building up for some time. Might I suggest you've been giving him too much junk food and not nearly enough fruit?"

I have to confess that I derived a cruel satisfaction from that scene: all that expensive high-tech equipment on standby, a team of experienced nurses, and a highly qualified doctor—all waiting for Margaret's son to have a "movement." You'd think it was difficult enough for William, who was lying there with an enema protruding from his buttocks. Yet the most uncomfortable and embarrassed-looking person in the room was Margaret herself. It was a moment I will always savor.

13

Nuts

It was easy to miss the transition from summer to autumn because the days remained hot and sunny. Although the overwhelming temperatures had gone, it was still more like summer than any summer I'd had in England. Our neighbors began to talk about The Crop and The Rain. We were told to make sure we'd dealt with the first before the second came along. Since we'd had little else to do for the last few months except wait for The Crop, we figured we must be ready. Watching almonds grow had been less than riveting. Our efforts to prune and mulch had as much visible result as a gnat biting an elephant.

With so much in the lap of the gods, I began to see why rural types were big on religion.

We hadn't helped matters by buying our almond farm without even reading a book on the subject. Everything we knew, we learned in broken translation from our neighbors. I hadn't seen any books on their shelves either. Some of the older ones couldn't even read. While their Californian competitors exchanged tips via dedicated almond websites, the locals sat around the fire and swapped their grandfathers' secrets. Certainly there was more to know than I imagined. For instance, I was surprised to learn that we had four varieties of almond on our farm alone. Language difficulties didn't help either, especially at the start. Apparently, Emilio told me about the basic distinction between bitter and sweet almonds when we first moved in. Unfortunately, at the time I thought he was saying the life of an almond farmer was bittersweet. Come to think of it, he did look at me strangely when I offered sympathy.

Our almonds fattened so slowly that we failed to notice when their outer skins finally opened and the odd one or two fell to the ground. Early one morning, long before I'd contemplated getting out of bed, I was woken by a menacing noise. I don't know if you've ever seen the film *Zulu* with Michael Caine, but at one point a small British contingent in Africa is surrounded by thousands of Zulu warriors. The sound I was hearing was identical to that made by the warriors as they thumped their spears threateningly against their shields. It was impossible to get back to sleep with the danger of massacre by irate tribesmen hanging over me. Peering cautiously from our upstairs window, I was baffled to see some people encircle a tree and begin viciously attacking it with long sticks. Being only half-awake, I couldn't fathom what the tree had done to deserve this. I rubbed the sleep from my eyes and looked again. All over the valley, similar groups consisting of my neighbors and their extended families were beating the living daylights out of trees. The time of The Crop had arrived.

Hitting trees with sticks was the sort of behavior I was discouraged from as a child, and I had to overcome a deeply ingrained sense of guilt in order to approach the task wholeheartedly. By now you will have guessed how straightforward cultivation was. Large sheets of material or plastic were placed under a tree and its nuts were knocked off. Then the sheet was gathered together and the contents emptied into a sack. That's it. The keen ones then put the nuts into shelling machines. The really conscientious did the shelling by hand. If you've ever come close to breaking your fingers over a handful of unshelled nuts at Christmas, you can imagine confronting dozens of agricultural sacks brimming with them. We took the lazy option and decided to sell our nuts complete with shells, even though they fetched a lower price that way.

It takes longer than you might imagine to crop over four hundred trees sagging under the weight of ripe nuts. Especially if you don't have an army of aunts, uncles, and cousins in the vicinity to give you a hand. Our usually helpful neighbors were too busy cropping their own. Consequently, our bodies were finished off long before the work was. Despite our exhaustion, we were both relieved that nature had been gracious enough to deliver the goods. The urge to open some wine and indulge in a little thanksgiving was irresistible. We felt we could at last allow ourselves to fantasize about spending the vast sum of money this was going to bring in.

I say our neighbors were too busy to help, but they did drop over from time to time to check that we were coping all right. Since all their own young folk wanted to be pop stars or football players rather than farmers, they were grateful that we were at least trying. In fact, some of these simple country people, like Pepe for instance, not only tolerated our naiveté but actually rel-

ished treating us like the simpletons for a change. He even insisted on showing me how to hold a stick. You couldn't blame
them for crowing a little. As usual, we showed ourselves to be
hopeless amateurs. We were there to avoid regular jobs and because we'd made a bit of money from building a database. We
were not there because farming ran in the family and certainly
not because of a lifelong fascination with almonds. The differences between us were plain to see. They wore rugged overalls
and sturdy boots. We wore T-shirts with shorts and tiptoed
through the prickly grasses with sandals on our otherwise bare
feet. They wore straw hats to shield their heads and eyes. We
didn't bother with hats but wore sunglasses, from which we
were forever wiping sweat. They heaped sacks onto trailers
pulled by a tractor. We loaded a sack at a time into our little car.
When they'd finished bashing a tree, they quickly moved on. We
stood around handpicking every last almond. Need I continue?

After months of sitting around thinking that farming was
pretty cushy work, Helen was finally getting her wake-up call.
By the end of two days of cropping, our hands were covered in
blisters and we were bent double with back strain. She was in a
worse state than I was. So far that year, the only time she'd had a
spade in her hand was when we were playing cards. When it was
all finally finished, there was a party atmosphere in the valley.
From all directions our neighbors began to inundate us with
gifts of a local nougat dessert made with almonds. Simona and
Theresa even brought around one each. The sisters jostled at
the handover and then each pestered me to try *hers* first. It was
only Helen ushering them out the door while thanking them
that saved me from an impossible choice.

At first we were convinced that no almonds in the world had
ever tasted as good as ours. We were determined to keep a lot of
them for personal use. For dinner we had chicken served with

our own almonds. The next day we had almonds on our cereal, almonds as a lunchtime snack, and pork with almonds in the evening. It was the same story the next day and the one after that. Funnily enough, as the days wore on, we decided to keep less and less of them aside when the dealer came.

I can only thank God that old Emilio was around when the dealer did finally stop by the farm to buy our nuts. I got confused and agreed to sell them at 150 pesetas a kilo, when he was already offering 200. It took Emilio several minutes and a good deal of stick waving to drive him back up to 200 again. Part of the problem was not having any idea how many kilos a sack of almonds weighed. It didn't help that there was no paperwork and no measuring equipment brought into play. The whole transaction was worked out by guesswork and using finger marks in the dirt. Only when it was all over did the true state of our financial situation become clear. After all, this was our main crop, the economic safety net for the adventure we were living. As our entire almond harvest bumped its way toward the road on the back of a truck, we could tell that the Caribbean vacation and new car would have to wait. We were left holding the equivalent of less than a thousand dollars.

"I did warn you that we'd need to diversify," said Helen.

"It's a disgrace," I said. "Have you seen how much a tiny bag of almonds costs at the supermarket? The middleman is making a fortune."

"If we had goats and pigs, we'd be laughing now," she continued.

"Next year I'm going to bag them up, stand outside the supermarket, and sell them myself," I said.

"This is your fault," said Helen. "We need to diversify. Are you listening to me?"

"Yes, yes. I'll start digging for oil tomorrow."

"This is serious," she said. "Perhaps we should make the farm into a tourist attraction. We could take in paying guests who want to experience the country."

"I can see it now," I said. "People would flock here to see trees with nuts on them. A farm with a real live dog on it. We could offer miles of hilly countryside in which to get snared on prickly grasses. Or better yet, we could advertise the place as an authentic failing farm. They'd come from all over the world to see us—the authentic failing farmers with our authentic bank overdraft. We could call it the 'nut house.'"

"You could be more positive," she said. "I'm sure that if you put your mind to it, you could think of something that would get us out of this situation."

"Sell the house and get a real job?" I suggested.

"What about a coffee shop?" she said. "We could sell the homemade pastries that Maria makes, and Anna's sausages."

"Who to?" I said, surveying the empty landscape. "We're lucky if we see one car a week down here, and that's usually Diego after he's had a few brandies and missed his turn. A tourist would have to be lost to wind up in town, let alone down a dirt track six miles outside it."

Until this point, owning over ten acres had given us the delusion that we were up there with the royal family and the Ewings of Dallas. The humbleness of our almond crop brought us back to earth with a thud. But life was the same for our neighbors, who worked five times as hard and still only just managed to keep their heads above water. Their cheerfulness kept us going when any sensible person would have considered hara-kiri. Virtudez and Diego senior had us over for dinner and served *Gazpacho Andaluz,* a cold spiced tomato soup that is one of the classics of Spanish cuisine.

"Local people first prepared this dish when they were starving during a famine," said Virtudez. "They couldn't even afford wood to cook with and all they had to eat were tomatoes, but instead of crying about it they made something new. Now it's considered a specialty." I'm sure she was trying to tell us something, but I never figured out what.

With The Crop over, the main topic of conversation in the valley became The Rain. Helen and I found this highly amusing. As two people raised in England, we felt we were experts on rain. It was a well-known statistic that this part of Spain enjoyed over three hundred sunny days a year. By contrast, we were used to over three hundred days of cloud and drizzle. Surely only someone who considered precipitation a rare and alien concept would go on about it as much as these people. We looked at the deep blue sky and the dry Mediterranean hills and shook our heads. After our humiliation with the almonds, we got an unhealthy pleasure from being able to scoff at our neighbors for once. "Any time now and The Rain will come," the younger Diego said, looking sagely at a clear sky.

"They don't know what rain is," said Helen when he'd gone.

"They're all mad," I said. In a few days it did begin to cloud over, but it was nothing we hadn't seen a million times before. The natives grew more and more restless. When we stopped at Vicente's store to collect our mail, the place was full of people stocking up on canned food, as if the end of the world were nigh.

"Be careful—The Rain is coming," he said, looking concerned.

"Yeah, Vicente, sure," I said. That night there was a terrific thunderstorm away in the direction of the coast. The wind picked up, the sky flashed white, and a distant rumble could be heard. We were fairly impressed, and it did rain a little overnight, but by morning the whole thing seemed to have blown over. The sun shone strongly through breaks in the clouds, birds sang, and all there was to show for The Rain was a couple of puddles.

"I guess that's it for another year," said Helen with a chuckle. "I do hope everyone managed to survive without running out of food."

"Or getting their hair wet," I added. Even without rain, we'd once more been plunged back into the Dark Ages because clouds were obscuring our solar panel. This was no minor hassle to us as it also stopped our running water, and all our conveniences sat idle as if they'd never been installed. The ancient Romans enjoyed better facilities than we had during cloudy weather. We penned a couple of letters to send back home. Helen created a lengthy epistle to Rita, making excuses for all that had happened during Simon and Margaret's visit. I wrote to my friends, ridiculing the locals for being afraid of a little water. Then we drove into town to mail them at the post office. It was overcast but dry when we went in. As usual, the line moved slowly as each customer chatted amiably with the woman behind the counter. The first thing to grab my attention was the door banging open and closed behind us as a series of people ran in off the street. They were wet and full of good humor as they dashed in to avoid a downpour. Then a drumming started on the roof that made Helen and me look warily at each other. Although there was a general buzz of excitement in the room, it was the turn of the locals to appear comfortable and us to sweat a little. We mailed our letters and joined a crowd gathered in the doorway. It was raining so hard that visibility was down to less than a hundred feet.

"It's bound to pass in a minute," I said. "Shall we make a dash for it?" Helen took my hand nervously. The other people in the doorway looked at us with surprise.

"Where are you going in this?" said one man.

"Home," I said with as much confidence as I could muster,

and off we ran. After two yards our clothes were soaked. After four it was like we'd fallen into a swimming pool and after six we were drowning. We just made it to the car and sloshed into our seats. The engine must have been well sealed because it actually started. Even with the windshield wipers on full speed, the road was just a blur. We inched along.

"Er, Shaun, I think you should know the water is up to the door," said Helen. I wiped condensation from the side window and peered out. Sure enough, we were already driving through two feet of water.

"We're at the bottom of a hill," I said. "It's a flash flood. If we can only get out of this part of town, I'm sure it won't be so deep."

"I don't want to worry you," she continued, "but have you seen what's behind us?" I turned to look. We were miles from the sea or any river and yet there was a boat closing on us rapidly. One of the occupants paddled while the other bailed out with a bucket. Just then the car's engine coughed and died. We climbed out of the windows and stood knee-deep in water. As the boat approached, I stuck out my thumb for a ride. We were delivered back to the post office to derisory cheers from the huddled crowd.

There was nothing we could do except watch urban flotsam sail by like prizes on a game show conveyor belt. Before long, the heavy downpour calmed to a steady drizzle and within half an hour the waters quickly began to recede. Nevertheless, we were stuck in town for the rest of the afternoon, waiting for our car to dry out. Finally that evening, to the accompanying rumble of another approaching storm, we loaded up the car with cans and set off for home. It was to be an epic journey.

Trees were down in several places, and when we reached our dirt track it was a fast-flowing river. We pointed the car upstream with the growing feeling that perhaps coming home was not such a bright idea. The other people we'd seen on the roads were making a dash for town. We were the only ones desperately fighting our way through to a remote location, where we would surely be stranded. I was getting pretty tired of people staring at me like I was a lunatic.

We were determined to get home. Partly because we were soaked to the skin and shivering from a twenty-degree temperature drop. But above all we were worried about Bobby. When we got there, he was trembling under the porch and looking put upon. Fortunately, Pedro García's ancestors had built the house on a slight rise, which now appeared like an island in a shallow lake. Nevertheless, when we got inside we found a good two inches of water on the floor—more than there was on the porch outside. At first this puzzled us but gradually we noticed drips coming from several points on the ceiling. The rumbling in the sky was getting louder, so I clambered onto the slippery roof to inspect the damage. Had I listened to my neighbors, I would have dealt with the roof weeks ago. There were several broken tiles and enough soil in the cracks up there to grow vegetables. We had plenty of spare tiles, but I could see that in order to reach one broken tile, I could quite easily break several more and perhaps a bone or two. It was a bad time to remember that I suffered from vertigo. In the end, I had some success by doing a tightrope walk up the ridges and then crawling flat on my belly to the appropriate location. By the time the storm was overhead, I'd fixed all the obvious holes and was covered in moss from head to foot. At this point, the lightning was awfully close and I didn't feel that standing on top of the highest building in the area was particularly sensible. I dropped from the roof and dashed into the house, looking like a monster from the swamp. Bobby growled at me from his hiding place under the table.

Within minutes the rain drummed down and the windows shook with thunder. Despite my repairs, we had to race around placing buckets under the drips until we ran out of them, and had to move on to pots, pans, and Tupperware containers. The mop was in constant use as water poured in through loose-fitting windows. Naturally, there was no electric light to alleviate the gloom or offer comfort at night. Our log pile was soaked and useless, so we huddled together under a big quilt to keep warm. When we finally went to bed, we put everything as high off the floor as we could and hoped for the best. It wasn't a good night's sleep.

The Rain came and went for an entire week. Then one morning we woke up and the sun was shining in a clear blue sky again. There was little indication that a year's rainfall had just fallen in seven days. The only real change was that the usual screech of cicadas was silent and the air was full of birdsong instead. Rain had washed the dust off our solar panel and it was beginning to charge the battery nicely. After a couple of hours I went to try the tap at the side of the house. Nothing happened. So I strolled over to the well with a flashlight. I expected that, as usual, I'd have to peer into the dark depths to see anything. I suppose I shouldn't really have been surprised when I opened the little wooden door and was confronted with water lapping against the brim. It would be a couple of days before the pump had dried out enough to work again. Being submerged for a week was definitely not recommended in the manufacturer's instructions.

In a few days, green shoots began to appear all over our land, and soon the ground was covered in lush grasses and colorful wildflowers. Nature had taken a cold shower after the heat of summer and seemed to be giving us a second spring. It was hard to believe, but I began to feel optimistic again. We might not have gotten rich off our almonds but, if we lived cheaply, we had enough money to keep us going a few more months. There was still the smaller olive crop to look forward to. Then the returning expats began to call us in for a number of jobs relating to flood

damage. Two houses needed repainting, one needed new cup-
boards, and another required some replacement roof tiles—
something I was becoming expert at. For the time being, even
our economic drought had come to an end.

The autumn also brought a renaissance of my hopes that we
could get connected by the electric company. A retired Spanish
army colonel owned a little farm in the valley, not far from
Diego and Virtudez. He lived in Murcia most of the time but
could occasionally be seen strolling in his fields on weekends.
He'd taken an interest when we first applied for electricity many
months before. Like the other locals, it hadn't surprised him to
hear that installation was prohibitively expensive, even if everyone in the valley teamed up to pay for it. However, the colonel
was not as easily defeated as the rest of us. He'd been quietly
making inquiries through contacts at the local town hall. Then in
the autumn he visited everyone in the valley, seeking our signatures on a petition. Apparently, there were government grants
available for installing electricity in remote areas. The knack was
to phrase the application correctly and then make a small "gift"
to the relevant official to ensure things ran smoothly. It all
sounded highly suspicious to me, but the other neighbors went
along with it, so I did too. Thereafter, conversations with fellow
valley dwellers always included cryptic references to electricity,
accompanied by winks and nods. I nodded and winked back
without the faintest idea what was going on.

A certain amount of mystery is the least you can expect if you
move to a foreign country with a language still largely beyond
your understanding. Occasionally, this mystery can become a little scary. The concern that almond croppers might be a horde of
savages after our scalps is a case in point. However, on the whole
we'd just about got used to living in an isolated location without

fear of attack from crazy people. Then one morning I was again
lounging in bed when Helen called me to the window. There
was a slight tremble in her voice and for some reason she
stepped back cautiously. "What is it?" I said.

"I think you'd better look for yourself," she replied. Moving
across our land toward the house was a group of half-a-dozen
rough-looking men, armed to the teeth. They each held shot-
guns, poised and ready. Knives glinted from their belts. Questions ricocheted around my head. Perhaps we'd inadvertently
offended someone dangerous? Or perhaps the natives were just
sick of foreigners drinking their beer and stealing the best spots
on the beach. "What's going on?" said Helen.

"I don't know," I said, "but I think we'd better get ready to
run for it."

"Why don't you go see what they want?" she suggested. I
looked at her suspiciously.

"They're not something to do with you, are they?" I said. "If
you don't want me around anymore, we can just call it off amicably you know." The look she gave me suggested that if she
wanted to kill me she was capable of doing it herself—and it
would be slower and more painful than being shot. On the face
of it I decided her suggestion wasn't too bad. The sooner I
gauged the intentions of these men, the better. I leaned dangerously out of the window and waved in their direction. They
waved back. "They don't seem too aggressive," I said.

"Go out and talk to them," she said. I threw on a ghastly multi-
colored T-shirt that Rita had sent me for Christmas, and prayed
that it wouldn't be what I would die in. But by the time I got
outside, it was clear the men were skirting the house by at least
a hundred yards.

"Good day," one of them called out cheerfully. At last I recognized that I'd once seen him in Vicente's store. "The hunting

season starts this morning," he told me. I recalled that only fenced land was off-limits. Later, as we sat on the patio and ate breakfast, a thought suddenly occurred to Helen.

"Oh my God, we'd better make sure Myrtle hasn't had a heart attack!"

"You're right," I agreed. "If she thinks a nightclub is an alien invasion, what's she going to make of this?" In ten minutes we pulled up outside Myrtle's house. All the shutters were closed and it seemed she must have gone away. But when she heard our voices, the front door slowly opened a crack. Myrtle cautiously emerged from the darkened interior, wielding a pitchfork in one hand and a trash can lid for a shield in the other. Best of all, she wore a steel cooking pot on her head.

"Have they gone?" she said, looking quickly to left and right before coming out into the sunlight. I realized how much I had to thank Myrtle for. Without her I would have been without competition as the fool of the *campo*.

A couple of days later, the younger Diego came to see if I wanted to hunt with him. He didn't even think to ask Helen, because in our area not a single woman ever hunted. It was a strictly male pastime, like being in charge of the barbecue or pissing by the side of the road. I wasn't going to ask her myself, because I knew she'd probably shoot *us* if it meant saving the animals. So the two of us set off alone with a dog each, a crate of beer, and one shotgun between us. They say dogs take after their owners, and Bobby turned out to be as hopelessly unaggressive toward animals as Helen, and as aloof as I was to anything that resembled work. Meanwhile, Diego's dog was grossly overweight and only interested in lying down for a rest at every opportunity. Despite the dogs' lack of enthusiasm, the tension when we set out was terrific. As we slowly moved through the grasses, we scanned the fields ahead. But pretty soon it became apparent that there wasn't much wildlife to hunt. By lunchtime we'd only seen a couple of pigeons and a wild rabbit. As a rabbit breeder, the last thing Diego needed to bring home was another rabbit, but he still had a shot anyway. "The idea of the hunt is to shoot anything that moves," he explained. I guessed this was why there didn't appear to be any wildlife left.

We stopped on a grassy knoll and I drank a warm beer while he consumed three. Then we turned up a long dirt track where he assured me there was good hunting. The farther we went, the narrower and more overgrown the track became. Sure enough, we saw a buzzard, suggesting that we were heading the right way. The route was too rutted for a vehicle to pass. Despite this remoteness, there were a few farmhouses scattered around. Most were abandoned, but occasionally we saw places where there were still old folk living there, who always dressed in black. These people already looked similar to one another, but the fact that they all dressed the same made it impossible to tell them apart. I knew that if something happened to Diego, I'd be lost out here on my own. I already wondered if we were going in circles and if the old folk looked the same because they *were* the same. Was it my imagination or was that buzzard actually circling over *us?*

At one stage we thought we'd cornered a fox that went into hiding on a rocky crag. I got Bobby's attention and pointed at the rocks. He wagged his tail and trotted off casually in the opposite direction. We stopped for more beers. Judging by the amount Diego put back, I thought by now he must be seeing two of everything. As the day went on, he was getting more trigger-happy. He started shooting at nothing but still managed to miss. Finally, he decided the gun was getting too heavy to carry and it was my turn to have a go. As soon as I had the weapon, I prayed that nothing would show itself. I didn't want to kill anything and I certainly didn't want to have to skin it and cook it.

Diego urged me to practice. "The sights aren't too good," he said. "My advice is to aim a couple of feet above your target." Taking his counsel, I tried to hit a rock. When I fired the gun, it kicked back and nearly dislocated my shoulder. A hundred yards beyond the rock a branch fell off a tree. Fortunately, the wildlife still wasn't showing and we decided to head back. A couple of times there was movement in the grass and I dutifully blazed off into space. "Now you're getting the idea," he said. For the first time, I began to relax, perhaps because the gun was no longer in the hands of a drunkard—well, someone a lot drunker than I was, anyway. Besides, I realized that Diego and the dogs were having a great time and I was no real threat to wildlife. Or so I genuinely believed. We were nearing our valley when Diego spotted a pigeon in a tree beyond a cluster of bamboo. "Have a go," he said, pointing his unsteady hand. I turned the gun vaguely in the direction of the bamboo and fired off a shot. The bird dropped like a stone. Diego stared at me in amazement. I started looking around to see who else might have fired. Having actually hit something, no one knew what to do about it. Both Bobby and Diego's dog were too domesticated to do anything but sniff. I felt ashamed. "Bravo!" Diego said, handing me the splattered pigeon. As soon as we split up, I found a quiet corner on the edge of our land and buried it. I knew better than to take it home.

14

Horsing Around

In a declaration of astounding optimism, Myrtle said she was ready to take her driving test. By careful planning, her driving was no longer my problem, unless I happened to be on the road at the same time she was. Her decision followed the resignation of the local driving instructor I'd persuaded her to hire. He'd developed a heart condition and been advised to retire. "Don't look at me like that," she told me. "It wasn't my fault." Those who'd recently seen her behind the wheel said she had a better chance of winning the lottery than getting a license. Nevertheless, she was confident of success when she heard she could take her test in England, because any European permit was valid in

Spain. The driving itself was obstacle enough without having language difficulties as well. If you asked her to turn right in Spanish, she'd probably do an emergency brake. Mind you, there was a good chance she'd do that even if you asked her in English.

She planned to attend a one-week intensive course that guaranteed to give her money back if she failed. While she was in England, we would move into her place and look after her menagerie of animals. There was a tearful farewell as she threw her arms around Silver's neck and tried to give the old horse a kiss. His response was to bolt across the field and leave her flat on her face in the dirt. "He's upset I'm going," she bawled.

After dropping her at the airport, we were left with the task of baby-sitting two dogs, three cats, a goat, a horse, and a jar of earwigs. At first I didn't realize about the earwigs. Admittedly, I was puzzled why there was a whole jar of them as I tipped it out onto the fire. It was only when Helen started hitting me that I realized Myrtle actually collected them.

"I'm sure they'll soon breed back to their former numbers," I said in an uncertain tone as I replaced the depleted jar on its shelf.

It should have been an enjoyable time for us. The house was certainly comfortable, with its stylish decorations and commanding view. It was possible to sit on the arching trunk of her olive tree in the afternoons and feel a breeze that blew unimpeded across the whole plain. I could sit for hours watching the town twinkle in miniature in the distance. Occasionally, a tractor would slowly traverse one of the fields in the middle distance. However, any hope that the week would make a nice romantic break was soon dispelled by our determination not to get along with each other. Even the gas lamps failed to produce the right ambience. By this time, gas lamps had as much novelty for us as an almond snack. A week in a New York housing project would have seemed like more of a vacation.

During this break from our place, I got the feeling that things between us were coming to a head. By now even a couple of stubborn procrastinators like us had been given enough time to contemplate our futures and were starting to consider the next step. How long would we remain here? Would *we* even be together? I was beginning to realize that Helen wasn't kidding when she said she could happily herd goats the rest of her life. She still hadn't seen the light. As far as she was concerned, it was *me* that hadn't seen the light. I was thinking the farm had no long-term future. Apparently she was starting to think *I* had no long-term future. Friendship or no, it looked like we both wanted something more enduring than we felt the other could provide. The answer to at least one of life's immediate questions seemed to be drawing near. But as if neither of us really wanted to face up to it, we kept giving each other one last chance. Maybe, just maybe, when we looked at each other we were looking at our destinies.

The subtle way we sounded each other out was through seemingly academic disputes over whether El Águila was a place where someone—*anyone*—sane would possibly choose to grow old. It didn't help when Myrtle persuaded Helen that the only reason I didn't want to die on the farm was because I was a man, and therefore incapable of commitment. Apparently the absence of basic facilities, let alone income prospects, had nothing to do with it. Lack of commitment became a catchall explanation whenever I was reluctant to be pushed into something. If I wasn't keen on her choice of café, then it was because I feared commitment. In fact, if it was too hot, it was because of my lack of commitment. Helen also accused me of not listening to her. She must have been right, because I failed to hear the tone change when her constant complaining about me stopped being in good humor. She still ran off to the bedroom after we had a big bust up, only now she slammed the door shut behind her.

I was a little peeved with Myrtle for always taking Helen's side. Especially as I was forsaking my nightly dose of the Cartoon Network in order to muck out her smelly, fly-ridden horse. It's not as if her household pets were all little cherubs either. Given how sweet Myrtle was to them, they showed little gratitude in return. Her house was like a refuge for unreformed street urchins. The two malnourished cats had made a recovery and turned mean. We nicknamed them Corleone and Capone. They fought it out for dominance over the old dog, the blind-in-one-eye dog, and the cat with the limp. Throughout the day they enforced their rule over the house by hissing and scratching. Even humans had to engage in a battle of wits to get a good seat in the lounge.

What destroyed the status quo was the introduction of Bobby. Like any strong, healthy dog, he showed a keen interest in cats. He only wanted to sniff them to see what they were made of, but was prepared to pursue them at high speed in order to do this. Corleone and Capone began by arching their backs and spitting in the usual way. They didn't know how to take it when Bobby just stood there wagging his tail at them. Baffled by this new form of insolence, they thought they'd better retreat, and the chase was on. Vases were toppled, dried flowers trampled, and curtains torn to shreds as cats clawed their way up them. We were supposed to be looking after the place but it soon started to look ransacked. The only real winners were Myrtle's two dogs, who were enjoying a resurgence of canine confidence. They demonstrated this by barking or growling every time one of the cats stuck its head into the room. Bobby was their messiah.

The interspecies tension in the house was such that we didn't dare go out without taking the dogs with us. We were slightly wary about this, as I'd already been cautioned once by the local police for having Bobby in the car. I'd been driving through town with him on the front seat next to me when a cop waved me down. He was the same bearded policeman who'd caught me and Myrtle swatting at a wasp while stalled in the middle of the main street. He stuck his head in through the window and said that it was illegal to have animals in the car if they couldn't be controlled. I looked at Bobby sitting there peacefully and wondered what he was talking about. "The dog should be in the back," he said, "and preferably behind a window or wire screen." I thought he was being pedantic and was about to argue the point when Bobby tried to lick his face. The cop hit his head on the door frame in his rush to get out of the way. In the end, I was grateful to leave the scene without a ticket.

In any case, we had to go into town to do some shopping, and bringing the dogs seemed better than giving them and the cats free rein to smash up Myrtle's place. Bearing in mind our car wasn't much bigger than a golf cart, you can imagine how crowded it was with two people in front and three big dogs in back. It was impossible to see anything behind me because the animals kept moving from window to window to check out the view. The windows also began to steam up with condensed drool from the panting of three canine tongues. It was market day in town, so we had to drive painfully slow because the streets were full of people. I was inching my way forward through the milling crowd when the dogs suddenly went berserk. What had set them off was a horse. What set me off was the bearded cop sitting on top of the horse—and now looking at our car to see what the commotion was. While I yelled threats at the dogs, they leapt from back seat to front and clambered over me and Helen. The veering car and sudden frenzy of loud barking sent pedestrians fleeing in all directions. All this activity startled the horse, which began turning in circles. Fortunately for us, it tore off down the street, with the cop fiercely hanging on for dear life while trying to look in control. We cut short our shopping trip and sped all the way home before he could call in reinforcements.

I'd be willing to bet those police horses weren't used to the pampering that Silver got. Silver certainly appeared baffled by it. Myrtle had left us a punishing schedule that had us out in the field or barn from dawn till dusk. The day began with the preparation of a feast of grains and sliced fruit that was better than anything I'd eaten for breakfast since I left for college. I was tempted to stick my head in the trough and go for it. In the cramped conditions of the barn, it was essential to place this meal in front of the horse as quickly as possible. This was the only way of preventing him from kicking us to death while we carried out the rest of our tasks. Only by distracting him with food could we remove his night blanket, clean out his hooves one by one, and then brush him down. It was the sort of treatment you'd think he would be thankful for. But, invariably, while I was standing there immobilized with one of his rear hooves in my hand, he would lift his tail and fart in my face.

Myrtle had warned us that it was vital to finish grooming Silver before he'd stopped eating and she had the bruises to prove it. Once he was suitably presentable, the barn door was opened so he could run out into the field—where he immediately rolled around to become scruffy and dirty again. We then had to fork out the bucket loads of fresh manure this diet was responsible for. It was the sort of early morning task that softened memories of commuting. Then the old bedding had to be tossed and fresh straw added. This compounded our misery by inducing an allergic attack in both of us. When we'd recovered from our sneezing fits, we had to hang up a net stuffed with hay for him to snack on. Our eyes had barely stopped streaming when it was time for his mid-morning carrot, and not long after that we had to prepare his lunch. In the evening, the trough of delights was again used as a lure to get him back into the barn and a distraction while his night blanket was reattached. Another net of hay and then it was out into the fading light with a wheelbarrow to collect up all the fresh, fragrant manure he'd blessed the field with during the day.

I'd often wondered how Myrtle managed to fill her days and now I knew. As for Silver, he still spent the whole time with his head draped over the railings, pining for the grassy fields beyond. The fourth day began like all the others. I emerged from the stable with streaming eyes and grasping at my throat in the usual way. Helen was bent double over a bale of straw that she was dragging in. When the mist cleared, I noticed that Silver was standing around quite casually, but *outside* the enclosure. "Silver's escaped!" I cried.

"You must have left the gate open," she said accusingly.

"You were the last one through it," I replied.

"No, I wasn't."

"Can we finish this argument later? Right now I think we'd better get him back inside." Actually, there wasn't much cause for alarm as all he was doing was standing there staring stupidly off into space, as horses do.

"I'll get a rope," said Helen.

"Is that necessary?" I asked. "Let's try to shoo him back in." Ignoring me, she went off in search of something to put over his head. Ignoring her, I tried to maneuver him back in on my own. I circled him, clapping my hands and clicking my tongue as I'd seen the peasants do. Silver kicked his hind legs in the air and ran off. After about three hundred yards he stopped to munch some grass.

"What the bloody hell have you done?" said Helen when she emerged. "I ought to stick this rope around *your* neck."

"Okay then, wise guy, *you* do it," I said, and sat on a rock with my arms folded. Helen approached the horse on tiptoe. All the while she was talking to him in a baby voice.

"Who's a naughty boy then?" she cooed. "Come to mommy." When she was finally a few yards off, she stopped suddenly in her tracks and turned. "How do I put this on?" she said, looking at the rope as if she'd never seen it before. I got up and walked over there at a normal pace, which deeply irritated her. "Slowly," she hissed. "You'll frighten him." But Silver was catching up after months of grass deprivation and didn't even notice me. We made a loop in the rope and tried to slip it over his head when a rare gap opened up between his teeth and the field. Our attempts to do this finally got his attention. For a while all three of us stared at the rope with puzzlement. Then I swear he laughed at us. He bared his big, ugly teeth, whinnied, shook his head, and moved off somewhere else where we wouldn't bother him.

At first he walked, but when he realized we were following, he began to canter. Before long we were running to keep up. "Do something, Shaun!" cried Helen. We tried to get in front of him to start driving him back toward the house but he broke into a gallop. Soon he was disappearing out of sight and heading for the hills.

"I'll go get the car," I said. When I turned back to the house, it was already half a mile away. Then as I finally got in our tiny vehicle, I saw that Silver had run off across fields too rutted for its feeble suspension. Although I found tracks that circled the area, I couldn't find *him* anywhere. Eventually I saw Helen waving her arms at me. I stopped and waited for her to walk over. She was furious.

"Where have you been?" she said, pinning me back against my seat with a look that would have stripped the hide off a weaker man. "He could be halfway to Portugal by now. I thought you were going after him in the car."

"What do you think this is, a moon buggy?" I said. "Anyway, I thought you were staying on his trail so we'd know where he's gone."

"I lost him over there." She waved her arm vaguely in a gesture that encompassed most of the Spanish interior.

"You haven't got your glasses on," I observed dejectedly.

"I can still see things moving," she replied indignantly.

"Yes, but you can't tell if it's a horse or a tractor." We decided to start looking in the direction he'd last been seen heading. Undulating fields covered in a forest of almond trees stretched away for miles. As we progressed, we stopped in at all the farms we could find to enlist help. At the first place, we met one of Myrtle's neighbors. She had once likened the man to a statue because of the way he stopped still and gawked whenever he saw her. We found him affable enough and he certainly knew the old horse in question. He appeared delighted to help with our predicament, perhaps anticipating the mileage he would get out of it at the village bar that evening. The folklore about us was already less than flattering before being outrun and outwitted by a long-in-the-tooth nag. With his help we gathered a small posse that searched right through siesta time. I begged him to promise that if we found the animal, he wouldn't tell Myrtle it had ever gone missing.

After a few hours, the farmers gradually gave up and only the neighbor stayed with us. It was clear he remained only because he found our search for the horse a divertissement unequalled in the village since the last fiesta. He was particularly entertained when we fetched a bowl of Silver's regular treats and shook it loudly as we walked along. We knew the horse could survive on its own for weeks if it wanted to. The grasses were tall and there was still plenty of water to be found after the rains. Finally, he too felt the entertainment was beginning to repeat itself and went home. Darkness fell to the sound of our calls echoing through the hills. "What are we going to do?" Helen despaired. "Myrtle will be devastated."

"We've still got two days to find the damned creature," I said. "We could easily have missed him in all this countryside. There are so many trees to obscure the view and it's not like he's ever come when called."

"What if we find his dead body?" she said, becoming tearful.

"I don't know. He's hardly full of life as it is. If we lean him up against the railings in his usual spot, we could be long gone before Myrtle notices anything amiss." Helen's glare told me she wasn't amused. For the next two days, while the dogs and cats were tearing the house and each other to pieces, we searched everywhere. But by the evening of Myrtle's return, there was still no sign of him. We cleared up the house as best we could and took Bobby home before going to pick her up. We'd stopped blaming each other and resigned ourselves to the facts. Once again Myrtle had lost the love of her life. One way or another we were responsible this time, and the guilt weighed heavily on both of us. "We can always get her another one," I said. "Decrepit horses can't be too hard to come by. Perhaps if we wait outside the glue factory, we can intercept one on its way in."

"It wouldn't be the same." Helen sighed ruefully. "Silver was special to her."

"How are we going to tell her?" I wondered, imagining this would be the last straw for Myrtle.

"I'm sure it will all just come out at the right moment," she said evasively.

Somehow the right moment never did seem to come. We should've told her straightaway, but she was so pleased when she saw us at the airport. Then in the car on the way back she talked nonstop about her experiences. It was no surprise that she was carrying a full refund. The only mistake she hadn't made on the crash course was actually crashing. Although disappointed that she didn't have her driver's license, she seemed proud of one distinction. "I'm the first person to fail their course in two years," she said brightly.

Talking about the trip kept the conversation away from her animals. She did once ask how they were but was thrown off the subject when I responded by guiltily offering her more driving lessons. Helen cleared her throat as a signal that I should break the news. I remained silent as a signal that she could do it herself. She gave me one of her looks and I gave her one of mine. Still, we kept quiet as Myrtle prattled on. However, when we reached the house, her attention turned to her family of strays. As we got out of the car, Helen nudged me. I nudged her back. Then we heard the dreaded words. "I must go and see Silver," she said.

"Come into the house first and see the others," I suggested. The way the dogs cried at her you'd think we'd been abusing them the whole time she was away. With Bobby gone, Corleone and Capone had reclaimed their territories on the chairs in front of the fire. They acted indifferent to her arrival until she tried to stroke one of them and got scratched for her trouble. I realized how disheveled the house looked compared to when she left, but after a week away she didn't seem to notice. "The cat knocked over your vase with the Greek dancers on it," I told her, testing the confessional waters.

"Oh, that's all right," she said, nursing her hand. "Now I really can't wait to see Silver."

"I'd like to get you a new vase," said Helen sorrowfully. "And we'll help you move your manure pile to where you said you wished you'd put it."

Myrtle looked at us suspiciously.

"You know, your cesspool needs cleaning—I'd be happy to take care of it for you," I offered.

"I don't know what's come over you two," she said. "You're far too kind to me as it is." Before I could get between her and the door, she was gone. We raced after her. The night air smelled of the pig farms down the road. In the darkness we heard her gasp. "My God! Whatever have they done with you?"

"This is it," I said. "Do I shoot myself now or wait for her to do it?"

"How *could* you?" said Myrtle in a voice that was beginning to crack. Then as we rounded the barn to join her, I saw something I never thought I was going to see again—Silver. He was standing in his enclosure and staring off into space in his usual way. I could only imagine he'd been hiding nearby and waiting for her to come back. She turned on us in bewilderment. "Why is the enclosure gate open?" she asked. "Someone could've taken him, or who knows what might've happened? There's no hay net up, and look at him scratching in his trough—it's empty." She was petting his neck like he was a wounded bird. "This is unbelievable. Just look at him. He's filthier than when I first took him in. Here you are, offering to do all kinds of things for me and you can't even take proper care of dear old Silver. Well, in that case I'm going to take you up on your offer to clean out the cesspool."

Helen had started covering our tracks by saying we must've left the gate open by mistake in our hurry to get to the airport. But the relief of seeing Silver was already fading as I considered the long list of unpleasant jobs I'd guiltily volunteered to do. As I glowered at him, he bared his teeth, shook his head, and gave out a whinnying laugh.

15

Making Connections

Helen spent hours trying to redeem herself in Myrtle's eyes. She went around bearing gifts like a new vase and a grooming brush for Silver. But even though she did everything short of wearing sackcloth and whipping herself, Myrtle was still "disappointed" in us. As for me, guilt had already given way to regret. I was furiously backpeddling on my offer to clean out her cesspool and move the manure pile. This was seen as yet another demonstration of my lack of commitment. Fortunately, I had a good excuse. Colonel Burgos had enlisted me in his campaign to bring electricity to the valley. He was a balding man with a typically upright military posture. The chief interest for him in his retirement was his little farm. It was a weekend amusement that didn't produce anything for sale but gave him enough olives to make oil for his family and friends. He was a man who thrived when he had a project to sink his teeth into, and my application for electricity had given him something to chew on.

I had sensibly given up hope after I found out that building our own nuclear power plant would be cheaper than connecting to the utilities. But since then, he'd unearthed an obscure government subsidy for bringing electricity to outlying areas—and learned that these funds could actually be accessed through the bureaucracy of our own nearby town. Where this grant went would be decided by the town hall and in particular the mayor, because he was also the chief of the local ruling party. Officially, the money would be spent on the most needy area; *unofficially,* the colonel had learned through a friend with contacts that the mayor was a "reasonable man." By this he meant that the grant could be secured by anyone who was prepared to give the mayor a cut. I wanted electricity badly, but due to the English influence in my upbringing, I didn't like the sound of this at all.

I liked it even less when the colonel's "friend," the shifty owner of a building firm in Murcia, said that I should play a key role in the bribery. I realized immediately that it would be academic to me whether the farm had electricity or not if I was locked up in a prison somewhere else. Reluctantly, I went to meet the builder, an overweight man with several chins, in a café in town. The builder, called Javier, had taken the project under his wing as a favor to the colonel—and in the expectation of his firm doing any associated building work if we were successful. To reassure me, he explained that the transaction would be as straightforward as a poker game; "like in your Westerns," he said. Most of the poker games in the Westerns I'd seen had resulted in at least one person getting shot. He told me we'd be fine as long as we picked the right moment to show our hand. However, it was also important that the mayor believed we weren't bluffing. An appeal from a group of dusty peasants wouldn't fill him with confidence in our ability to be discreet, or to come up with the necessary cash. The presence of a well-dressed businessman and a foreigner would suggest that the financial credentials of our bid were sound. He would do all the talking except at one fundamental point. "You must be the one who offers him money," he said. "Then if it turns out that my information is wrong and he calls the police, you can just say you're a foreigner and you didn't understand what was going on." It sounded like a sure thing—for him.

For my part, I wondered what the punishment was for trying to bribe a public official. In the grand scheme of things it seemed a triviality, but my proper British schoolboy conscience was still nagging at me. My sense of self-preservation was screaming at me. Meanwhile, my neighbors, fearing that I would bow out, went to great lengths to tell me that what we were doing was normal practice; it happened all the time. "Okay," I asked, "then why does a foreigner have to do it?" It was so much easier, they explained blandly; no family embarrassments, and besides, this had to do with money from the national government—it was much more appropriate that a foreigner do it rather than a local. None of this was very convincing to me; but they made it sound as clear as $E=mc^2$.

Apart from old Emilio, who wanted nothing to do with it, they all came around to visit and each had his or her own corroborating tale of official corruption. Even Emilio didn't object to a little bribery. It was the electricity he was opposed to, because it was too newfangled for his liking. My favorite story was Pepe's account of how a local landmark came to be built on the hill that dominated the town. A local truck company owner, who made his fortune shipping lettuces and tomatoes to northern

Europe, had built the mansion twenty years ago. What I didn't know was that it had been illegally built right smack in the middle of a national park. It seemed the two men responsible for enforcing building regulations were also "reasonable men." Nevertheless, the knack in these matters was to be subtle, or else there would be a public outcry. It would ridicule the authority of the government too much if they tore down the woodland and built a house in one go—so it was done in barely perceptible stages. First a few trees had rings cut in their bark so that they died and could legitimately be chopped down. Then a year later a shack was built that could quite easily have been for forestry workers. Bit by bit more trees were lost and the shack was added to and upgraded. Finally, four years later, the finished mansion towered over the town. Apparently, this approach was considered subtle enough to give everyone amnesia about the protected woodland that had been there before.

The real reason no one complained was that locals were as relaxed in their attitude toward the law as they were about everything else. Some blamed this irreverence toward authority on the fascist dictatorship that had run the country from the time of Roosevelt until 1975. Who could be criticized for breaking the rules under such a government? Indeed, it was considered heroic and everyone did it to some extent. Although that was all in the past, apparently the habit was hard to kick. Also, criminality in a backward area such as ours hadn't taken on some of the ugliness it had elsewhere. A couple of our expat friends were burgled. They were surprised to come home and find that, instead of leaving a mess, the burglar had put everything neatly away again after his search for valuables. In fact, the first thing to alert them that an intruder had been in their house was the unusual tidiness.

I still wasn't happy about bribing the mayor. However, I was sure that if anyone deserved electricity, it was my neighbors.

They'd certainly convinced me that if we didn't succeed in bribing him, then someone else would. As with so many important events in life, there was little time for consideration. A few sleepless nights later and the day of our appointment had arrived.

At the builder's request I put my suit on, but it was by now so full of holes that the effect was to make me look more down and out than I did in a T-shirt and shorts. The white inner lining showed through the navy blue material like a bad case of dandruff. Before leaving I quickly filled in the holes with a blue pen. This was passable from a distance but looked even more disreputable up close.

When we arrived at the town hall, I was very nervous. "Remember," said Javier, "we don't just blatantly say 'have some money.' The codeword around here for a bribe is 'paella,' got it?"

"Got it," I said, all the while thinking that the famous rice dish was an odd thing to choose. "What do I do—invite him for dinner?" Javier's face told me he wasn't in a joking mood. The town hall was an imposing place that looked like it dated from the time of the Inquisition. Large arches along the front of the building were lined with cypress trees groomed into tall columns. Not only was I intimidated by the grandeur inside and out, but to my horror, the builder appeared to be too. His eyes darted about and his chins wobbled nervously. The building also housed the main police station for the town and was crawling with cops. To get in you had to pass through forbidding wooden doors as massive as those of a medieval church—or perhaps a medieval dungeon. At least if we got caught, it wouldn't be a long walk to the cells. "Shall we cut out the middleman and turn ourselves in now?" I suggested in a whisper.

We reached the administration area, which was full of the

clack clack of typewriters. Sunlight fell in shafts through thick
tobacco smoke. Judging by the haggard appearance of those on
the benches, they'd been waiting half their lives to be seen. A
baby cried and a man ranted at a shrugging official. Javier anxiously scanned faces in the front office, looking for his contact. I
noticed his hands were shaking. A man slipped from behind a
desk and sidled up to him. They spoke in low tones and then the
man pointed to a glass window by a security door. A bored policeman sat on a plastic chair beside the door. We approached the
window and spoke to the woman on the other side.

"We have an appointment with the mayor," Javier said in a
weak voice. "Here's the name." He'd written *my* name down on
a piece of paper. When I went to protest, he quietly explained
that the general petition for electricity had been tacked on to my
original application in order to backdate it by several months.
When we finished our discussion, the woman went off to check.
The builder whispered in my ear and gestured behind us.
"That's the Spain where you have to fill out forms in triplicate
and then wait months or even years to hear anything," he said.
Then he nodded at the door in front of us. "This is the Spain
where anything is possible if you have the right connections."
The woman returned and said that an appointment had been
confirmed but oddly the diary did not list all those who would be
attending.

"*Señor* Briley here," said Javier, "and myself."

"I'm afraid I have to know who you are," she said.

"My name is Javier."

"Javier who?"

"Just put Javier," he said cagily. She raised her eyebrows, and
with a look of reluctance, pressed a buzzer that unlatched the
door. I wanted to tell her to cross out Mr. Briley and just put
Shaun. But we were quickly ushered into an anteroom where

the mayor kept us waiting for three-quarters of an hour. I think we were supposed to be impressed with how busy he was. All his secretary did was file her nails. Ironically, there was a poster on the wall outlining government proposals to deal harshly with corruption. A lot of the vocabulary was beyond me, but then I figured I was probably better off not knowing. Asking the builder to translate didn't seem appropriate under the circumstances. When the secretary's phone rang, I nearly leapt out of my seat. It was the cue to show us in.

The mayor's office was suitably impressive, with flags flanking a large polished desk that was completely empty. If any work had gone on there, then all trace of it had been removed and a fine layer of dust put in its place. The mayor himself was about forty and spoke with a squeaky voice that didn't fit with a grown man. But at just over five feet tall, he hadn't really grown that much. He compensated for this lack of stature with a pompous manner and strutting walk. After shaking hands, he sat down and nearly disappeared behind the desk. Through the window behind him we could see a man in tattered peasant clothes who was sweeping the yard with a broom made of sticks tied together. It was impossible not to notice the contrast with the mayor, who wore a very smart suit and a gold watch. I realized that Javier also looked very dapper. Meanwhile, I was sitting with my hands on my knees to cover the moth holes in my trousers. I'd have preferred to be with the guy in the yard.

To start off with, Javier and the mayor made light conversation, as if the purpose of the visit was an informal social chat. I waited patiently for the banter to come around to food so that I could mention paella. "Is anybody hungry?" I said helpfully when there was a lull. Javier glared at me. Finally, the mayor asked how he could help and the builder mentioned our hopes of winning the grant for electricity. He didn't correct the mayor

when the latter jumped to the conclusion that we were both residents of the valley. A folder was sent for and the mayor sat and
read it with an occasional shake of the head.

"To be honest with you," he squeaked, "it's not a very strong
application. I think the council is likely to favor another area.
Between you and me, it's an area that traditionally supports the
Party. Their representatives have a lot of influence."

"But you know you can rely on their support," Javier said per-
suasively. "By connecting this area, you'll win new votes."

"It's already decided," said the mayor. "There's nothing I can
do."

"I know what I could eat right now," I said desperately. The
mayor looked at me as if to say "who is this?" Javier's face registered panic and his eyes pleaded with me to shut up.

"It's because the council doesn't favor us that we've come to
appeal to you," he said. "Everyone knows your fine reputation.
I'm sure you could persuade the council."

"You mustn't overestimate me," said the mayor. "I, too, have
people I must answer to. It would be difficult. It's the sort of
favor I would only do for my friends, and how do I know you're
my friends?"

There was a long pause while the mayor studied his hands. I
didn't understand why the conversation had suddenly faltered.
Had they finally run out of trivia? Then I realized that Javier was
looking at me. When he saw he had my attention, he nodded
frantically, chins aquiver. "We would like to offer you a paella," I
spurted. This time the pause was terrifying. The mayor continued to study his hands, but for a second his face looked flush.

"You'll have to make it a good one for this favor," he said. For
the first time, he looked up at me and the balance in the room
had shifted. Now I was the player.

"Oh, it'll have all the toppings," I said. "Chicken, prawns,
mussels—you name it. And no gristly bits either."

"How do I know that your paella will be enough to satisfy someone of my appetite?" he said, looking a shade irritated.

"Do I look like I don't eat enough?" I said. "I can assure you, we'll lay on a three-course meal in your honor." He took a pen and wrote something down on a slip of paper. Then he reached out to hand it to me. I didn't want to get too close in case he noticed my suit was full of holes, so I edged forward and then snatched it off him. It was blank apart from a number. Converted into money it was a sizeable figure, but a small fraction of what it would cost us to pay for an electricity transformer.

"I'm sure we can arrange a dish of those dimensions," I said. I was wondering how far I was supposed to take the paella reference when the conversation abruptly changed tack and became casual again. Javier and the mayor spoke about sports and the weather, as if they were sitting at the café. I found in their behavior a strange denial that anything out of the ordinary had taken place. The only clue that anyone was nervous was the way all three of us were overeager to laugh at the slightest upbeat remark. Soon we shook hands and left, as if it had been just a normal meeting with the mayor. For all I knew, maybe it was.

"I think your application has promise," he said at the door. "I can't guarantee anything, but I'll see what I can do."

"We've got him," Javier said later. "Now it's down to how much influence he really has at the town hall. Let's hope he doesn't get a better offer in the meantime."

For weeks we heard nothing. Then at last the mayor's office contacted Vicente's store and asked for a meeting with all the joint-applicants. It was agreed that Diego senior and Virtudez would host the gathering at their house. There was no word as to whether we should expect good news or bad. Nearly everyone had made arrangements to raise their share of the bribe. Usually the valley was so quiet that the passing through of an unknown car had people talking for weeks. So you can imagine what a stir something of this magnitude created.

I'd half expected Helen to oppose the whole scheme, but she got swept along by everyone else's excitement. Her attempt to embrace a primitive life was finally wearing her out. She was starting to realize that it was a lot easier to appreciate nature if it didn't take up your whole day. I could also tell that she was feeling defeated. Not only had we failed to be self-sufficient, but our almonds were more of a cash flop than a cash crop. Mother Nature had proved to be a deadbeat parent. It was a betrayal she never quite recovered from. Furthermore, she could argue with me about modernizing and moving on, but it was hard to take a moral stand against a valley full of impoverished peasants. It turned out that even Myrtle wanted electricity.

So the relentless forces of modernity finally won the battle we'd fought on our farm—just as they were winning the same battle in the world at large. Whatever other conflicts were still undecided, she told me graciously: "If we do get electricity, I guess I'll learn to live with it." Had she decided to oppose this momentum of progress, then her only ally would have been Emilio. This was little comfort to her. First of all, he was widely denounced as senile. Also, she'd never forgiven him for saying that she should obey me as "head of the household." Even though she knew I didn't see it Emilio's way, it bothered her that he and I had become firm friends like her and Myrtle. Through his daily coffee visits, he had become my mentor. Mostly we talked about life in the *campo*. This was particularly irksome to her as it was supposed to be her specialty, not mine. Yet she avoided these conversations because Emilio tended to find her rosy view of nature hysterically funny. His mockery was particularly hurtful as it came from someone who really knew what it was like to live off the land. Meanwhile, back in England, Helen's mother heard that electricity could be coming. Rita saw it as a chance to rescue her daughter from her folly, and offered to lend us our share of the cost. Helen accepted.

By the day of the meeting, she had wormed her way sufficiently back into Myrtle's good graces that we were allowed to pick her up. Since she had just about forgiven us for Silver, I was surprised to be greeted by a face that was bright red, as if with anger. "Have you caught the sun?" I asked her.

"No, its a goddamned skin cream I bought that doesn't agree with me," she snapped. "I knew I should never have trusted something from that store. I got it in the hippie place in Mojácar; the one that sells all those risqué bathing suits. " She handed a jar to Helen. "Can you read what it says on the label? You know my eyes."

"It says Emotion Lotion," said Helen and then she stopped. I could tell by her face that something was wrong. "Have you tried washing it off?"

"Yes, why?"

"Oh, nothing; I'm sure it'll be all right—but I wouldn't use it again if it causes a reaction." While Myrtle was getting in the car, Helen took me aside and showed me the jar. "It's for women to put on their private parts," she said, "for stimulation, if you know what I mean." Poor put-upon Myrtle. Her face looked like a beet. When we got to Diego's, she drew even more stares than usual. There were about a dozen households there, including her neighbor who'd helped us look for Silver. Seeing him worried me. To turn Myrtle from red to green he'd only have to say something innocent like "I see you found the mule." Luckily he played the gawking statue until she'd passed him. Then he winked at me and a smile cracked at the corner of his mouth.

There was no room for all these people in the small white house, so we sat around under the olive trees out front. It was a warm day and the flies were bad, but not as bad as they'd been in the height of summer. Virtudez put out a table with a fresh cloth for the mayor to sit at. For the rest of us she made pot after pot of her gritty coffee, which was so strong it left half an inch of tar on the bottom of the cup. Meanwhile, groups and conversations formed, broke up, and reformed in different combinations. Pepe rubbed his fingers together and speculated how much electricity would add to the value of his farm. His daughter helped Virtudez in the kitchen. We could hear Maria's loud goatherding voice boom from within. Diego senior was too preoccupied with the welfare of his guests to concentrate on anything else. He flitted between groups, filling up coffee, and drawing attention to the fine new paintwork on his barn. Meanwhile, his son grew increasingly drunk and emotional. "He's coming here, to my house," he said, thumping his chest and looking teary eyed. "The mayor is coming to the house of Diego, son of Diego. What an honor!" Emilio told anyone who would listen that electricity would ruin the valley and, furthermore, he was quite happy without it. Since no one would listen, the ninety-year-old ended up mumbling it to himself.

"It's all very well being sentimental about candles and wood-burning ovens," Colonel Burgos argued, "but you people have lived through enough hardship." The colonel was happy to take credit for leading the valley into the twentieth century just as the rest of the world started the twenty-first. He felt it was best not to say too much about his absent builder friend, Javier. But as time dragged on, he began to look less commanding and started glancing nervously at his watch. Meanwhile, I was going out of my way to ignore the friendliness of Theresa and Simona because of Helen's unfounded belief that we were plotting a sordid three-way relationship. However, Helen was already jealous enough to ignore me too, so I ended up on my own between Emilio and a silent old lady with the features of a prune. Red-faced Myrtle sat at the back and looked fearfully at the gathering, as if it were a gang of bandits poised to rob her.

First of all, the mayor's arrival was fashionably late. Then it was predictably rude. Finally, even the most laid-back began to wonder if he was going to show up at all. Someone suggested he'd been detained elsewhere. "With his godlike nature, you'd think he'd be able to be in two places at once," the colonel muttered bitterly between his teeth. The younger Diego was just beginning to make threatening remarks about slights to his family's honor when the mayoral Mercedes was seen heading our way. It turned out his driver had got lost on the dirt tracks and they'd been driving around in the wilds for an hour.

The mayor looked particularly short that day, despite holding his head up high off his chest. I think it was the presence of so many people of normal height. If he thought he was looking down his nose at the peasants, he actually gave the effect of trying to look up their trouser legs. Nevertheless, he was as close to a celebrity that this crowd had ever seen and he knew it. After inspecting the chair distrustfully, he sat on the edge of Virtudez's table and gave a short speech about the importance of returning favors. I didn't know how any of them could stomach what he was saying. These were people who survived day to day because they shared favors for which a return was never asked.

They didn't seem to care, because it was obvious what he was building up to. We were to get our electricity. The mayor told us that work would start before the end of the year. Throughout his talk, while everyone else was reverently silent, Emilio kept up his mumbled protest. Occasionally, he got too loud and someone would shush him and then look apologetically at the mayor. When that happened, Pepe laughed his toothless laugh, which invariably turned into a hacking cough. I was overjoyed with the news. We'd be able to live in comfort and were back on track to sell the house for a profit some day before I became a toothless old man myself. However, I was also preoccupied with a troubling thought. The whole business back at the mayor's office had gone a little over my head. What if the mayor really was expecting a lavish paella for lunch? In the end, I got my answer when he looked right through me as if he'd never seen me before. This was in marked contrast with the slick intimacy he shared with the rest of the crowd. Even Myrtle's face seemed receptive to his charm, or perhaps it was just the Emotion Lotion. Naturally, there was no open mention of the payment that would be made to him personally. The only visible sign of debt collection came at the end of the talk, when his driver went around signing people up for his political party. Then the mayor was whisked away and the noisy and jubilant crowd began to disperse. Only Emilio shook his head sadly and said, "Shame, what a shame."

16

Moving with the Times

Emilio was the one person we saw every day because he always came for coffee after lunch. I think he did this partly for the novelty of talking to people so different from himself. Having never been very far from the valley, he found a couple of foreigners pretty entertaining. Some of his views might have been as dated as he was, but when you got to know him, you could feel very secure in his company because he was so honest and dependable. He loved to share his knowledge and did so in a demonstrative manner. "This is how it's done," he would say, not allowing that it might be done differently elsewhere. For instance, anyone who wasn't a Catholic must be a heathen. But

when he told us we were going to burn in eternal hell, he did so
with a chuckle, which let us know that if God was half as forgiv-
ing as he was, then we might be all right.

I've seldom met anyone so poor who was such a total gentleman. Emilio really had a touch of class. He always stood upright
and dressed smartly, even though his suits were threadbare and
dusty. I suppose it says more about me than it does about Helen
that I could tolerate his traditional outlook on gender roles and
she couldn't. But I knew he never intended any insult. Indeed,
in the light of his charm, and obvious respect for the women
around him, it was hard not to forgive him. I simply had to remind myself that when he was born, the horse and buggy were
still the preferred means of transport, even in London and New
York.

What really astounded me was the way he used to recite po-
etry, often of his own composition. He would lower his cup of
coffee and with a dramatist's flourish announce that he was
going to speak. Some of the poems were about the civil war,
some about crops, but mainly they were a mystery of vaguely
rhyming noises. To us it would go something like "the turn of
the seasons, blah blah, leave your wheat field fallow, blah blah,
the coming of the rains, blah," and so on. The knowledge that
we could barely catch half of what he said was no deterrent to
him. As he got more senile, he began to tell us the same ones
over and over as if they were new. Rather than break his old
heart, we would try to act as astonished as the first time we'd
heard it. The truly amazing thing about these poems was that
Emilio couldn't read or write. The skill to recite in rhyme had
been handed down to him by his parents in the early days of the
twentieth century.

We were accustomed to not understanding him as he jab-
bered away. What surprised us was learning that most of the

Spanish couldn't understand him either. Although the elderly knew and respected him, he tended to be mocked by the young. Once a week we'd give him a ride into town to do some shopping. A group consisting of two young foreigners and a ninety-year-old peasant drew a few looks. He had very little money to buy anything and was too proud to accept any charity from us. The trip to town was more of an outing for him. By and large, he was self-sufficient on his farm. Everything was home produced, from the muscatel wine of our first drunken encounter to the fresh vegetables always available in his garden. His simple diet was enlivened by the addition of copious amounts of garlic to everything he ate. I believe this is how he kept the flies away, and perhaps also why he'd remained a widower.

It was through this kindly old neighbor that we learned much of what we knew about local customs. One such lesson was that in the country it was okay to eat other people's crops if you only took a little as you passed through. Often as he crossed our land on his way to Pepe's, he would take some figs or a handful of almonds to break open with a rock and eat. The miserly puritan part of us never quite got used to this and Helen used to complain that he should ask first. Nevertheless, as time went on, we started to help ourselves to lemons from a tree in his orchard. He had what he called a "lunar" lemon because instead of one large crop a year, it produced a small number of fruits each month. He never used them all and most of them fell to the ground and rotted. Even so, we weren't comfortable about taking them from his land despite the fact he'd given us permission to help ourselves to anything. In our embarrassment we used to go up to his orchard in the cover of twilight to pick one. Then one day, after recent rains had turned the soil muddy, we saw him with his head bent to the ground—following a trail that seemed to be leading our way. It was a set of our footprints going back and forth to his orchard. When he realized what it was, he fell about laughing. From then on he would regularly bring us a lemon and it was always the best one on the tree.

Having been born into a life based around nuts, Emilio was gradually diminishing his stock of almonds by turning them into plums, apricots, and nectarines. He was determined to demonstrate that anything with a stone could be grafted onto any similarly stone-seeded plant. The legacy he left the valley would be this little forest of fruit trees all around his house. Having failed miserably to grow much in the way of fruit ourselves, we invited him to show us how to graft a plum onto one of our almond trees. It was a delicate procedure that involved cutting back most of the tree, so that the sap would rise strongly in the young shoot chosen for grafting. Preparing the sprig of plum and attaching it to the tree shoot with a little bandage of bark involved greater dexterity and patience than I possessed. Time after time, my attempts ended in failure until, in the end, I was put to shame by the quick fingers of a supposedly arthritic old man.

One of our more harebrained schemes was to introduce Emilio to Myrtle. The American woman had such a solitary and paranoid existence that we felt we should try to smooth her introduction into the local community. We could think of no better way to build her confidence in the natives than meeting an unobjectionable gentleman like Emilio. Her Spanish was so bad that he could say what he liked about the role of women and she'd be none the wiser. The language barrier wouldn't deter him though, and there was no disguising the warmth and sincerity of his personality. No one could be more polite or more harmless. We suspected Myrtle would be too frightened to agree to such a meeting, so we decided to take him with us unannounced. To minimize the confusion, we briefed him ahead of time.

On the day, he showed up at our house in a clean shirt, his

suit brushed down and his silver hair apparently slicked back
with olive oil. On our advice he'd laid off the garlic the night before. We drove over to Myrtle's and introduced him. After they
shook hands, she wiped hers on her overalls and looked at us
suspiciously. I did my best to translate his convivial chatter, but
she kept her attention determinedly focused on Helen and me.
He was ignored apart from an occasional worried glance, as if he
were a ticking box we'd left in her lounge. Helen could see there
was no rapport building between the two of them, so she whispered a plan into my ear.

"What's the matter?" said Myrtle.

"We've just remembered we have to go to Vicente's store to
get a butane bottle," I said. "We promised we'd pick it up this
morning." Without hesitating, Helen and I rose and went out
the door.

"Wait a minute," said Myrtle in panicked tones. "What about
him? You can't leave him here."

"I'm afraid we'll have to," I said. "He won't fit in the car with
the gas bottle. Don't worry, we'll come back for him in about an
hour." We drove off down the track with Myrtle running after
the car, calling us back. "Are you sure this is a good idea?" I said
as she disappeared out of sight behind us.

"She'll be forced to confront her guest now," said Helen. "It'll
do her good. We couldn't have left her in safer hands."

"I've got a feeling they won't be dancing around the porch to
the sound of one of his serenades when we get back," I said.
Indeed, when we returned an hour later, the place was eerily
quiet. I knocked but there was no reply. The door was still open,
so we went in. We eventually found Myrtle locked in the toilet,
where she'd been the whole time we were gone. Emilio was still
in the lounge, fast asleep in a chair.

Fortunately, he wasn't offended by the experience, but it
taught us the limitations of trying to help Myrtle with her social

life. Actually, he told us that visiting her house was less strange than coming to ours. Her place was decorated in a traditional Spanish style and only had those gas lamps. Ours was painted in bright colors and was full of baffling objects like a vacuum cleaner called R2D2 and a coffee machine, neither of which could be demonstrated working. Emilio was as lost with modern gadgets as we were with the odd-shaped wooden farm implements and religious mementos that littered his place.

I loved going up to his farm and trying to figure out what everything was for. Just as he was always smart, the exterior of his place was grandly dressed, with its fruit orchard laid out in squares and a stately line of tall pines leading to the door. He told us he'd planted those pines as a young man when the trees were only a foot high. The inside was like ours had been before we'd started bashing holes in walls to fit things like lights, kitchen appliances, and bathrooms. Apart from the one bedroom that he'd left untouched since the time of his wife's death, the rest of the house was very basic in its decoration and smelled sooty from the fire. The white walls were brushed with lime and had never seen paint. It was like a museum of an earlier time.

It dismayed Emilio that no one would take seriously his opposition to the coming of electricity. He watched with sadness as the valley he'd lived in for nearly a century began to transform. Apart from one or two of the trees, he was the oldest living thing there. After the mayor's announcement, the value of houses doubled overnight. Abandoned buildings were snapped up by people that no one knew. Long-lost relatives appeared from oblivion to claim their stake in family property. The news even resurrected those who'd been gone so long that everyone was sure they were dead. It was a mystery how word had spread so fast and so far—apparently even to the netherworld. There was a bustle of activity never before seen in the valley and a glint of greed in every eye.

I hoped that if electricity made our lives easier, we would suddenly get along much better. But after the neighbors cooked up a cash paella for the mayor, Helen seemed unhappy and started to lose interest in the things she used to live for—strolls among our trees, planting new flowers, and even her vegetable patch. Emilio, on the other hand, was not about to give up on the magic of this land that he loved. Ironically, it was just as Helen had thrown in the towel that his influence began to make me understand what all the fuss was about. It was typical of the way things were going between us that we couldn't synchronize our feelings on the matter. If you'd put us in a boat with an oar each, we would've immediately started rowing in opposite directions. When I informed her of this belated and admittedly hypocritical change of heart, she cried out "Men!" and stormed out of the room. Nevertheless, I began to see what she'd seen before the defeat and cynicism set in. The absence of roads, vehicles, and lights did make the place special. The valley bordered on virgin wilderness and was itself only lightly caressed by man. Standing within those surrounding hills was like being in the palm of nature's hand. You felt you were a part of everything alive and somehow connected to all that was around you. The place wasn't exactly lush, but the greenery that was there was even more special because of this.

"There's nothing more beautiful than a flower in the desert," Emilio said, holding up a poppy. It was just a plain red poppy but he was right. In the sun-bleached landscape, that speck of color was the richest jewel you could imagine.

Before I had time to appreciate the valley's oneness with nature, it was broken. Instead the connection was with a world of wires, of power stations, and the great teeming masses of industrial Europe. It felt like we'd been snatched from nature and plugged into a machine. First of all, access had to be created for the electricity company. Great noisy tractors belching fumes widened and smoothed our track. Soon gravel was laid and it was only a layer of tarmac short of a road. Already at this stage some of the isolation of the valley was lost forever. The new link with the road network brought curious strangers. Even Antonio, who had refused to endanger his little town car on our bumpy track, began to pay us short visits and comment that the place might turn out all right if we could get a few beers and some music out there. Until then, any car that entered was a strange sight in our world. Now we were the spectacle in theirs. Most of my neighbors had never had a lock on their doors, but for the first time things began to get stolen.

Swathes of inconvenient trees were felled and huge unsightly pylons stacked in fresh clearings. There were new and unwelcome sounds in the valley. The clanking of metal on metal, throbbing generators, traffic, and music thumping from the radios of workmen. The weird practices of Spanish laborers were not confined to showing up after siesta to work in the dark. At the other end of the day, they had the unpleasant habit of doing all their noisiest work just as the sun was coming up. Diego's cockerel wasn't the only one put out by this. Every day at six in the morning, we'd be shaken from our beds by a banging that caused plaster to fall from the ceiling. Then after a couple of hours, when it was quite clear that no living creature could still be asleep, they stopped for a lengthy breakfast and thereafter proceeded to take things easy. Indeed, this irritating stop-start approach was applied to the project as a whole. After several weeks of intense activity that turned the valley upside down, the work was suddenly abandoned. With the first flurry of preparation finished, it would be months before we saw the workmen again. The pylons were left where they lay to get rusty for the rest of the winter.

I felt guilty when I looked at this disruption through the eyes of Emilio. In a way, our infatuation with the charms of his valley had ultimately destroyed it. After all, it was our intrusion that got the ball rolling. My application for electricity set things in motion, and I played an incriminatingly prominent role in winning the grant that was paying for it all. I had to wonder if things might've been different if only I'd been a little less lazy about my chores. A very high price was being paid for a few conveniences. But even before electricity, we'd unwittingly ushered in a new interest in the valley. When we first moved there, the locals had mocked us because everyone else wanted to move out. But once they realized we weren't on the run from an asylum, they began to think again. The determination of foreigners to live there challenged them to reconsider the possibility that it might be a desirable spot after all. Soon after the utility company started work, we heard that the regional authority had voted to install a new irrigation system for crops, and running water for the houses. No bribes had changed hands—they just felt we ought to have these things since we were getting electricity. It was a domino effect. The coming of electricity caused Diego junior to change his mind about moving to the town. Before long, he and Anna announced they were to have a baby. It would be the first new birth to join the valley's aging population in twenty years.

Choosing between staying a peasant and moving forward was not a difficult decision for the vast majority in that poor area. Believe me, the charms of a life without any modern appliances are overrated. Very few stopped to think what they were leaving behind or how perhaps a higher standard of living might have come at less of a price for nature. I couldn't help thinking of the billions that governments spend figuring out how to kill people, with missiles and nuclear weapons, and I wondered if the valley might have progressed differently if a fraction of that money had gone into research on solar power instead. But our own eye-strain and erratic water supply had proved that even here, in the sunniest part of Europe, the dawn of a solar age was a long way off. So we all raced headlong toward the death of this last vestige of old Spain, of old Europe even. "I promise you that in a few years the valley will be full of roads, pollution, and streetlights, just like any other place," said Emilio as we sat on our porch one night. He looked sadly up at the cosmos. "The stars remind us how small we are. Soon we won't be able to see them anymore."

If people listened to what he was saying, they pretended not to hear. We were caught up in a stampede. Some dealt with his protests by being unkind to him. He was written off as a mad old man who cooked over twigs. "What's wrong with cooking over twigs?" Emilio would say, angrily waving his walking stick. "People have been cooking over twigs since the beginning of time. If you can't do that anymore without being called mad, then it's the whole world that's gone crazy." It wasn't just nature that was being lost, he insisted, but a way of life that could exist side by side with it. In the end, it was too overwhelming for him and his health and sanity really did start to deteriorate. Most people thought he talked such garbage anyway that it took awhile for them to realize he'd changed. He became more repetitive than ever and his voice weakened. One day he didn't show up at the usual time for his coffee visit. We imagined he was just late, but Maria walked up to see if he was all right. He wasn't. He was dead.

I can't express the shock, the disbelief. I felt an incredible pity for him, thinking of how lonely he must have been at the very end. When she told me he'd died, there was a voice in my head saying I was going to take it in my stride because after all, who was he to me? But my lip began to quiver and my eyes to fill. I would miss him and that distinctive warm sigh he used to utter when he beheld the landscape we'd shared. It said so much more than words.

I knew I was closer to him than Helen was, but I was still surprised by how calmly she took the news. Perhaps it was her own manifestation of shock. She tried to console Maria and me, but I only found her words glib. At that moment her company was the last thing I wanted, so I went off to be alone. In the supreme confrontation with truth that comes with a death, I finally realized that our relationship had itself already died.

In the days that followed, the hour of Emilio's coffee visit came and went conspicuously. His son drove up from the city, piled that long lifetime of mementos into a Dumpster, and took it to the municipal dump. The place was left empty, with a "for sale" sign up where its driveway met the smooth new track. Even so, there was no escaping painful reminders, like the new growth that soon appeared on the plum he'd grafted to our almond. One day I noticed the path he'd worn through the grasses walking from his house to ours. On a whim I strolled up it to take one last look around. I didn't expect to see his two dogs there because I knew Maria was feeding them. But apparently they refused to leave the place, and spent all their time in the shade of those tall pines he'd planted as a youth. They sat with their heads on their paws, waiting for his return.

One thing that had been drummed into us by Emilio and the other old-timers we knew in the *campo* was the importance of family. Among those who still lived the peasant life, there was a deep respect for this fundamental bond. Of course, they'd never met *my* family. Both of us were adamant that our own families must be a throwback to some period of evolutionary instability. How else could these people be related to us? Generally speaking, psychopaths out on parole were more welcome as house-guests than our relatives were. But something in the Andalusian water must have brought on a kind of amnesia that in turn resulted in nostalgia. Most remarkable of all was that over the year, Helen tried hard to patch things up with her mother. I'm sure that if they'd actually had to speak to each other, the whole project would never have got off the ground. However, through the carefully phrased wording of their letters, it finally worked and they began to grow closer than ever. My memory of events told me that one of the reasons we'd left England was so that we could escape living with her mother. However, by the end of the year, they'd found a convenient scapegoat for the distance between them—me.

One of the other subjects of this correspondence had been how wonderful it was at our farm. This was a little harder for Rita to swallow. She hated the very idea of the farm, but news of the coming of electricity finally persuaded her to visit. Since she'd paid for our share of the connection costs, she wanted to check up on her investment. Back in England she worked in government bureaucracy, doing something like sending back forms because the signatures were outside the box, or because they'd been filled in with the wrong color ink. It was the sort of work she'd have enjoyed doing even if they hadn't paid her. But an additional reward for this vitally important tax-funded posting was several weeks of leave every year. Rita had saved up five weeks of vacation and planned to spend some of it at our place. Even at this point, there was a hint in her letters that she considered our purchase of the farm on a par with running off to live in a Russian commune with a bunch of Bolsheviks. Helen had gone to great lengths in several letters to reassure that it hadn't been done out of spite, just to ruin her mother's reputation.

Her initial plan was to stay in a hotel in town because Simon and Margaret had convinced her that our place was only fit for snakes and scorpions. We'd stayed in the only hotel in town one time when we came to look at the house. It appeared all right from the outside. There was a big entranceway leading into a lovely plant-strewn interior courtyard. The centerpiece of the courtyard was an armless goddess sitting atop a defunct fountain that had become overgrown with ivy. A sweeping stone staircase led up to the second floor. But it also had cockroaches and mold on the walls. The toilets were a hole in the ground to squat over, with a footprint on either side. There were bloodstains all over the place from squashed mosquitoes, and the beds sagged so much that one wondered if a Spanish trampoline squad had ever passed through the establishment. Motor scooters with no mufflers raced up the street day and night. Breakfast was a stale roll and dinner was a greasy stew made with fatty lumps of un-certain mammalian origin.

Helen persuaded her mother that the unreliable comforts of our house were a marginally better bet. Whatever spark we'd ig-nited may have burned itself out without starting a fire, but we still had one thing in common—the farm. Encouraged by her mother's imminent arrival, we worked together as a team. It was turning once more to winter when Rita finally came, and we went through the usual rigmarole of cleaning and overdoing the fumigation. Again it was a spur to finally finish a number of out-standing jobs. Not a day went by without a workman's truck being parked outside the house of one neighbor or other as they got their homes ready for electricity. Modernization and renova-tion were being carried out all over the valley now. I found a workman who was not averse to a bit of moonlighting in return for a couple of beers during siesta, and together we managed to plumb sinks in the kitchen and bathroom. With Helen being un-usually helpful, I even connected pipes to a shower through one of those instantaneous gas-fired water heaters. Unfortunately, there wasn't enough water pressure from our solar pump to ignite the heater. We were going to have to wait for electricity from the utility company to get a warm shower. After a year of pouring bottles over my head, I still thought it was pretty neat. It just involved a slight reversal of the usual practice. Instead of leaving the bottles in the sun, you had to lay out there yourself until you were hot enough to find a cold shower bearable.

Helen and I put tiles on the bathroom floor and walls—as evenly as the floor and walls would allow. We even put lampshades on the lights in anticipation of the day when we could have stronger bulbs and more than one on at once. All we needed was connection to the utilities and we'd have a modern house. By any standard we'd finally completed the farm's renovation.

We got the place finished about two weeks before Rita came and took over. After a year's hard work, it wasn't long to appreciate the fruits of our labors. Out of politeness we let her have our room and took the blow-up bed in the spare room for ourselves. Within twenty-four hours, the situation had reverted to the way it had been in her house in England. I don't know how she did it, but we ended up living almost entirely in the one room while she laid claim to the rest of the house. If you wanted a break from her, you had to go to bed. Had she been staying for only a week it wouldn't matter, but after a couple of days she announced she'd be spending the full five weeks with us. You see, after moaning about the place all year, she'd fallen in love with it at first sight. She behaved as though she'd never seen anything so delightful in her life. Of course, it was a very different El Águila to the one we'd fallen for a year earlier. She hadn't been around before the road and electricity pylons got there to know what she was missing. And it was certainly easier to appreciate the rugged life if you could have a shower—even a cold shower—at the end of the day.

Our neighbors decided to treat the coming of Helen's mother

as a major event. One by one they came to welcome her, bearing
specially prepared gifts. Everyone tried to be friendly, but it was
hard to build a relationship when they didn't speak English and
she had no intention of learning any Spanish. Unless we were
there to translate, their coffee visits were half an hour of awk-
ward silence punctuated by smiles, nods, and the clink of cups
on saucers. I soon got the impression that Rita was less than en-
amored with the natives. After all, if you took away the dialogue,
you got a different picture. Diego came across as gruff and was
clearly drunk whatever time of day it was. Meanwhile, Maria always kept one eye on her misbehaving herd and was likely to
leap unexpectedly from her seat at any moment and shout a
string of expletives.

However, none of these idiosyncrasies were enough to break
Rita from her enraptured spell. Meanwhile, it seemed that
wherever we went, she was there. The farmhouse suddenly
seemed very small. Sensing mutiny, she played the parent card
on her daughter. "Helen, my dear, you wouldn't throw your own
mother out in the street, would you?" she would say. "Could you
afford electricity here if I hadn't put up the money to pay for it?"

"No."

"Is the place worth double now because of electricity?"

"I suppose so."

"Then you could say I'm entitled to half. Certainly you
shouldn't grudge me a small visit. Not after you lured me out
here with those letters." It was at this point that I would leave to
viciously attack some firewood with the chain saw. I was beginning to wonder whether it was England that I'd been allergic to,
or Rita. Later on, Helen came into our room and threw herself
on the bed.

"Mom's driving me up the wall," she said. "I can't take it anymore."

"She'll be asking *us* to leave next," I said.

"We could take a vacation and go away for a while," she suggested. I had the feeling I'd heard this line before.

"Wasn't *this* supposed to be a vacation?" I said. "I don't know if I dare go on vacation with you again. We'll probably end up breeding lamas in the Himalayas." Instead we devised a plan to put Rita off. We sat outside at the time of day when the bugs were at their worst and swatted flies like three African natives. "If you think this is bad, you should see it in the summer," I told her. "You can't open your mouth in case they fly in."

"Oh, I'm sure it'll be much better soon when the irrigation water comes and makes it less of a desert," she said cheerily.

Our next plan was to cut down some more prickly pear. I took Bobby over and pointed at the felled cactus.

"Fetch the snakes, there's a good boy," I said. He just cocked his head at me quizzically and whined.

"Oh, I'm glad you cut those dreadful things down," said Rita. "If only you could get rid of these dirty peasants too. They're so incomprehensible. If there were normal people living here, it could be rather wonderful." So we decided to introduce her to Sir John and Lady Cynthia and show her just what "normal" expats were like. The plan backfired. I've never seen Rita drunk before but it wasn't a pleasant sight. By the second bottle, she and John were in agreement that Spain would be so much better if it were run by the British. I had to get up and leave. While I was away, he set about persuading her that she should buy a vacation home for herself.

Whatever we did, she seemed to love staying at our place all the more. Apparently, it offered just the sort of retreat she'd been desiring for years. Our second approach, since we couldn't get rid of her altogether, was to at least move her a few miles away. Feigning support for the vacation home idea, we proceeded to show her some of the run-down farms that had been on our list before I abandoned real estate due to moral qualms.

I figured that when I got to the pearly gates, I'd be able to justify unloading one of these troublesome properties on to her, on the grounds of extreme provocation.

However, something was to happen that changed the political situation altogether. Pretty soon Helen and her mother would be teaming up to get *me* out. It was no secret in the valley that our relationship had fallen apart over the year in inverse proportion with our progress in putting the house together. Our answer to this problem had been simple—we ignored it in the hope it would go away. This was easy to do while we were juggling so many projects, but once we'd finished the house, it became hard to overlook. Even Rita had noticed that I spent more time talking to Bobby and that most of Helen's conversations were with the plants.

The last straw came one day when I was out inspecting olives at the far end of our land. When I heard the cicadas go silent and the grasses rustle, I assumed it was Bobby or perhaps Helen, since she was going to cut my hair that afternoon. Actually it turned out to be Simona. We chatted for a while about the olives, and then she came and stood next to me as I showed her a broken branch that had been puzzling me. In fact, she wasn't so much standing next to me as standing on top of me. With typical obliviousness, I'd completely failed to notice that she was coming on to me. By way of excuse I'd like to say that it's hard to tell when someone cross-eyed is trying to make eye contact with you. Before I could do anything about it, she'd rested her head on my shoulder. "I know you and Helen aren't getting along," she said. "I just want you to know that you can always talk to me about your problems." She smiled at my dumbfounded reaction. "It's okay," she continued, "my mother found out from Helen that you're attracted to me."

"What?"

"I think you're very special too."

"That's very decent of you," I stammered, trying to extricate myself from her arm as it snaked around my waist. Tempting as the feel of her body was, I could hear someone else coming. Simona heard it too, kissed my cheek, and ran off in the other direction. I looked about guiltily, expecting Helen, but it was Theresa.

"Have you seen my sister?" she said.

"I believe she may have passed this way," I said, looking embarrassed, "but she's gone now."

"Good," she said, and flashed her buckteeth at me. "I wanted to see you alone."

"You did?" I eyed her suspiciously. She fluttered her eyelashes and stepped closer.

"I just wanted to let you know that if things don't work out between you and Helen, well, I'm not seeing anyone at the moment."

"That's very—er—interesting," I said weakly. Clearly, the choice of eligible young men in the valley was extremely limited. Once again I was saved by the cicada alarm and movement among the trees. "It's busier down here than Times Square on New Year's Eve," I said, turning in time to see Helen approach.

"I thought as much when I saw Simona running out of here," she announced. Her lip was quivering with rage.

"It's not what it looks like," I said.

"Oh, yes it is," she replied. Theresa wasn't helping by assuming a defiant stance. Helen stormed off and I was grateful to follow.

"You realize this is your fault," I said.

"Don't be pathetic," she spat. "Why is it always the woman's fault when the man is unfaithful?"

"If you hadn't gossiped to Maria about your unfounded suspicions of me, then none of this would've happened," I said. "Now everyone's got the wrong end of the stick."

"Is that really the best you can do?" she said in a sarcastic tone. "Aren't you going to regale me with some story about falling out of a tree with your trousers down just as they happened to be passing by?"

It was no use. The time to face facts had arrived. I learned that she, too, had already concluded our relationship was running on empty, and this mishap only served to bring it sputtering to a halt. It's not like we'd seen eye to eye on anything right from the start. Apparently, she'd given up the visions she'd had for both me and the valley at about the same time. "I've had as much luck cultivating you as I've had growing vegetables," she said. If you'd seen our vegetables, you'd know that she wasn't mincing her words.

Ironically, this formal pronouncement that we were finished lifted the pressure that had built up between us over recent months. "Thank God you both feel the same way," said Rita, who was pleased as punch that her daughter had come to her senses about me. "The way you were arguing all the time, I felt sure you were going to get married." Helen showed all the signs of being greatly relieved herself. She was smiling again and even laughed at my jokes. In fact, she wasn't nearly heartbroken enough for my liking.

I decided to give her time to show a little more remorse and went into town to get a haircut. Over the year, she'd cut my hair but she hated doing it, and under the circumstances I didn't really want to ask her to do it that day. In any case, by the time she'd finished, it usually looked like someone had stuck a bowl over my head and cut around the rim. For some reason, my hurt pride—and the uncertain future that now beckoned us—made me determined to have a haircut that wouldn't make me look stupid for a change. The problem was choosing the right barber. All the men in town appeared to have one of three hairstyles: short, very short, and bald. At that time, I preferred slightly longer hair, but in an area like this I might as well have worn a dress for all it suggested about my sexuality. Unfortunately, I'd already reached the point when I could wait no longer without getting wolf whistles from the local men.

I picked the youngest-looking establishment, where the barber seemed to be a man who would at least listen to a request for something different. Even here the photographs on the wall seemed to date from the time of the Generalísimo, but they at least implied that someone with some skill with scissors had once worked there. Perhaps that heritage would count for something. I gave the man detailed instructions about layering my hair and where to put the part, emphasizing that above all I didn't want it too short. "Sí, sí," he said, nodding confidently. I couldn't figure out why he needed to plug in that sheep-shearing implement, but I suspected I was in trouble. By the time he'd finished, even a Buddhist monk couldn't complain that it was too long. Helen didn't say anything about it and was clearly determined to pretend that she hadn't noticed I'd got someone else to do it. However, it would be several hours before she stopped doing a double take each time she looked my way.

Later that evening, she came to me while I was out wandering aimlessly with my thoughts among the trees. She told me her mother wanted to buy our house as a vacation home for herself. "I'm selling her my share," she said decisively. "So that leaves you with a choice: You can be part-owner with her or else sell too. She's offering to give us everything we've paid into the place."

"You mean she's offering us next to nothing," I said.

"It's up to you," said Helen. "I've already made up my mind. She's going to help me get started again in England. On my own." I can't say the news was unexpected but I was still stunned. I quickly reviewed my options and decided there was no way I was sticking around if Helen left. A partnership with

Rita wasn't exactly appealing. Considering the situation with Simona and Theresa, it probably wasn't safe for me to stay anyway—however I played things. Given the passionate temperament of the rival sisters, the chances of the whole affair ending in bloodshed were just too great—and it would probably be *my* blood.

"What about the farm?" I said. "Your mother only likes farming as long as there's no mud involved."

"If you go, then she plans to lease the land to a local farmer. She's only going to come here a couple of weeks a year."

"You were right all along," I said. "We should have left the place as it was."

"No, you were right." She lowered her eyes. "This could only ever be an investment or a vacation home for people like us. Connecting electricity was the right thing. Who were we trying to kid?"

"I can't lay a brick the right way up," I admitted.

"And I can't even kill a chicken."

So we sold the house to Rita. I'd always planned to sell it to a foreigner one day, but she was the last person I had in mind. It was all over so quickly. We were a couple of friends searching for ourselves who ended up looking in each other's hearts. I suppose it was inevitable, given the isolation and the adventures we shared. Our biggest adventure turned out to be each other. We'd also come looking to enrich our lives with "something more." Certainly, we'd found peace and quiet for a time, but we wanted more than that too. We were too spoiled to settle for the peasant life. Personally, I came out to Spain thinking it was a way to avoid work. I didn't want to struggle with the rest of them. I certainly ended up with something more than I bargained for there. I'd never worked so hard in my life as I did on that farm. It wasn't just the valley that lost some of its innocence that year. I learned that if you don't chop that wood you'll freeze, and you don't even want to think about leaving the chemical toilet unemptied.

Strangely, it was in these necessary struggles that I finally found what I was searching for. While harvesting crops and making essential renovations, I accidentally discovered a sense of purpose that I'd sorely lacked. Although I was more than averagely incompetent at these things, I felt I'd still somehow managed to achieve something. Renovating a house with my bare hands, eating food I had grown, and working for myself in a foreign land gave me maturity and a sense of fulfillment. So what if the renovations were lopsided, the food inedible, and the business at times illegal? What I learned on that farm was that "hard work" was not necessarily synonymous with a loss of personal freedom—at least if you didn't get caught bribing the mayor. I saw that endeavor could actually be liberating and fun when directed toward a desired accomplishment. Most people make this sort of discovery in kindergarten. I guess I was a late developer. The upshot was that I woke up one day and finally realized that it was more than just the treadmill I'd been fleeing. I was at last ready to face up to some of the challenges I'd been so keen to abdicate. Instead of just wanting to run away, I started looking for a direction to run in.

The time I'd spent with Emilio had something to do with this awakening. I used to think that it was Emilio's philosophical approach and the way he took his time about everything that I admired. At first I believed that what we recognized in each other was a desire to take life as easily as possible. He might have been as old as time but he was still cool. But after a while I realized he wasn't special because he liked to sit in a field and feel the breeze. Sure, he lived close to nature, but unlike Helen, he never expected it to be an all-providing friend. Nature for him was a temperamental god, to be feared and respected. Life had never been easy for Emilio, and in the end he'd lost his struggle to be a part of it. But he'd fought his battle with incredible dignity, as a poet and a gentleman, always ready with a smile. I finally realized that here was someone who earned respect not by evading struggles, but by the way he took them on. Now *that* was cool.

Being away a long time also made us begin to see the value of home and family, and the cultures that molded us. A couple of months later, Helen went home to England and I understand she has gone on to be a very successful computer programmer. Eventually, I returned to America, the home of my parents. Before going, I would spend a few more years in Spain, mostly working with foreigners on the coast in a different part of the country. But in the end I would crave those aspects of a culture that are hard to attain when you don't speak the language like a native. I spent too much time with the English and Americans and was too successful at simply getting by to really push my Spanish. Okay, I admit it—I was just too lazy about it. In fact, the "culture" reason for leaving is phony too. I left for love, or rather lack of it. The only Spanish women I attracted were those with a vocabulary as limited as mine. Meanwhile, most of the English-speaking women were old enough to be my grandmother. If I'm being honest, this is probably the only reason I'm not still there, because even "new" Spain is one of the nicest places to live in the world. In my desires, I'd finally caught up with where Helen's heart had been. By then we'd lost touch, but I often thought of her and wondered if she also thought of me.

The time went quickly between that fateful day when she came to me among the almonds to say she was selling, and the day I left the "old" Spain of El Águila behind me. There was no room for Bobby in back with my bags, so he got to sit on the front seat next to me. I took Helen's hands in mine, expecting that one of us would say something meaningful about the amazing experiences we'd shared. But with nothing left to argue about, we were strangely silent. As usual when words failed, we let touch speak our feelings. We kissed softly and sadly for the last time. Then I got in the car and she and her mother waved me off. I guess they were waving to me but it could have been Bobby, I suppose. Although the new track was smooth, I took it slow. Progress might be coming to the valley but everyone still knew everyone else's business. At each bend there was someone waiting to say a last farewell and hand a bunch of grapes or a bag of figs through the open window. Pepe and his two disappointed granddaughters, the two Diegos, Anna, and Virtudez—all our neighbors came to say good-bye. All except one. As I reached the summit of the hill, I stopped the car, switched off the engine, and looked back one last time. I could hear Maria calling to her flock away in the distance where I'd left her minutes before. The whole valley was laid out before me. I could see the scattered white houses among the trees and the cluster of deep green at the spring. The hot air smelled of thyme and made the far-off hill fort shimmer in its mountain cradle. The sky was so blue and the scene so still and peaceful. Then a breeze swept through the valley, and in the stirring of the grasses I heard the warm sigh of Emilio. It was the farewell I had been waiting for.